Cycles of the Sun, Mysteries of the Moon

The Calendar in Mesoamerican Civilization

by

Vincent H. Malmström

UNIVERSITY OF TEXAS PRESS, AUSTIN

Copyright © 1997 by the University of Texas Press

All rights reserved

Printed in the United States of America

First edition, 1997

Requests for permission to reproduce material from this work should be sent to Permissions, University of Texas Press, P.O. Box 7819, Austin, TX 78713-7819.

♾ The paper used in this publication meets the minimum requirements of American National Standard for Information Sciences — Permanence of Paper for Printed Library Materials, ANSI Z39.48-1984.

Library of Congress Cataloging-in-Publication Data

Malmström, Vincent Herschel, 1926–
    Cycles of the sun, mysteries of the moon : the calendar in Mesoamerican civilization / by Vincent H. Malmström — 1st ed.
        p.   cm.
    Includes bibliographical references and index.
    ISBN 0-292-75196-6 (cloth: alk. paper). — ISBN 0-292-75197-4 (pbk.: alk. paper)
    1. Indian calendar—Mexico.   2. Indian calendar—Central America.   3. Maya calendar.   4. Indian astronomy—Mexico.   5. Indian astronomy—Central America. 6. Maya astronomy.   I. Title.
    F1219.3.C2M25   1997
    529'.3'0972—dc20   96-11638

In commemoration
of the native genius
of the people
of Mexico

CONCORDIA UNIVERSITY LIBRARY
PORTLAND, OR 97211

Contents

Illustrations

Figures

Tables

Preface

Any reconstruction of the knowledge or belief systems of a preliterate people must of necessity be at least somewhat imaginative. Even though our research may have uncovered *what* an early people knew, without an eyewitness description or a written record at hand we can never really be sure *how* they came to know it. What the stimulus or motivation or accidental discovery may have been that led to such and such an idea or to this or that custom or practice, we oftentimes can only speculate. And, in so doing, one is obliged to seek the most conservative and credible solution possible, while at the same time realizing that the true explanations for some human thoughts and/or actions may well border on the bizarre and irrational. This book, then, is both fact and fiction. In it, I not only recount what I and other researchers have learned through the decades about the pre-Columbian peoples of Mesoamerica and their impressive cultural achievements, but I also attempt to posit what I hope are rational hypotheses concerning where, when, and how many of their innovative breakthroughs and discoveries were actually made. Thus, while most of the facts I present are immutable, some of my interpretations and explanations are admittedly conjectural, and the reader is invited to decide for himself or herself whether more credible answers yet can be given. This, then, is really an invitation to join me in solving not one but a whole series of mysteries. As we go along, I will tell you what the clues are, and give you my best arguments for what the "motives" may have been. Hopefully, by the time my case has been made, you — the jury — will have been convinced beyond a reasonable doubt, and can render an impartial verdict, namely that the pre-Columbian peoples of Mesoamerica were among the most precocious and ingenious of any on our planet!

Among my companions on this quest into the origins of the Mesoamerican intellect have been half a generation of field assistants drawn chiefly from my students at Middlebury and Dartmouth Colleges. To each and all of them I owe a special debt of thanks for their patience, understanding, and unflagging good spirit under what have oftentimes been trying and difficult conditions. Beginning with Aaron Kiley, they include Linc Cleveland, Rob Walkinshaw, Karin Malmström, Bruce Keogh, Jay Harter, Paul Dunn, Warren Whitney, Juan Carlos Navarro, and Alex de Sherbinin. Though the questions of some of the 100-odd students who took part in my Foreign Study courses in Mexico through the years helped to guide my own thoughts into new directions, I must make special mention of at least one, Sarah Kotchian, whose independent research project led to the accidental discovery of what was then probably the oldest magnetic artifact in the world. (Four years later, Paul Dunn became the first person to recognize the magnetic properties of the yet-older "Fat Boys.") On some of my later Foreign Study Programs, when I chose not to both drive and lecture at the same time, I depended on the iron nerves and steady hands of such stalwart chauffeurs as John Corbett, Steve Mines, and Tony Hartshorn; to all three of them I say "thanks again" for bringing all my student charges and me home again in one piece. To my friend and professional colleague of nearly two decades, Professor J. Rowland Illick, I owe the warmest of thanks not only for his cordial and supportive encouragement through the years but also for his valuable participation in my final field program sponsored by Middlebury College in 1975.

Fortunately, my change of venue to Dartmouth College resulted in increased interest in and expanded support of my Mesoamerican research from both administrative and alumni quarters. Professor of history Gregory Prince, then provost at Dartmouth and now president of Hampshire College, became an energetic proponent of my hypotheses and was instrumental in introducing me to Dartmouth alumnus Guido H. Rahr Jr. of Minneapolis, whose strong dedication to the cause of geography is matched by his deep commitment to Native American Studies. Because both of his "loves" happened to come together in my research, Guido Rahr made a generous financial gift to Dartmouth, establishing a Mexico-oriented field program in the Department of Geography. I also owe a special word of thanks to Dartmouth alumnus Robert C. Dorion of Guatemala, whose financial support made possible, among other things, one of my wide-ranging "expeditions" to South America and Polynesia. Without such assistance I could never have carried out the research described in the following pages.

As these various field studies culminated in a growing series of journal articles, the idea was born to incorporate my findings into a single comprehensive volume. It is to Shannon Davies of the University of

Texas Press that I owe the inspiration for preparing this book; as my sponsoring editor, she successfully shepherded the manuscript between the Scylla and Charybdis of editorial committees and critical reviewers with tireless patience, good humor, and energetic determination. I am deeply grateful to her. To John Clark of Brigham Young University's Department of Anthropology and Archaeology I owe a special debt of gratitude for his careful reading and critical evaluation of the manuscript at the earliest stages of its preparation. And to Deborah Nichols, a colleague in Dartmouth's Department of Anthropology, I wish to express thanks for helping me to update my acquaintance with the recent literature and philosophical trends of a sister discipline. Without their help, the completion of this book would not have been realized. I alone am responsible for any shortcomings which the finished volume may have.

By the same token, without the patient, long-suffering forebearance of a tolerant and forgiving wife, my many seemingly capricious forays into jungle, mountain, and desert would never have been possible. For the many months of absence and neglect which my obsession with the sacred calendar has occasioned her, I can only apologize belatedly — and lovingly dedicate this book to Ruth.

Hanover, New Hampshire
December 1995

Chapter 1

Questions, Hypotheses, and Assorted Detours

All research begins with a question — often a host of questions. I suppose that the first time I asked the question that resulted in this book was when I was a sophomore in an anthropology class at the University of Michigan back in 1944. "How," I queried my professor, "did the Maya ever come up with a calendar that had only 260 days?" His answer was as honest as it was unsatisfying: "No one really knows."

This was, of course, not the kind of question that one loses any sleep over or that begs for an immediate reply. After all, if it hadn't been answered in over a thousand years, the solution to this enigma, intriguing as it might be, could probably wait a while longer. As it turned out, it did not capture my own attention again until nearly thirty years later when, quite by accident, I stumbled onto what seemed to be a credible answer while leading my first student field trip to Mexico in the winter of 1973.

In the meantime, the checkered course of my evolution from university undergraduate to professor of geography, then at Middlebury College in Vermont, had taken me through a series of episodes as a cartographic researcher with the Army Map Service in Washington, D.C.; a pilot cadet in the U.S. Air Force; the first graduate student in geography at the

University of Texas; and a Fulbright grantee to Norway. Along the way, I had married a lovely Norwegian woman, fathered two attractive daughters, and settled down in a charming 200-year-old farmhouse replete with a mountain view and a nearby covered bridge to teach at a prestigious New England college. By that time, most of my research and writing had found its focus in Europe.

The field trip to Mexico was my first real opportunity to visit a region which had been the primary object of my earliest academic interests. In addition to majoring in geography, I had taken minors in both anthropology and geology, and immersed myself in the study of history as well as the Spanish and Portuguese languages to prepare myself for a career in Latin America. Now, given the opportunity to develop a brief but innovative inter-session course, my long-latent interest surfaced once more in an offering which I titled "Civilization and Environment in the American Tropics."

For five eventful weeks I drove a vanful of excited students from Vermont to the Yucatán and back. In that hectic itinerary we included visits to as many archaeological sites in as many different natural settings as we could possibly reach. And at all of them we examined the various aspects of the ceremonial center's location, as well as its surrounding patterns of landforms, climate, soil, and vegetation. However, when it came to an interpretation of the artwork and architecture of the site itself, we invariably deferred to the local guide or a tourist's handbook.

One morning in late January, 1973, as my students and I lounged in the shade of "El Caracol" — the snail-shaped observatory at Chichén Itzá — my unanswered undergraduate question suddenly flashed into my mind. We were listening to a Mexican guide explain the dramatic interplay of light and shadow on the façade of the great El Castillo pyramid at the time of the equinoxes. As he spoke, I wondered if the strange 260-day calendar of the Maya might not have marked the interval between two successive passages of the vertical sun somewhere here in the tropics.

There was no way to test that hypothesis — at least none that suggested itself to me during our grueling drive back to Vermont. But once I had returned to campus, I immediately made a dash to the college library. The first question I had to answer was at what latitude such a phenomenon would take place. And the second was whether such a latitude lay anywhere in the vicinity of where the Maya lived.

Getting out a solar ephemeris (a volume published annually by the government for astronomers and navigators which provides the latitude of the sun for each day of the year), I quickly discovered that a 260-day interval can in fact be measured in Central America at latitude 14°.8 N, as well as at the same distance south of the equator in the general area of southern Peru and Bolivia. Of the two options it was naturally the first that interested me most, for I found that the parallel of 14°.8 N ran across the southeasternmost corner of Mexico and the entire width of the countries of Guatemala and Honduras.

What the ephemeris also revealed was that such a 260-day interval could only be measured between the time that the sun passed *southward* over that line until its next crossing in a northerly direction. Thus, in the sun's apparent annual migration from tropic to tropic, it took 260 days for it to travel from 14°.8 N latitude to the Tropic of Capricorn and return, whereas only 105 days were required for the sun to go up to and return from the Tropic of Cancer. Most intriguing of all, however, was the *date* on which this 260-day interval commenced. It was August 13 — the day the Maya believed that the present age of the world had begun!

While this seemed too fortuitous to be a coincidence, the very location of the critical parallel also left me in stunned disbelief. It ran right through Copán, the great ceremonial center in the mountains of western Honduras which had served as the Maya's principal seat of astronomical studies. Was this, too, just a coincidence?

Additional library research soon provided some answers but also raised some new questions. The archaeological literature told me that Copán dated to the fifth century A.D., whereas it also revealed that the sacred 260-day calendar was in existence at least as early as 400–300 B.C. (The actual occupation of the Copán valley by early farmers had begun at least by 1000 B.C., but the first evidence of an advanced level of "civilization" in the area is a stela with a date equivalent to A.D. 426.) Thus, while the astronomy of Copán was correct, the ceremonial center had been founded about 800 years too late to have served as the calendar's birthplace.

Continuing my readings, I encountered an observation made by a German naturalist, Hans Gadow, that made especially good sense to me as a geographer. Writing about the turn of the century, Gadow, like so many researchers both before and since, was intrigued by the origins of the strange 260-day calendar. He was convinced that it had to have been the product of a lowland tropical setting, because its days were named for such animals as alligators, monkeys, and iguanas, which do not live in highland environments. I knew that such creatures would certainly not be found amidst the pine and oak forests surrounding Copán, so now I had the additional reason of geography for rejecting what had seemed at first glance to be both a facile and obvious solution. (Only later did I learn that several earlier researchers already had fallen into what I soon came to label the "Copán trap" because they had overlooked both the historical and geographical constraints of the sacred calendar.)

Of course, to answer my original question, I now had to return to the map of archaeological sites to see if I could find one that not only lay *along the parallel of 14°.8 N*, but that also was *situated in a lowland tropical niche* and that was *in existence at least as early as 400 B.C.*

Zeroing in on the "lowland ecological niche" was easy, because it could only exist in one of two places: it was either to be found on the western (Pacific) coastal plain of Mexico or on the eastern (Caribbean) coastal plain of Honduras. Because the parallel of 14°.8 N ran through the mountainous core of Central America for most of its length, the only lowlands it crossed were on either end of this line. Deciding which of the two lowland areas it might have been — Pacific versus Caribbean — was also quickly resolved, because only a few Indians inhabit the swampy, trade wind–soaked rain forests of eastern Honduras even to this day. On the other hand, in the narrow coastal plain of southernmost Mexico my map of archaeological sites showed what was described as an "important ceremonial center in Late Pre-Classic times": a place named Izapa that had never been mentioned in any of my anthropology courses, and that certainly was unfamiliar to me. Nevertheless, what mattered was that Izapa had the "right" astronomy, the "right" geography, and the "right" history; indeed, it was the only site in all of the pre-Columbian New World that did! I was excited enough by this striking convergence of clues to dash off an article describing my hypothesis and submit it to the magazine *Science,* which published it in early September 1973.

CONFRONTATION AND CHALLENGE

Among the many letters which poured in congratulating me on my deductions and asking for reprints of my article was one postmarked in England. It was a note from the dean of Maya archaeologists, Sir John Eric Sydney Thompson, and he was clearly unhappy with my conclusions — so unhappy, it appears, that in an exchange of letters later published in *Science* one of his disciples accused me of having been "anticipated" by earlier, subsequently "discredited" researchers whom I, perhaps knowingly, had failed to acknowledge.

Naturally, I was taken aback by the hostile, almost vitriolic tone of this response, and I began to wonder what sensitive nerve I had touched to elicit such a harsh indictment. After all, to my mind I had simply put forward an original hypothesis which seemed to make sense and deserved to be debated in a broader academic forum. I could not imagine why the "big guns" in the field of archaeology found my reasoning so distasteful.

As time went by, several facets of the confrontation became clearer. The contention that my hypothesis had been "anticipated" by earlier researchers was accurate in only one particular. I found from a review of the literature that the conclusion that the 260-day calendar derived from the interval between zenithal sun passages near the 15th parallel of north latitude had been reached by at least three scholars: Zelia Nuttall in 1928, Ola Apenes in 1936, and Rafael Girard in 1948. The first two had fallen into the "Copán trap," as I nearly had myself, while Girard, as a nationalistic Guatemalan, had insisted that the calendar had been developed in the highlands of his country and not in neighboring Honduras. Thus, none of these researchers had truly "anticipated" me by pinpointing the locus of the calendar's birthplace in Izapa, even though the same facts of history and geography should have been known to each of them as were known to me.

Moreover, I found that in 1945 Robert Merrill had pointed out the correspondence between the date of the sun's southward zenithal passage over the latitude of Copán and the beginning date of the present epoch of the Maya world. But I also learned that Merrill's observation had been summarily dismissed as a "coincidence" by Thompson. Thus, even this early in the "confrontation," I sensed that the latter's response seemed to be part of a definite pattern—to wit, anyone at odds with J. Eric Sydney Thompson could obviously expect trouble!

It was only much later that I realized how accurate my initial perception was. Some years after Thompson had passed away, the distinguished Yale anthropologist Michael Coe candidly admitted in print how fortunate he counted himself for not having invoked Thompson's "caustic criticism," even though he had dared disagree with him as a graduate student. (Thankfully, the discipline of geography has never had so chilling a father figure in its cast of characters.)

There was another reason for the cool reception my hypothesis had received from the anthropological fraternity. At the time my *Science* article appeared, I had no idea that an internecine struggle was raging within the discipline over one of the most divisive issues imaginable: the question of which people had been the true founders of civilization in Mesoamerica—the name by which the region of high culture in Mexico and Central America is defined. Was it the Maya, who without question represented the ultimate in pre-Columbian cultural sophistication within the region, or was it the still somewhat shadowy people known as the Olmecs? The anthropologists and archaeologists were polarized into two opposing camps with strong antagonisms for each other's point of view. The "Mayanistas" were led by such notables as the Englishman Thompson and the American Sylvanus Morley, while the "Olmequistas" were comprised chiefly of Mexican anthropologists. Unbeknownst to me, by arguing for the calendar's birthplace in Izapa, I had inadvertently joined the Olmec camp, and if for no other reason than that, I found the entire "Mayanista" faction of the discipline arrayed against me.

Even though I somewhat belatedly came to understand how Thompson's domineering personality and the internal struggle between the "Mayanistas" and "Olmequistas" had both conspired to generate such negative reactions to my hypothesis, I should have been aware at the outset that my real transgression was not being a card-carrying anthropologist or archaeologist. Here was I, a geographer, invading the turf of "their" discipline and daring to suggest a solution to a problem that had engaged them in more than a half century of research and debate.

Although I was scheduled to spend the spring term of 1974 doing research at the United Nations Food and Agriculture Organization in Rome, in view of the antagonism which my *Science* article had generated I decided that I must devote at least six weeks of that time to a field reconnaissance of southern Mexico and western Honduras. Only in that way could I actually see for myself the place where my deductions had told me the sacred calendar had been born. And, only by making a pilgrimage to Copán could I confirm my conclusion that the calendar had given rise to it, and not the other way around. Indeed, by now it had become a "matter of honor" for me to determine whether I could have been so misguided in my deductions, or if the problem lay with "them." Certainly, I was under no illusion that the anthropologists or archaeologists had any more of a corner on the "truth" or on logic than a geographer did. If what I found failed to support my hypothesis, I would say so, and put the matter to rest once and for all. But if I was reassured that I was "onto something," I vowed to keep looking for the proof for as long as it took me to make my case.

PIECING TOGETHER THE PUZZLE:
A PRE-COLUMBIAN "WHODUNIT"

So many new, exciting, and unexpected discoveries emerged from my first visit to Izapa that even before I had left that awe-inspiring site I was convinced that I really was "onto something." However, little or nothing of what I learned at Izapa had ever appeared in print. Indeed, apart from a few cursory digs which had been carried out there in the 1940's, its systematic excavation had begun only in 1962 under the auspices of the New World Archaeological Foundation, funded by Brigham Young University. Just wandering amongst Izapa's 130-odd mounds and pyramids, experiencing firsthand its tropical rain forest setting, and trying to imagine what the carvers of its flamboyant, enigmatic sculptures were trying to commemorate was something that a lifetime in a library carrel or a classroom could never duplicate.

As I stood musing over the site from the summit of its highest mound, I realized as never before that what the geographer looks for in the field and the kinds of questions he or she asks are entirely different from those that the archaeologist or anthropologist is trained to investigate. The latter seek to establish a temporal context into which to fit the various artifacts which their excavations uncover, and for most of the history of these disciplines that has meant using stratigraphy — working out the age of a site by a careful examination of the layers of soil which have accumulated over it. More recently (beginning in the 1950's), radiocarbon dating replaced stratigraphic analysis as the primary tool in establishing chronological horizons, in many instances resulting in substantial revisions of dates fixed by stratigraphic means. (Indeed, as my own research progressed, it was both ironic and reassuring that where my findings initially appeared to be at odds with the generally accepted, stratigraphically determined chronology of a site, once the radiocarbon results came in, they invariably served to lend additional support to my hypotheses.)

Moreover, when it came to understanding the spatial context of a place, where it was located, and how it was related to its surroundings, I found that there was little helpful information to be gleaned from the literature of our sister disciplines. Nowhere, for example, would I have discovered that the entire ceremonial center of Izapa was aligned to a towering volcano on the northern horizon, or that from its main pyramid the length of the solar year could be calibrated at the summer solstice against the highest volcano in all of Central America. Seeing at the edge of the jungle clearing a statue of a man on his knees worshipping the mountain and along the side of the ball court a bas-relief depicting a seaborne visitor to the site told me that Izapa was a very special place indeed.

But now I also realized that I would have to carefully reexamine most of the ceremonial centers I had so hurriedly visited on my earlier reconnaissance, because only now was I beginning to ask "the right questions": What was the site's spatial relationship to the surrounding topographic features? And was there any significance to the internal design and layout of the ceremonial center or to the orientation of its principal structures? So, even before I said my first farewell to Izapa, I was already making plans for my next research trip to Mexico the following winter.

My 1975 junket to Mexico produced two more exciting discoveries — one which confirmed my basic hypothesis regarding the origin of the 260-day calendar as nothing else could have, and the other which added an entirely new and unexpected twist to my research. Since the buzzwords of that expedition were *alignments* and *orientations*, when my students and I arrived at Teotihuacán, I immediately put them to work trying to decipher the layout of the great metropolis. At its peak, this immense ceremonial center on the outskirts of modern Mexico City had been the largest urban center in the New World, and for a time it was one of the three largest cities on our planet. When we discovered that it was oriented to the setting sun on August 13, that could only mean that the city's founders — although they were over 1000 km (600 mi) from Izapa — had already been engulfed by a "wave of calendrical diffusion" a couple of centuries before the dawn of the Christian era!

The second discovery was made at Izapa itself, while checking the alignment of a couple of freestanding sculptures off to the side of one of the main pyramids. Although the first sculpture, a representation of a rattlesnake's head, produced no surprises, the second (which my students and I identified as the head of a turtle) proved to be strongly magnetic in its snout. Had its sculptor not been aware of its magnetic lines of force, its pole of attraction would probably have been randomly situated in the eye or the ear of the creature instead. My paper reporting the discovery of what was probably the oldest magnetic artifact in the world was published by the British science journal *Nature* early in February 1976.

By the time of the article's publication, my own professional evolution had taken a new turn, for at the beginning of that year I had accepted a position as professor at Dartmouth College in Hanover, New Hampshire. Making such a career change in the middle of the winter had one drawback: It prevented me from carrying out further fieldwork in Mexico in 1976. On the other hand, an important compensatory trade-off was in gaining access to Dartmouth's impressive computer facilities. I therefore decided to write a computer program incorporating those parameters of the Maya calendrical system on which there was the most general agreement and then proceed to run it "backward" — from Spanish colonial times to whenever — to see if I could establish when each of its components, the 365-day secular calendar and the 260-day sacred almanac, had come into being. In the process, I also thought that it might be possible to determine when the Maya had undertaken a reform in their calendar by selecting a new new year's day, as well as to establish when their so-called Long Count had come into being. The latter was an extremely sophisticated innovation whose European counterpart was not developed until the sixteenth century!

One of the results of this computer exercise — the date of the origin of the Long Count — proved to be not only "credible" but also confirmative of one of the many researchers who had earlier run afoul of Thompson; however, the other three seemed to leave me even further out "on thin ice" than I had been with my initial hypothesis and would surely open me up to an additional barrage from the archaeological community. I therefore held off publishing my findings, because in one instance I was projecting a calendar reform among the Maya 600 years before the city at which it supposedly took place had been founded, and in the other two instances, my calculations showed that both the secular and sacred calendars were about a millennium older than Izapa was supposed to be! (In each of these instances, newer radiocarbon dates ultimately came to my rescue, and all of my far-out computer results have subsequently been vindicated.)

The winter of 1976 was also a time for intense map research, and the results of that exercise proved fully as rewarding as my computer project had been. As I pored over large-scale maps of the major ceremonial centers of Mesoamerica, I found that time after time they replicated the locational principle which I had first discovered in Izapa: Their solar orientation at one of the solstices invariably aligned with the highest mountain within view. (In other words, the location of the ceremonial center had been consciously chosen so as to align with the highest point at sunrise or sunset on either June 22 or December 22.) It was as though the sun-god himself had decreed the location of native American cities, for each of them employed a commanding topographic feature to calibrate the march of time. When I sent a couple of research papers describing my computer reconstruction of the Maya calendar and the locational principle of pre-Columbian cities to the editor of the *Journal for the History of Astronomy* in Cambridge, England, he encouraged me to combine them into one longer treatise, which I did, and this was published in 1978.

In the meantime, I had made a further research trip to Mesoamerica in the winter of 1977. Although my student assistants and I had ranged from the far northern desert of Mexico to El Salvador and Honduras on our journey, our principal accomplishment was to visually confirm many of the alignments I had first measured on the maps.

The following winter I was back in Mexico again, and this time my primary focus was the site of the supposed Maya calendar reform. Not only did I find the proof I was looking for, but I also confirmed that the Maya had used the August 13th sunset to orient the first great city which they had constructed. Exciting as these discoveries were, I also identified what is probably the oldest lunar observatory in the New World — a totally unexpected bonus!

The year 1978 also marked my first research trip to South America. Its mission was to locate possible antecedents to the calendars of Mesoamerica; here, a negative result proved reassuring. In the autumn of the same year, while leading a Dartmouth Foreign Study Program to Sweden, I had occasion to identify a monument on the south coast of the country as the Swedish equivalent of Stonehenge. Composed of some 200 tons of mammoth stones arranged in the shape of a ship, it stands on a morainic bluff overlooking the Baltic Sea. (By this time, of course, I couldn't even take my wife on a Sunday picnic without looking for alignments and orientations.) The Swedish antiquities board had described this monument as a "late Iron Age burial" (i.e., A.D. 400–1050). This unplanned detour into megalithic astronomy lasted another year, for the autumn of 1979 was again spent in Scandinavia attempting to find other calendrical monuments attributable to the same culture. (This brief foray into European archaeoastronomy did generate an article for a Swedish scientific journal which managed to stir the pot on the far side of the Atlantic as well.)

The Swedish discovery had come in the wake of an especially productive expedition to Mesoamerica in the winter of 1978. My field assistant and I had finally "cracked" the formula which the early town planners had used to lay out their cities, and we had repeatedly confirmed its presence throughout the Yucatán Peninsula and the highlands of Oaxaca. We had likewise worked out the astronomical properties of the spectacular Maya capital city of Tikal, and by now the final bits of evidence for how the calendar had diffused throughout Mesoamerica were almost all in place. One element of "static" in the whole picture was that we also had discovered nearly a dozen more magnetic sculptures, this time in Guatemala, which were probably even older than the turtle-head at Izapa. The latter find was reported on the science page of *Time* magazine, while the astronomical matrix of Tikal and the evidence of calendrical diffusion were published in a symposium report issued by the Center for Archaeoastronomy.

In 1981 a more extensive journey to western South America and Polynesia took my field assistant and me to such varied sites as San Agustín in the jungles of Colombia, Cerro Sechín in the desert of Peru, Tiahuanaco near the shores of Lake Titicaca in Bolivia, and Easter Island. While we uncovered several intriguing bits of evidence, subsequently described in a comprehensive paper dealing with Mexico and Sweden as well, again the fact that no credible antecedents for the calendars of Izapa were uncovered in any of these possible "donor regions" simply reinforced the likelihood that the calendars were the products of the native genius of Mesoamerica.

With the calendars' origins and diffusion now so clearly established—in my own mind at least—I saw my further research taking a somewhat different tack. By making Izapa the centerpiece of my argument, I knew that even most of the "Olmequistas" were wary of me. Half a century of their work had turned up so much evidence of the Olmec presence in the Gulf coastal plain of Mexico that for anyone to suggest that the "real" geographic center of innovation had been instead on the Pacific coastal plain was totally flying in the face of the "Olmequista" camp.

Many different geographic foci have been suggested as the cradle of the Olmecs, with some lines of reasoning being based on environmental evidence and others on the stylistic evolution of art forms. For example, in his classic study from 1949 titled *Mundo olmeca* (*The Olmec World*), Ignacio Bernal identified the hearth of their civilization as the "Olmec metropolitan area"—that part of the Gulf coastal plain lying to the south and east of the Tuxtla Mountains. Michael Coe, writing in 1965, essentially agreed, arguing that the core area of Olmec culture lay in the heartland of southern Veracruz and western Tabasco, most probably at San Lorenzo because the earliest radiocarbon dates stem from there. However, Coe conceded that the original home of the Olmecs may have been in the Tuxtlas since this is where most of their building stone came from and it was probably one of the many volcanoes in that region which served as the inspiration for the fluted-cone pyramid at La Venta. Of course, if such were the case, their true origins might lie buried forever beneath deep layers of lava and ash — which would certainly account for no earlier evidence ever having been found.

Alfonso Caso tended to agree, in part at least, contending that the Olmec civilization, like those of the Near East, was the product of the great alluvial valleys that one finds so prominently in evidence on the Gulf coastal plain of Mexico. It was their fertile soils, he argued, that made possible the food surpluses that in turn gave rise to the great urban developments of the Olmecs. Of course, Caso made no distinction between the environments through which their respective rivers flowed, those in the Old World being deserts and that in the New being a rainforest. To him, the "hydraulic" parallel was close enough.

William Sanders disagreed, pointing out that all the Old World civilizations were based on irrigation techniques developed in arid lands; therefore, the urban origins of the Olmecs, if they paralleled those of virtually every other known civilization — and there was no good reason to believe that they didn't! — must have been in the semiarid basins of the Mexican plateau. In short, it was quite inconceivable to Sanders that the Olmecs should have been such an exception to the "rule" that they could have developed the necessary agricultural surpluses in a tropical rainforest environment, when no other culture in the world appeared to have been able to do so.

Roman Piña Chan agreed in part with Sanders, suggesting the likelihood that, because of the relatively numerous Olmec finds which had been encountered in and around the state of Morelos, this area must have been the cradle of their civilization. Using much the same line of argument but stressing a stylistic progression, Miguel Covarrubias believed it was on the Pacific slopes of the states of Oaxaca and especially

Guerrero that the origins of the Olmecs should be sought; it was in the latter areas, he said, that "[Olmec culture's] most archaic forms appear." Charles Wicke essentially seconded Covarrubias's motion, specifically zeroing in on the Mixteca-Alta region of western Oaxaca where a particularly primitive monument had been discovered at the village of San Martín Huamelulpan. Edwin Ferdon used much the same rationale to argue for the primacy of the Tehuantepec region, having discovered a fairly early representative of Olmec sculpture at Tonalá, whereas S. W. Miles wanted to push the Olmec heartland even farther south into the Pacific coastal plain of Chiapas and Guatemala, likewise on the basis of "archaic" sculptures.

At first glance it might seem an exaggeration to attach so much importance to the sacred calendar. Yet, anyone familiar with its role in the life of pre-Columbian Mesoamerica realizes that bound up with the calendar are many if not all of the more sophisticated aspects of the region's early intellectual life: the awareness of a cyclicity in the movement of celestial bodies, the evolution of mathematical skills by which they could manipulate the numbers derived from those cycles, and the development of a system of hieroglyphics for recording the results. Thus, if and when the calendar diffused from Izapa to the Olmecs, the Maya, and the other peoples of the region, with it must have come most of the trappings of civilization — astronomy, mathematics, writing, urban planning. So, too, should there have been some transfer of material culture, witnessed in types of pottery and styles of architecture. And certainly one of the most reliable of trace elements in pinning down the diffusion of peoples is language. If I could find evidence that cultural traits such as these had paralleled the movement of the calendar, my hypothesis would be immeasurably strengthened.

Accompanied by another student assistant in the spring of 1983, I was off to some of the most remote mountain areas of southern Mexico to visit remnants of a linguistic group who I hypothesized were the original bearers of civilization in Mesoamerica. Our results not only confirmed what earlier researchers had argued for in terms of the interrelationships of the languages they spoke, but they also provided a coherent spatial context by which to explain their present scattered distribution. So confident was I of my findings that I titled my resultant paper, published in 1985, "The Origins of Civilization in Mesoamerica." (Concurrent and subsequent studies by linguistic specialists have confirmed the linguistic identity of the Olmecs, though my hypothesis for the present geographic distribution of these languages has yet to win their endorsement.)

Confident that I had at long last pulled together about as much evidence as I could regarding the *origins* of civilization in Mesoamerica, I decided to turn my attention to the situation which existed in the waning days of pre-Columbian civilization. What, for instance, had been the contribution of the peoples and cultures of the region who were the *last* to fall into the embrace of the sacred calendar—peoples like the Nahuatl-speaking nomads from the northern desert, the Toltecs and the Aztecs, and the Purépecha, or Tarascans, who live in the southwestern Mexican state of Michoacán? And how does the explanation of one much-repeated Maya date at Copán now make it possible for us to confirm positively the correlation of their calendar with our own? In the pages which follow, these are some of the themes I will explore as I chart the achievements of the "Mesoamerican intellect."

Chapter 2

Humans and Environment in the Americas

The human presence in the Americas most likely began some 30,000 years ago with the advance of hunters across the Bering landbridge from northeast Asia into Alaska. By 23,000 B.C. they were seeking shelter in caves in western Nevada, and by 15,000 B.C. they were hunting woolly mammoths in the marshes of the Mexican plateau. Certainly by 10,000 B.C. their descendants had occupied much of South America, and a few millennia later had reached even the remotest outliers of Tierra del Fuego.

This 30,000-km (20,000-mi), 20,000-year trek was the epic of hundreds of generations. Through this vast expanse of space these peoples of Mongoloid origin had encountered environments ranging from polar to tropical, from desert to rain forest, from featureless alluvial plains to lofty volcanic peaks. And during this vast expanse of time, they had experienced the disappearance not only of the great ice sheets but also of many of the larger game animals adapted to the glacier's fringes, followed by a marked warming of the climate and a rising of sea levels. Thus, although their sustenance had initially depended almost exclusively on their fortune as hunters, whether on land or in the adjacent coastal waters, as they advanced into the warmer, more vegetated regions of the Americas their diet increasingly came to embrace edible plants as well. Their economy was essentially one of "collecting" — that is, living off whatever animals, fish, or birds they could kill and gathering whatever roots, berries, or fruits they could find. Yet, even under these circumstances they were quick to realize that "all places were not created equal," for some regions afforded them a bounty of foodstuffs whereas others were niggardly in the extreme.

About the time that the first hunters and gatherers were reaching the southernmost outposts of the Americas (i.e., ca. 7000 B.C.), peoples in the Amazon basin, the foothills of the central Andes, and the mountains of southern Mexico and Guatemala were beginning to modify the environments of certain of the food plants which they had come to favor. At first, these modifications entailed little more than plucking away competing, unwanted vegetation or supplying water to a desired plant in time of drought. Gradually it likewise came to involve consciously selecting and planting seeds in areas that had been specially prepared to receive them. Thus, from such humble origins evolved the process of plant domestication which we term "agriculture" — or perhaps more properly "horticulture," because of its initial gardenlike scale. Certainly, for the early peoples of the Americas this was no "revolution," but rather a painfully slow evolution which saw the proportion of their diet based on domesticated plants increase from some 10 percent about 5000 B.C. to just over 35 percent about 1500 B.C. (MacNeish, 1964, 531–537). Chief among the plants which were being cultivated relatively early in the Mesoamerican region were squashes, chile peppers, avocados, beans, and amaranth, with maize making its initial appearance as a cultigen sometime around 3000 B.C. (Long et al., 1989).

Because of the overwhelming importance of maize to the subsequent development of civilization in Mesoamerica, a brief recapitulation of the history of its domestication is in order. Through the researches of Paul Mangelsdorf and his associates, the transition of what was a singularly unpromising plant, whose initial cob was no larger than a thumbnail, to the large golden-eared type of grain we know today, has been meticulously traced. Wild forms of maize grew both in Mesoamerica and along the west coast of South America in Peru and Ecuador. Somehow — most likely, it would seem, through the human agency of trade—the primitive domesticate from Mesoamerica was crossed with its counterpart in South America, resulting in a genetically improved form of corn which was crossed again with an Andean grass known as tripsacum. This second crossing resulted in a much altered and enlarged ear of corn which, when traded back to Mesoamerica, crossed a third time with a native grass of the Mexican highlands called teosinte. From this union a further explosive increase in size took place, resulting in the whole spectrum of maize types found throughout the region today. It was from these, in turn, that the modern hybrids we are familiar with in the North American corn belt were derived (Mangelsdorf, 1983).

The beginnings of agriculture, slow and uneven as they were, nevertheless had a profound geographic significance. For the first time in human history, the natural world had been divided by a cultural dichotomy: Unlike hunting and gathering, which could be practiced everywhere, agriculture was possible in some areas but not in others. Although the specific parameters of given plants were certainly not understood at the outset, by trial and error would-be farmers found that there were spatial limits to where they could grow their crops of choice. In a tropical setting, adequate warmth was scarcely a concern, but adequate moisture, at the appropriate time, definitely was. Differences in drainage, exposure, and productivity of the soil were no doubt observed but probably not identified as factors of consequence in their own right.

In North America, the most critical cultural boundary demarcating the hunting-and-gathering cultures from the agricultural cultures was the climatic limit of maize, or corn, cultivation. (In South America, on the other hand, the potato permitted the expansion of cultivation into regions far cooler than those in which corn would ripen.) Where maize would grow, a people could become farmers; where it would not, they were destined to continue to subsist as hunters and gatherers. This was not a matter of human will, intelligence, or energy; it was a decree of nature which not even the most determined, dedicated, or capable individual could defy. In northeastern North America, where warmth was the limiting factor, the Iroquois of central New York state could and did become maize farmers, whereas the Algonkians, farther north in the St. Lawrence Valley, could not grow corn and thus were denied that option. In the American tropics, the limiting factor was moisture, and in the south and east of Mexico where the rains were adequate to nurture maize, farming societies developed and throve, whereas on the plateau in the north and west, only nomadic collecting was possible. As we shall see, in large part it was this boundary between two environments and between two economies which marked the northern limit of Mesoamerica—the region of high native cultures on the North American continent.

The shift to an agricultural economy in those geographic areas of the Americas where such a transition was possible was also accompanied by a change in the spatial patterns of behavior of the peoples involved. Whereas a hunting-and-gathering society was almost of necessity a nomadic one, with its members following the migrations of game or the seasonal variations in the fruiting of plants, a farming society—at least one based on such higher-order plants as maize, beans, and squash—tended to become more geographically fixed. The investment of time and labor in clearing land, planting seeds, weeding, watering, and fertilizing, and ultimately harvesting the mature crop meant that agricultural peoples became more settled in place. Moreover, because farming entailed an active "partnership" in the production of food, rather than just a passive collection of whatever bounty nature provided locally, the food supply usually became not only more secure and dependable but also capable of supporting larger numbers of people. Population densities began to increase and, depending on the land-use patterns which developed, more and more people tended to live together in small villagelike settlements. This inevitably resulted in greater social interaction, with all the positive and negative consequences that such contact brings in its wake.

Where agriculture was practiced under especially favorable conditions—and usually such geographic areas were discovered by accident rather than by conscious design—it was even possible to produce more food than the local inhabitants actually needed at any given time. The significance of being able to produce surplus food can scarcely be overemphasized, for by releasing some workers from the day-to-day chores of tilling the fields, it permitted a diversification and specialization of labor that had never before been possible. In the Old World, such specially favored areas of food production had been found in the so-called exotic river valleys of the Near East, such as the Tigris and Euphrates, as early as 4500 B.C.; in the Nile Valley of Egypt by 4000 B.C.; the Indus Valley of Pakistan by 3500 B.C.; the valleys of the Amu and Syr Darya in Central Asia by 3000 B.C.; and the Wei river valley of North China by 2500 B.C. In every instance a desert climate with cloudless skies, 12 hours of daily sunshine, the absence of frost, little or no vegetation cover to clear, and rich alluvial soils coincided with a continuous supply of water from the adjacent river — true "Gardens of Eden" in which only the totally lazy and indifferent could have failed to enjoy the blessings of plenty. Indeed, each of these exotic river valleys was either the cradle of a civilization in its own right or, at least, the beneficiary of a diffusion which first began in Mesopotamia and was later emulated elsewhere under remarkably similar environmental conditions.

It should also be pointed out that in the wake of surplus food production and the concomitant necessity for food storage, a couple of modifications in the material culture of the peoples concerned were almost inevitable hallmarks of such an advance. Vessels for storage, such as baskets and pottery, now became part of the inventory of the average household. And the latter, in particular because of its relative imperishability, has become a favored diagnostic tool of the archaeologist in tracing the economic evolution of a culture. Although examples of preagricultural ceramics do exist, the more usual case is that they are evidence of a settled, farming society of greater complexity and sophistication. We shall return to the role of ceramics somewhat later.

There is good evidence that in the New World the model of "hydraulic" civilizations described above was first replicated in the Atacama Desert of Peru where about 40 short exotic rivers cut their way from the Andes to the Pacific. However, in the region which we have called Mesoamerica, no such exotic river valley environment exists, though a somewhat similar lacustrine setting eventually gave rise to the region's largest metropolis, Teotihuacán, and later to its most sizable heir, the Aztec capital of Tenochtitlán. Nevertheless, in the latter region, archaeologists have been unable to pinpoint any single, well-defined cradle for the rise of civilization in the same way as they have in most of the other great cultural hearths of the world. While most archaeologists are now agreed that the oldest, or "mother," culture of the entire region is that of the misnamed Olmecs, who these people really were and where they came from are still matters of some dispute.

As originally defined, Mesoamerica was a region whose boundaries embraced the geographic core area of the pre-Columbian civilizations of the North American continent. As such, it was a cultural concept whose unifying characteristics were the very hallmarks of the more advanced indigenous societies, among them a hierarchical political structure, an urban way of life, monumental architecture, a highly developed religious pantheon, a sophisticated calendrical system coupled with a knowledge of astronomy and mathematics, and the use of a hieroglyphic form of writing. But, because it was primarily a region defined by human achievement, its boundaries have tended to fluctuate through time; thus, the frontiers of Mesoamerica in the distant past were quite different than they were on the eve of the Spanish conquest. Indeed, the region as it is generally defined today represents the culmination of a long, slow process of geographic diffusion throughout southern Mexico and northern Central America.

Although Mesoamerica was essentially a cultural concept, its dimensions had a very real physical basis. It was a region in which maize not only could be grown but within which it also became the staple foodstuff of civilization itself. Everywhere the warmth and moisture were adequate, though the latter was only seasonally so because of the monsoonal nature of the climate. Over most of Mesoamerica, the rains were associated with the summer, or high-sun, half of the year, whereas during the winter, or low-sun, period, the amount of precipitation received fell considerably short of what most plants, wild or domesticated, required for active growth. As a result, much of the vegetation demonstrates an adaptation to drought, whether in size of plant, density of plant cover, loss of leaves, or modification of leaf structure to retain moisture. Where the total annual precipitation is especially heavy and/or the seasonal drought is relatively brief, the resultant vegetation is a tall and luxuriant rain forest, or *selva*. Elsewhere it grades into a lower deciduous forest and in northernmost Yucatán into a scrub forest of relatively short thorn trees. Some interior upland valleys border on being steppe.

The productivity of the soil varies both with the nature of the bedrock from which it has been derived and with the wetness of the climate. Without question, the region's most productive soils are the alluviums laid down along the major rivers, especially of the Mexican Gulf coastal plain, but the limestones which underlie the Yucatán and much of southern and eastern Mexico and the northern highlands of Guatemala also contribute to the fertility of these areas, even where the rainfall is relatively heavy. On the other hand, because limestone is porous, most such areas have no surface streams, all the rainwater having drained down into the water table which often lies at a depth of many feet. As a result, water is in short supply and where there is a paucity of rainfall to begin with, as in the northern Yucatán, much of the original limestone surface is so little weathered that the farmer's fields are almost nothing but bare rock. However, in addition to the areas with alluvial soils and lime-rich soils, areas of recent volcanic activity such as central Mexico and the southern highlands of Guatemala contain mineral-rich soils which have supported a dense settlement of sedentary agriculturalists for literally hundreds of years. On the other hand, in some of the mountainous areas of western Mexico where the bedrock is composed largely of igneous intrusive rocks such as granite or metamorphic rocks such as gneiss and schist, the resultant soils tend to be sandy, porous, and relatively sterile, and crop yields tend to be low and farming populations consequently small.

Thus, the challenges posed to the would-be farmer in Mesoamerica varied markedly from place to place, with soil fertility and adequacy of moisture being the most critical factors determining the success of agriculture in the region. And while no people or society set out consciously to find the "magic" combination of geographic factors which would allow them to produce a surplus of food which would then in turn set the wheels of civilization in motion, in at least one place within the region a fortuitous natural endowment had favored such a development even before farming had become a viable option. This was in Soconusco — that part of Mesoamerica which lies in the Pacific piedmont of Guatemala and the adjacent area of southernmost Mexico.

SOCONUSCO: A SPECIAL PLACE

Perhaps few other regions of the Americas demonstrate as great a physical and ecological diversity within such a limited area as does Soconusco.

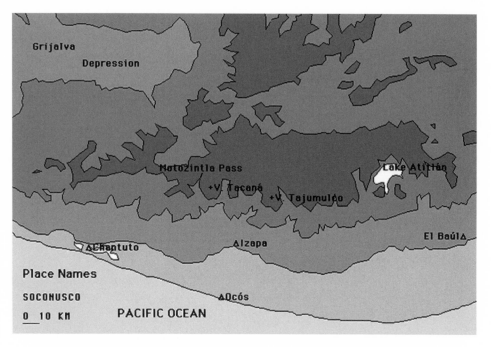

Figure 1.
Topography is shown by increasing intensities of shading, with areas from sea level to 200 m (650 ft) in the lightest tone, areas from 200 to 1000 m in the next darkest tone, areas between 1000 and 3000 m darker yet, and areas above 3000 m (10,000 ft) in the darkest tone. The height and ruggedness of the mountain wall backing Soconusco insured the region a measure of isolation and protection from the interior in the earliest stages of its cultural evolution and have continued to complicate inland communications to the present day.

If we are generous in its dimensions, we can say that it extends for roughly 300 km (200 mi) northwest-southeast along the Pacific versant of Mexico and Guatemala, beginning around the present-day town of Tonalá and extending to just south of Guatemala City. Because its inland boundary coincides with the continental divide, its overall width is nowhere more than about 50 km (30 mi). Thus, its total area is less than 15,000 sq km (6000 sq mi), or smaller than the size of the states of Connecticut and Rhode Island taken together.

Within this small area the topography varies from sea level to over 4000 m (13,000 ft) in elevation. Indeed, the highest mountains in all of Central America are found in Soconusco — Tajumulco (4221 m, 13,845 ft) lying in Guatemala about 30 km (20 mi) from the Mexican frontier, and Tacaná (4094 m, 13,428 ft) itself forming part of the boundary. Yet, even the mountains themselves contribute to Soconusco's diversity, for from Tacaná south they are all of volcanic origin whereas on the Mexican side of the line they are chiefly composed of granite. Consequently, the resultant soils differ as well, those in Guatemala being relatively fertile while those in Mexico are primarily sterile sands. However, two factors combine to mitigate the essential poverty of the soils in the Mexican coastal plain. First, the deposits of volcanic lava, ash, and dust have weathered more rapidly and more deeply than have the granites, with the result that a vaster amount of alluvial material has been brought down in the Guatemalan sector of Soconusco than in the Mexican. Consequently, the Guatemalan coastal plain is wider than that in Mexico. Second, because the predominant long-shore current in the Pacific is from the south, the alluvium derived from the volcanic debris has been swept northward along the Mexican coast so that most of the outer lagoon areas have become the recipients of finer, more productive soils than those found farther inland near the granite foothills.

Because of its latitude (i.e., 13–17° N), Soconusco has a distinctly tropical climate with a very small temperature range throughout the year. The coldest month averages 27° C (80° F) while the mean for the warmest month does not climb above 30° C (86° F). Warmth, therefore, is both constant and essentially unvarying in Soconusco, unlike parts of eastern Mexico where the occasional passage of *nortes* (northers) from December to February can brusquely drop temperatures into the lower teens C (50's F).

On the other hand, in common with all of Mesoamerica, Soconusco experiences a decidedly monsoonal pattern of rainfall. Whereas the constantly high temperatures mean that on average 130–160 mm (about 5–6 in.) of moisture could be theoretically transpired and/or evaporated into the atmosphere every month, in at least five months of the year the average precipitation fails to reach that amount. Thus, from December through April there is a steadily growing moisture deficit within the region, totaling a shortfall of over 550 mm (about 22 in.) by the time the summer rains begin. However, once the rains commence, they are so heavy that the total dry-season deficit is more than made up by the end of June, and thereafter the surplus continues to grow. The maximum

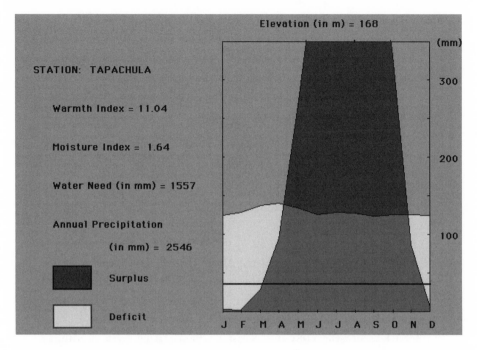

Figure 2.
A water budget diagram for Tapachula, the main city of Mexican Soconusco today. Two curves are seen in the diagram—one relatively even line running across the graph which depicts water need and a second, very uneven line running off the top of the graph which shows monthly precipitation. Water need is a direct function of temperature, and in every month of the year the warmth is such that about 125 mm (5 in.) of precipitation is required to meet the needs of growing plants. From November until April—the low-sun, or winter, months—the actual precipitation falls below this threshold, resulting in a deficit of moisture (the areas shown in white). However, the rains begin with a vengeance in late April and far exceed the water need of the region until early November. This seasonal shift from low-sun drought to high-sun surplus (the darkly shaded area) is typical of what the geographer calls a "monsoonal" climate. The fact that the accumulated warmth—i.e., the warmth index—totals more than 8.0 means that Soconusco is decidedly tropical, whereas the fact that the moisture index is well above 1.0 means that it is a humid climate that supports the growth of dense forest vegetation. (Data from Secretaría de Recursos Hidráulicos.)

monthly rainfall occurs usually in September when the onshore flow of moisture is reinforced by the occasional passage of a tropical storm or hurricane along the coast; in that one month alone the surplus normally totals more than 500 mm (20 in.). Although the rainfall tapers off rapidly in November as the winds begin to reverse their direction and blow off-land from the American Southwest, by the end of the rainy season the surplus of moisture has grown to more than 2200 mm (86 in.). Even after the deficit from the dry season is subtracted from this amount, it will be seen that Soconusco receives a surplus of over 1650 mm (65 in.) of rainfall each year, ensuring that the streams of the region run all year and that the vegetation over most of the area retains its character as a lush rain forest.

Naturally, the greatest climatic variations within Soconusco result from differences in elevation. Distinctly tropical species of trees, plants, and crops are found up to a height of just over 900 m (2950 ft), whereas typical subtropical plants climb to something over 1900 m (6200 ft). Warm-temperate types of vegetation, including maize, for example, find their ecological niche up to 2600 m (8500 ft), and cool-temperate species thrive up to 3000 m (9800 ft). Above that elevation, the predominant vegetation is composed of coniferous trees such as numerous types of pine and the fir. For all intents and purposes, the tree line is found at about 3250 m (10,700 ft), which means that the remaining 1000 m (3300 ft) before the crest is reached is characterized by a tundra, or páramo, type vegetation. (To be sure, all of these limits rise somewhat the farther one moves toward the equator.) Of course, through this entire climb not only does the precipitation *increase* with elevation but so does its effectiveness—because both the transpiration and evaporation rates *decrease*. Thus, the higher slopes of the mountains of Soconusco experience a super-humid climate; that is, the precipitation which they receive totals well over twice the amount which the plants or crops in the region require for their growth.

Reflecting this broad spectrum of habitats—ranging from brackish mangrove-laced lagoons at sea level to cloud forests and páramos on the mountain crests—is a richly diversified fauna of marine life, animals, and birds. With fish, shrimp, lobster, mussels, turtles, and aquatic birds inhabiting the coastal lagoons and deer, tapir, and peccary roaming the foothills, the earliest hunters-gatherers-fishers-and-fowlers who happened into Soconusco encountered such a richly diversified and bountiful food supply that it is likely that little more than 10 to 15 man-days per month were required to feed themselves.

Table 1 – Archaeological Chronology of Soconusco

Name of Phase	Dates	Characteristics
Chantuto A	4650–3400 B.C.	Hunters, gatherers,
Chantuto B	3400–2150 B.C.	fishers, fowlers
(?)	2150–1850 B.C.	
Barra	1850–1650 B.C.	
Locona	1650–1500 B.C.	Farmers
Ocós	1500–1350 B.C.	Pre-Olmecs
Cherla	1350–1200 B.C.	Olmec influence
Cuadros	1200–1000 B.C.	Olmecs
Jocotal	1000–950 B.C.	Olmecs
Early Conchas	950–850 B.C.	
Late Conchas	850–750 B.C.	

Source: "The Beginnings of Mesoamerica: Apologia for the Soconusco Early Formative," John E. Clark (director, New World Archaeological Foundation), p. 15.

Certainly, the needs for clothing and shelter were minimal. Indeed, the manner in which the local inhabitants saw fit to cover their nakedness was dictated more by modesty than by necessity. Protection from the elements involved little more than providing a place where the heavy rains and the broiling sun could be excluded, where foodstuffs could be stored, and where some measure of privacy could be obtained. If unwelcome insects and wild animals could be shut out as well, so much the better. For this purpose, the pole hut, or palapa, with its steeply pitched

Table 2 – Generalized Mesoamerican Chronology

Period	Dates	Major Sites
Preclassic		
Early	2000–1000 B.C.	San Lorenzo
Middle	1000–300 B.C.	La Venta, Monte Albán
Late	300 B.C.–A.D. 300	Teotihuacán
Classic		
Early	A.D. 300–600	Tikal, Copán
Late	A.D. 600–900	El Tajín, Uxmal
Postclassic		
Early	A.D. 900–1200	Tula, Mitla
Late	A.D. 1200–1500	Tenochtitlán

roof of palm fronds and relatively open-weave walls for ventilation was as basic and practical a solution as could be imagined.

To secure one's livelihood it was necessary to fashion both tools and weapons, and for these the fundamental raw materials were stone, bone, and wood. Although the granite ridges of southern Mexico afforded little workable stone for toolmaking, in the volcanic deposits of Guatemala were local outcrops of obsidian, which was highly prized for the razor-sharp edges it lent to arrowheads, spear points, and knife blades (Clark and Lee, 1984, 225). As people pushed their quest for sustenance into the water realm, at first they waded into the shallow lagoons on their own, and later ventured into deeper water buoyed by logs lashed together with vines and with casting-nets fashioned from the fibers of reeds or lianas. Still later they began making canoes by hollowing out large logs using either axes or fire or both. Thus, both on land as hunters and gatherers and in the coastal marshes and lagoons as fishers and fowlers, the residents of Soconusco were quick to develop a tool kit which allowed them to successfully exploit the rich variety of resources which they encountered. Thus, during even the earliest cultural horizon which the archaeologists working in this area have recognized — the so-called Chantuto period (4650–1850 B.C.) — it seems that the inhabitants of Soconusco enjoyed not only a freedom from want (i.e., a surplus of food) but also a considerable measure of leisure time. (See table 1 for the chronology of the Soconusco region as it has been developed by archaeologists of the New World Archaeological Foundation. In table 2 a more generalized chronology applicable to the entire Mesoamerican region is presented.)

Chapter 3

Strange Attraction: The Mystery of Magnetism

Some time about the beginning of the period which the archaeologists have called the Barra (1850–1650 B.C.), the people of coastal Soconusco appear to have developed a hierarchical society of sorts, for the construction of large, relatively elaborate houses on elevated, packed-earth mounds, apparently intended for the use of chieftains, was already being carried on (Clark, 1991, 13). The rise of an elite which could command the labor and no doubt the tribute of the working masses, even before a large-scale dependence on farming had evolved, suggests that the food supply was relatively secure, that an exchangeable surplus was available—at least for the favored few—and that a specialization of labor was under way. Population densities were high enough to imply that village life was commonplace and that a political superstructure, based certainly on genealogy but perhaps increasingly on wealth as well, was in the process of formation. Indeed, the peoples of Barra-phase Soconusco appear to have created the first ranked societies in all of North America.

There is some question as to when the first pottery appeared in Mesoamerica. Ceramic shards found at Puerto Marquez on the west coast of Mexico near Acapulco and dated to 2400 B.C. have recently been challenged by Clark and Gosser (1994, 1). They argue that the sophisticated Barra pottery found in coastal Soconusco represents some of the oldest dependably dated ceramic ware in Mesoamerica, but that two other pottery traditions were also in evidence within the region by 1600 B.C. One of these was in the central highlands of Mexico where Purrón pottery appeared, and the third center was in northern Veracruz where the so-called Chajil pottery has been unearthed. Although it is unclear whether these Mesoamerican complexes developed spontaneously and independently or whether they were influenced by ceramic complexes that are known to have existed in northern South America from one to four millennia earlier, it seems quite apparent that they owed little or no inspiration to each other. For example, whereas Purrón pottery was relatively austere and utilitarian, Barra was elaborately decorated and functionally specialized—the first typical of everyday housewares, the second of sophisticated luxury goods. Thus, if any conclusion can be drawn regarding the societies which produced these differing types of ceramics it must be that the Purrón, with its rather pedestrian plates, dishes, and cooking bowls, was far less affluent than the Barra, with its ornately slipped and highly burnished drinking goblets. Only with the passage of time did the two styles tend to converge, with the Purrón becoming more "fashionable" and the Barra more utilitarian (Clark and Gosser, 1994, 1–11).

Concurrent with the beginnings of their hierarchical social structure, the people of Soconusco also appear to have begun commemorating the likenesses of their chiefs in monumental sculptures. Not surprisingly, there is considerable difference of opinion among archaeologists regarding the relative age of the sculptures in question. Some contend that they date back to the Early Preclassic (ca. 2000 B.C.), while others assign them to the Late Preclassic (ca. 300 B.C.). Piña Chan, for example, saw them as "pre-Olmec" and dated them to 1200–800 B.C. (1981, 108), whereas Parsons confesses to being "slightly conservative" when assigning them a date about 500 B.C. (1989, 281). Because they can only be dated stratigraphically, it is not always easy to decide with which horizon they should be associated, especially when it is likely—as some authorities point out—that the sculptures themselves may have been moved and reerected in new locations. (The reader is referred to the arguments on this matter presented by John Graham [1989] and A. Demarest [1982].) However, due to the abrupt change in geology along the present Mexico-Guatemala boundary, virtually all such sculptures are found on the Guatemalan side of the line where the local bedrock is basaltic lava, in contrast to the Mexican side where it is granite. Thus, the very nature of the raw materials at hand was responsible for the geographic distribution of this art form, for the granite proved a more challenging and less rewarding material to work with than did the softer and more easily fashioned basalt. Consequently, large rounded boulders, often 1.5 m (5 ft) or more in diameter, were selected as the medium upon which either the rudimentary features of a head or a body were etched out in bas-relief. Only a minimal amount of carving was done, so in all cases the faces have a decidedly bloated appearance and the bodies are corpulent. Indeed, although no aspects of gender are depicted on these statues, archaeologists have called them the "Fat Boys" because of their apparent obesity.

Whether their rotundity is a reflection of the fact that the individuals being depicted were actually fat or whether it was simply a matter of laziness on the part of the sculptor in not carving away more material to make the representation more realistic, we can only speculate. What we do know is that clay figurines of obese chieftains were a stock-in-trade among somewhat later artisans farther north in Soconusco (i.e., the Mexican area), so, as in many early cultures, plumpness may well have been considered a sign of beauty and/or affluence (Clark, 1991, 21).

The heads that were depicted tended to have a fairly similar, generic appearance. If they were intended to highlight any individual differences, their sculptors appear to have been singularly unsuccessful, although a few of the heads do have some strikingly unique characteristics. One of them, for example, which is now in front of the little museum at La Democracia, Guatemala, bears a strong likeness to F.D.R., lorgnette eyeglasses and all. The bodies, on the other hand, almost invariably have the arms wrapped around them so the fingers of the hands nearly come together over the fullness of their abdomens, and the legs and feet often do a similar encircling act near the base of the sculpture.

Despite their crudity as works of "art," the "Fat Boys" have one char-

Figure 3.
One of the so-called "Fat Boy" sculptures located in the town plaza of La Democracia, Guatemala. Originally unearthed at nearby Monte Alto, it was labeled Monument 5 and is believed by Parsons to date to about 500 B.C. The magnetic properties of these sculptures were first discovered in 1979 by my student assistant, Paul Dunn of the Dartmouth class of 1981.

acteristic which lends them a true air of mystery: Many of them are magnetic! This discovery, made by my field assistant Paul Dunn and myself in 1979, took everyone, including the archaeological community, by complete surprise. If the sculpture depicts a head, it is often magnetic in the right temple. If it depicts a body, its magnetic pole is usually near the navel. However, no plugs of magnetic material have been inserted into the boulders at these points. Rather, at these places the sculptures appear to contain enough of a concentration of magnetite, or magnetic iron ore (Fe_3O_4), to attract a compass needle. Moreover, these localized zones of magnetism usually have an opposite pole of attraction situated scarcely more than 10 cm (4 in.) away. Thus, where the magnetic lines of force enter a head above the right ear, they usually leave it below the ear. And if the magnetic lines of force enter a body to the left of the navel, they tend to exit it to the right of the navel. Each sculpture, therefore, usually has two oppositely charged poles situated so closely together as to suggest a kind of U-shaped magnetic field.

Today, eleven of these statues are found in La Democracia, Guatemala, arrayed along two sides of the town's plaza, while the twelfth stands near the entrance to the museum. They reportedly were assembled from the newly cleared sugarcane fields surrounding the village sometime after 1950. Five of the statues depict human bodies, six depict human heads, and one is fashioned in the shape of a large bowl or receptacle. Of the humanoid figures, four of the five bodies have magnetic properties, as do four of the six heads. If we begin on the northwest corner of the plaza, we find the following patterns occurring in a counterclockwise direction:

West side of plaza:
    (1) Body; north pole to the left of navel; south pole to the right of navel
    (2) Head; north pole in the right temple; south pole below the right ear
    (3) Head; no magnetic property discernible
    (4) Body; no magnetic property discernible
    (5) Head; no magnetic property discernible
    (6) Head; north pole in lower right ear
East side of plaza:
    (7) Basin or receptacle; no magnetic property discernible
    (8) Body; north pole to the left of navel; south pole to the right of navel
    (9) Head; strikingly Olmec characteristics; no magnetic property discernible
    (10) Body; north pole on upper right side of body near waist; south pole on lower right side of body
    (11) Body; north pole in back of head; south pole on back of right side of head
On the front, or east side, of museum:
    (12) Head; a line of north polarity occurs along the middle of the nose, mouth, and chin; south pole at the bottom of the right ear

Of course, the enigma posed by the "Fat Boys" is really a double-barreled one. First, we must ask if their sculptors were actually aware of their magnetic property, and, if so, how they might have initially recognized it, especially in the presumed absence of iron. Or, on the other hand, might not the localization of magnetic poles within these sculptures have been simply a matter of chance? And second, if the magnetic property of each of these stones was indeed known, what prompted their sculptors to associate this mystical force with such localized parts of the body as the right temple and the navel?

Even if it does not take one magnet to detect another, at least it requires a sensitized piece of iron, such as the needle of a compass, to do so. Greek sources credit Thales of Miletus with having discovered the property of magnetism about 600 B.C., and the Chinese author Fu Chin mentions "a stone which can give a needle its direction" in a manuscript dating from 121 B.C. Yet, the Mesoamerican cultures, to the best of our knowledge, remained innocent of the use of metals until at least as late as the ninth or tenth century of the Christian era. Even then their acquaintance appears to have been limited to such metals as copper, silver, and gold, all of which have a lustrous appearance. Thus, how a Stone Age people familiar with chipping their primary tools and weapons out of materials like flint and obsidian stumbled onto the presence of magnetic iron ore in basalt boulders remains a mystery.

The most likely explanation which suggests itself is that the stone carver or sculptor may have noticed the attraction and/or adhesion of fine dust particles to the surface of the monument as he was cutting and polishing it. Naturally his curiosity would have been aroused as he observed that small fragments of the material he was working on were being drawn back to the stone from which he was trying to remove them. A less likely scenario for the discovery of magnetism might have been the chance placement of two small iron-rich boulders close to one another, causing them either to attract or repel one another depending on their polarity.

Whichever of these hypothetical reconstructions we favor, central to both of them is the notion of a stone carver working with a basalt boulder that is endowed with significant local concentrations of magnetite. Let us assume for the moment that, however the property of magnetism was first discovered in Mesoamerica, it is now known. The question which confronts us next is how and why it ever became associated with the right temple of the head or with the navel. What imaginative belief or line of reasoning impelled a stone carver to shape a carving of a head in such fashion that the magnetic lines of force came to a focus both above and below the figure's right ear? Or, when carving a massively rotund body, to make sure to position his subject in such a way that the magnetic lines of force entered and exited on either side of the figure's navel? Surely the sculptors' conscious repetition of this orientation in statue after statue cannot have been any more a matter of chance than if all the sculptures had been hit by lightning in precisely these same places. Clearly, something in the early Soconuscan culture seems to have dictated a linkage between the right temple and magnetism and between the navel and magnetism. What was it?

Naturally, one might conjecture that the connection being implied between magnetism and the head was the symbolization of a mental or spiritual link—perhaps the commemoration of creative thought. The fact that the right temple was selected rather than the left may simply have been a reflection of the overwhelming propensity of humankind for right-handedness; surely the ancient Soconuscan stone carver would not have been aware that control over the right side of the body is actually centered in the left hemisphere of the brain. Similarly, the association between magnetism and the navel may well have been a commemoration of the physical side of life—the continuity of the life-force from mother to child, despite the cutting of the umbilical cord at birth.

Had the "Fat Boys" been the only magnetic sculptures discovered in Soconusco, these speculations may have borne some semblance to the true nature of the thought processes which went through the minds of the ancient stone carvers. But, as luck would have it, the first magnetic sculpture found in the region (by the author at Izapa in southernmost Mexico in 1975) was not a depiction of a human head or body at all, but most likely the representation of the head of a turtle. (At least it was so identified by me and my student assistants, although we later learned that the personnel of the New World Archaeological Foundation who had initially excavated the sculpture had termed it a "frog.") Located some 30 m (100 ft) to the southeast of the ramped pyramid of Group F (on the northwest side of Highway 200), the turtle-head has a strong north polarity in its snout and an equally strong south polarity in the extreme back of its head. In addition, there is a weaker pole of south polar-

Figure 4.
The earliest magnetic sculpture discovered in Mesoamerica was this carved turtle-head located about 30 m (100 ft) off the main pyramid of Group F at Izapa, identified by the author in 1975. In the inventory of monuments compiled at the site, this was catalogued as A54.

ity located on the right side of its mouth directly under its right eye. Overall its magnetic attraction is such that it easily deflects a compass needle from 15 cm (6 in.) away, and the resultant field represents a good approximation of that demonstrated in a classic science-class iron filings experiment. In short, the turtle's head acts as a giant bar magnet.

Once the sculpture's magnetic properties had been identified and measured, I had my students undertake a survey of all the other exposed rock at the site to determine whether this was a unique or commonplace occurrence. When the survey revealed that this was the *only* magnetic sculpture which could be identified, I felt confident in concluding that its carver must have purposefully reserved this magnetite-rich boulder for his representation of a turtle. But then the question arose — what could have prompted him to associate magnetism with a turtle?

When I reported this discovery to the scientific community in the journal *Nature* in February 1976, the editor permitted me one sentence of speculation — to wit, might the carver have somehow come to associate the uncanny homing instinct of turtles with magnetism? At the time the article was published, such speculation had little supporting evidence to back it up. Indeed, one of the world's most eminent specialists on turtles, Archie Carr of the University of Florida, had only recently completed an intensive investigation of the navigational abilities of this reptile for the Office of Naval Research but was forced to conclude, after testing every conceivable hypothesis, that he still didn't know how they did it; when it came to magnetism, all he could say was that he could not rule it out (Carr, 1967, 171). Of possible relevance to the question at hand, however, was a reference which Carr made to a deep-carapaced black turtle that migrated from the Galápagos Islands to lay its eggs on a limited stretch of black-sand beach in Soconusco. Not only were other species of turtles well known within the region because of the periodic migrations of loggerheads and leathernecks north and south along the shore, but since time immemorial the turtle had served as one of the preferred sources of meat. Although Carr was of necessity cautious and noncommital, recent research in zoology increasingly suggests that not only turtles but also birds and even some worms may orient themselves by using the earth's magnetic lines of force, so what may have been a questionable speculation in 1976 has now become an area for serious inquiry (Seachrist, 1994, 661).

The "Fat Boys" assembled in La Democracia and the turtle-head found at Izapa do not exhaust the examples of magnetic sculptures found in Soconusco, however. Among the assortment of stone carvings brought together in the open-air "museum" at the El Baúl sugar plantation in Guatemala are not only the third-oldest known Long Count inscription (of which more presently) but also at least two statues possessing magnetic properties. One of these (discovered in 1979) depicts two men sitting cross-legged on a bench with their arms crossed on their chests. Both men have north magnetic poles where their arms cross, while under the bench upon which they sit are two south magnetic poles — the pole below the man on the left, as one faces them, being more pronounced than that beneath the man on the right. Nearby, a well-fashioned likeness of a rampant jaguar was found to have north magnetic poles in both of its paws, but no discernible south poles. (This discovery came to light when another student assistant and I revisited the site in 1993.) Finally, a small humanoid sculpture situated in the plaza of the village of Tuxtla Chica near Izapa was found in 1983 to be magnetic in the right side of its head.

Thus, the mystery of magnetism in Soconusco remains just that: Because the "Fat Boys" appear to have been the earliest of this collection of carvings, it seems that magnetism, however it was discovered, was first associated with human beings — at least in the cluster of statues found in the Guatemalan piedmont. Later, and in a different part of Soconusco — this time just over the present-day border in southern Mexico — another sculptor fashioned a carving of a turtle's head having a magnetic field focused on its snout. Does this mean that the local appreciation of magnetism had changed, or were the discoveries and associations of magnetism — first with people and later with the turtle — independent and unique? One can only continue to speculate. But what does seem certain, however, is that the property of magnetism had been identified in Soconusco, perhaps as early as 2000 B.C., but in any case well before the birth of Christ, and that it had been incorporated into the local statuary.

THE GEOGRAPHIC EXTENT OF
THE KNOWLEDGE OF MAGNETISM

Inasmuch as the property of magnetism came to be associated with statuary in Mesoamerica, it appears that the idea of its being useful or practical in any way seems not to have occurred to the native Americans. This may have been because it was never identified in any rock which was portable. Or perhaps it was never appreciated as being more or other than some kind of supernatural or magical force. Clearly, no understanding of its direction-finding properties — i.e., the principle of a compass — seems to have resulted from their discovery. However, some investigators have suggested — not too convincingly, it should be pointed out — that the alignment and layout of certain pre-Columbian ceremonial centers may have been carried out with such a device (Fuson, 1969, 504). Unfortunately, our knowledge of what the magnetic field was like at any given place on the earth's surface three thousand years ago is so sketchy that it would be hazardous to push such a hypothesis very far, especially in the absence of any kind of compasslike artifacts.

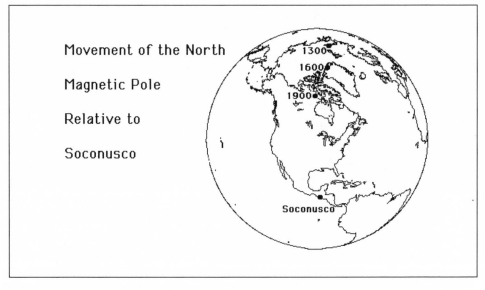

Figure 5.
Due to Soconusco's location almost in line with the historic movement of the north magnetic pole, compasses used in the region would have continued to experience a magnetic declination of virtually the same magnitude throughout the last 500–600 years, unlike those used at such a place as London, England. Whether the movement of the pole during prehistoric times followed a similar path is unknown.

In this connection, however, it is interesting to note that the known shift of the north magnetic pole has been from just north of the Russian islands of Novaya Zemlya sometime about the year 1000 to between Spitsbergen and Greenland about 1500 and into the Queen Elizabeth Islands of the Canadian Arctic by about 1900. While this shift represented a major change in declination for residents of the Old World—from about 15–20° east of north to the same relative distance west of north over roughly a thousand years—had this movement been viewed from the longitude of Soconusco (i.e., 90° W), it would have been hardly noticeable. In other words, a compass needle would have pointed almost due north throughout that entire time.

Finally, it should be noted that in Michael Coe's excavations at San Lorenzo in the late 1960's, a piece of magnetite measuring about 2.5 cm (1 in.) in length and a little less than a 0.5 cm (0.25 in.) in cross-section

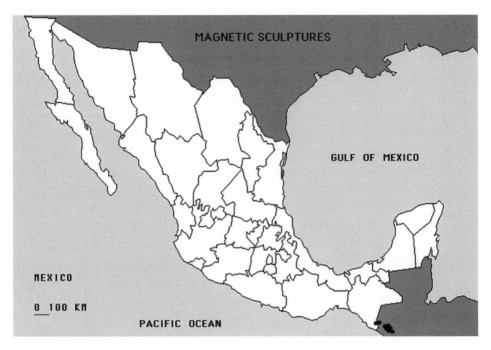

Figure 6.
All of the roughly dozen magnetic sculptures which are known from Mesoamerica are found within the volcanic bedrock zone of piedmont Soconusco. Several other areas of volcanic bedrock exist in Mesoamerica, such as in the Tuxtla Mountains and along the Transverse Volcanic Axis which runs across the center of Mexico from Citlaltépetl (Orizaba) in the east to Volcán Colima in the west; however, in none of them did the local inhabitants recognize the presence of magnetic iron ore as they apparently did in Soconusco. Because magnetism appears always to have been associated with relatively massive stone carvings which could not be easily moved, the knowledge of this force seems never to have diffused beyond the region.

was uncovered, prompting him to envision it as a part of a compass. Testing its direction-finding properties by floating it on a cork mat, Coe noted that it consistently oriented itself to the same point slightly west of magnetic north. More-exhaustive tests (involving the suspension of the magnetite bar on a thread) were later carried out by John Carlson, who reported that the object's orientational ability did not come closer than about 35° to the north magnetic pole (Carlson, 1975, 753). Thus, it could conceivably have been used as a direction-finder, but with scarcely more "preference" for north than for either east or west.

It appears, therefore, that the knowledge of magnetism never really diffused farther than Soconusco, and then only so far as the local bedrock remained basalt. With the possible exception of some localized use having been made of the magnetite bar found by Coe at San Lorenzo, it likewise appears that the potential use of geomagnetism for direction-finding was never fully appreciated by the early Mesoamericans. The author's discovery of the magnetic properties of first the turtle's head at Izapa and later the "Fat Boys" of Guatemala have served little but to add a dimension of "background static" to the whole equation of Mesoamerican intellectual development. This is because, apart from appreciating their awareness of the force, we know neither how they discovered it nor to what use they may have put it. My imaginative speculation that it may somehow have been associated with the homing instinct in the turtle leads me to insert one final footnote in passing: The Chinese, who are generally credited with having been the first culture to appreciate the direction-finding capacity of geomagnetism, use the term "black-turtle rock" as their description for basalt. Moreover, when they began fashioning compasses with which to navigate, many of their earliest models were made in the form of turtles. One hesitates to raise the question of independent invention versus diffusion — especially over such a vast expanse as the Pacific — but in any case the similarity or coincidence in thought patterns is rather striking. Thus, with no real answers at hand, we must conclude that, for the Mesoamericans, magnetism probably remained nothing more than an awe-inspiring marvel of nature.

Chapter 4

New Windows on the World:
Working the Land and Sailing the Sea

The first clear evidence of agriculture appears in Soconusco during the period which archaeologists have called the Locona (1650–1500 B.C.). What is not so clear, however, is whether the earliest cultivated plants were roots and tubers, such as manioc and sweet potatoes, or seed crops, such as maize, beans, and chiles. Certainly there is little question but that roots and tubers would have been easier for incipient farmers to cultivate because they are propagated from shoots and will grow under a wide variety of soil and moisture conditions, as Sauer has pointed out (1952); on the other hand, by the end of the Locona period maize definitely appears to have become the dominant crop, with various beans, chiles, and squashes supplementing the diet as well. (To commemorate the agricultural origins of the hierarchical society which arose in Soconusco at this time, Clark [1991, 13] suggests naming the people of the Early Formative cultures of the region the Mokaya, which is an anglicized verson of a Mixe-Zoque word meaning "corn people.") (See table 2 in chapter 2 for a chronology applicable to the entire Mesoamerican area.) It is also likely that by this same time cacao, a tree native to Soconusco, was being appreciatively exploited to prepare a "drink of the gods," at least for the noble elite of the society.

Although there is little reason to assume that the transition from a hunting-gathering-fishing-fowling economy into one where farming had become the main source of subsistence was anything other than gradual and unspectacular, during the Locona period cultural influences emanating from Soconusco began to spread northward and westward through the Tehuantepec Gap into the highlands of Oaxaca and the lowlands of the Gulf coastal plain. Archaeological evidence for this expanding sphere of interaction comes inevitably from such tangible artifacts as ceramics, but by no means were the cultural influences necessarily limited to them. We have already briefly noted that the earliest ceramics in Mesoamerica demonstrate three distinct geographic foci, only one of which was in Soconusco (the other two, you will recall, were in the central highlands of Mexico and on the northern coast of Veracruz); but if any of these foci was the recipient of influences from further afield, such as Central and South America, it would most likely have been Soconusco.

Now, while one does not have to predicate the beginnings of pottery in Mesoamerica on diffusion from South America, not to do so is to unnecessarily complicate its evolution in the Mexican arena. Indeed, in view of the complex life history of the maize plant as worked out by Mangelsdorf, it appears that regular and repeated contacts between Mesoamerica and the west coast of South America were already commonplace by at least 2000 B.C. (On the Atlantic side of the Americas, migrants from South America are known to have been island-hopping into the West Indies as early as 5000 B.C. (Adams, 1991, 43).

It would not be unreasonable, therefore, to suggest that sometime around 1500 B.C. the peaceful isolation of Soconusco may have been brusquely punctuated by the arrival on its shores of alien seafarers borne on large sail-bedecked log rafts. Although they came not as conquerors or religious missionaries, their arrival signaled the collision of two different worlds as surely as did the arrival of the Europeans on the opposite coast of the Americas some 3000 years later.

The newcomers may well have hailed from coastal Ecuador, which had access to timber resources for raft construction that were lacking farther to the south; in any case they were the cultural heirs of the civilizations which had arisen in the exotic river valleys of desert Peru perhaps some 800 years earlier. (The Cerro Sechín culture, now recognized as the forerunner of the so-called Chavín civilization, has been dated to 2300 B.C.) The ceramics which they brought with them—subsequently labeled as "Ocós" after the seacoast settlement near the mouth of the border river (Río Suchiate) between Mexico and Guatemala, which was first uncovered by the excavations of Michael Coe in 1960—were initially likened to the Chorrera pottery of southern Ecuador. Gareth Lowe, in his studies of Barra pottery somewhat later (1967), also saw South American antecedents for the Ocós ceramics. However, more recent research has called into question the dating of both the supposed South American donor cultures and the Mesoamerican recipient cultures, so the spread of pottery into the region may not have been as simple a south-to-north diffusion as first thought.

Whether or not the incipient, out-reaching civilizations of western South America provided the stimulus for sophisticated forms of pottery to the burgeoning chieftainships of Soconusco, it seems likely that these civilizations would have had other, perhaps even more earthshaking influences on these pullulant societies, for ideas travel as easily as objects or commodities. Similarities have been noted by some scholars in the religious motifs of the Andean area and the so-called Olmecs of Mesoamerica, so one cannot rule out the introduction of such influences. Indeed, it is not impossible that, interwoven in this religio-spiritual exchange, there may have been some measure of narcotic export, for Chavín was itself a key way station in the coca network emanating in the Amazon basin. Nor is it likely that these southern seafarers returned home empty-handed, for the timing of the Ocós contact coincides closely with the ultimate breakthrough of maize as the staple crop of the Americas. Thus, the return cargo may have included not only new and improved varieties of corn but also such highly prized commodities as cacao, quetzal feathers, and rubber, all of which Soconusco produced in abundance.

The Ocós phase (1500–1350 B.C.) may well have marked Soconusco's introduction to the world, at least to the expanding trade network of South America's developing civilizations. As such it was a period of unprecedented commercial activity and intellectual ferment. What

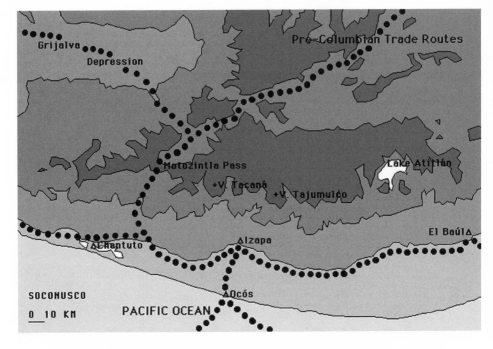

Figure 7.
Because of its wealth of exotic commodities, such as cacao, quetzal feathers, and rubber, Soconusco early became a nexus of trade routes on both land and sea. Undoubtedly one of the primary routes of movement since time immemorial has been along the Pacific piedmont, stretching northward into the heart of Mexico and southward into Central America. The rugged terrain back of Izapa most likely encouraged traders moving inland to utilize the Motozintla Pass, through which access to both the Grijalva Depression and the highlands of Guatemala could be gained. Sea contacts with South America had probably already been made ca. 1500 B.C. by residents from the Ocós area and northward along the coast as well.

had been a relatively somnolent, self-contained, and self-satisfied society whose horizons were limited by the mountains on the north and the unending ocean on the south had suddenly been thrust into contact with peoples of more advanced culture from "beyond the sea." Just knowing that they existed must have been a catalyst to engendering an entirely new "worldview" among the thinking elite of Soconusco. Surely, life could never again be the same.

Although it is impossible to assign an accurate date to it, there is a carved stone set into the middle of the north wall of the ball court at

Izapa (identified as Stela 67) which unmistakably portrays some aspect of Soconusco's early maritime contacts. (It should be noted that the archaeologists who excavated Izapa argue that *almost all* of the monuments found at the site were carved and set in place after 300 B.C. [Lowe, Lee, and Martínez, 1982, 23].) Whether these contacts were of an explorative or a commercial nature we will probably never know, but the depiction in question is both simple and graphic. It shows a (bearded?) man with arms outstretched standing in a boat crossing a body of water in which fish are portrayed beneath the waves and two long-nosed wind-gods are shown blowing from opposite directions. In the man's right hand is a cross. While some viewers of the carving are immediately tempted to see the latter as a Christian symbol, it could, of course, represent a cross-staff, which was an early navigational device. Naturally, how the carving is interpreted has a material bearing on the age which is assigned to it. In any event, it is obvious that the only navigable body of water within reach of Izapa is the Pacific Ocean (had canoe traffic through the coastal lagoons been depicted, it is unlikely that either waves or wind-gods would have played any part in the scene), but whether the carving testifies to a transpacific voyage or some coastal venture there is no sure way of knowing.

CALENDARS AND COUNTING

The 260-day sacred almanac

As long as the people of Soconusco gained their livelihood from hunting, gathering, fishing, and fowling, there was little need to take cognizance of the rhythms of nature, except in the most general way. Surely, everyone was familiar with the fact that the animals of the forest mated at certain times and not at others; that some of the trees of the forest flowered before the rains began; that sometimes the offshore current moved from the "left hand" and at other times from the "right"; that sometimes the sun rose over the sea and sometimes over the land; and that the migrations of the turtles along the coast or their trek up on the beaches to lay their eggs coincided with certain of these "signs" and not with others.

Even as they had consciously begun to collect the shoots of the

Figure 8.
In the middle of the north wall of the ball court of Izapa is this carving of a (bearded?) man
standing in a boat with a cross in one of his outstretched hands. In the waves beneath the boat fish
are depicted, and on each side of the boat long-nosed wind-gods blow from opposite directions. In
the inventory of monuments made at the site, this was catalogued as Stela 67.

manioc root or the sprouts of the sweet potato (both, by the way, of
South American origin) and stick them in the ground, it mattered little
whether they did so before or after the rains came. Manioc root grew
very readily, and as long as it was well cooked before it was pounded into
paste and made into dough-balls or tortillas, it could be counted on to
still the pangs of hunger whenever the hunters, fishers, or fowlers came
home empty-handed.

On the other hand, it was quite another matter when the serious cultivation of maize began (most likely around 1500 B.C.). Although there
never was a problem with adequate warmth in Soconusco, to have attempted to plant corn during the dry season was to flirt with disaster.
Even a mistake of a few weeks would mean that the seeds would dry out
and die before they could start to germinate. If, on the other hand, the
would-be maize farmer waited too long before planting his seed, the

rains would begin with a vengeance and then the likelihood of even getting the seed into the ground without having it wash away would be minimal. Thus, while maize held out the promise of a heavier yield and a
tastier and more nutritious foodstuff, it also demanded a greater awareness of the timing of the life-giving rains. To realize this promise, it was
now imperative, as never before, to understand the cycle of the seasons.

But where in the random chaos of Soconusco's nature could the
careful observer discern the first semblance of order or pattern? Certainly, changing directions of ocean currents and the migratory habits of
birds or turtles may have offered some clues, but they were too imprecise
a basis on which to establish an agricultural timetable. The answer most
likely had to be found in the movements of the sun itself, because it
could be seen to shift its positions of rising and setting from far out over
the ocean to well up beyond the mountains with a slow, day-by-day regularity. And, in the process, there were two days during this solar migration when the sun passed directly overhead — once on its journey from
the sea to the land and once on its way back again.

Anyone who made a conscientious effort to mark this rhythm — and
obviously some curious skygazer with the luxury of time at his disposal
did — would have realized that the most effective way to calibrate the
sun's zenithal passage was with a simple upright pillar or post (i.e., a gnomon). At noon on the days on which the sun passed directly overhead,
the pillar would cast no shadow whatsoever, whereas on any other days
of the year that would not be the case. Therefore, once the zenithal position of the sun had been ascertained, a precise "date" could be assigned
to it. However, either of the two days when the sun was directly overhead
was theoretically as good as the other on which to begin the count; why,
therefore, should the skygazer prefer one of these days to the other?

Of course, his choice could have been perfectly arbitrary. But more
likely, it was conditioned by another natural phenomenon of which he
could hardly have been ignorant. By sheer coincidence, a night or two before the southward passage of the vertical sun, the sky was literally bom-
barded with shooting stars which had their apparent origin in the northeast. This was the annual Perseid meteor shower, occasioned by Earth's
passage along its orbit through a rain of stellar debris which takes place
every August. Thus, our skygazer would have been witness to celestial

Table 3 – Dates of Zenithal Sun Positions within Mesoamerica

Latitude (°N)	Southward Passage	Northward Passage	Days Elapsed North-South	Days Elapsed South-North
13	August 18	April 24	116	249
13.5	August 17	April 26	113	252
14	August 15	April 27	110	255
14.5	August 14	April 29	107	258
15	August 12	May 1	103	262
15.5	August 10	May 2	100	265
16	August 8	May 4	96	269
16.5	August 7	May 6	93	272
17	August 5	May 8	89	276
17.5	August 3	May 10	85	280
18	August 1	May 11	82	283
18.5	July 30	May 13	78	287
19	July 28	May 16	73	292
19.5	July 26	May 18	69	296
20	July 23	May 20	64	301
20.5	July 21	May 23	59	306

Note: At the latitude of Izapa (14.8° N) the zenithal sun is overhead on August 13 on its southward passage and again on April 30 on its northward passage. These passages result in intervals of 105 days when the sun is north of Izapa and 260 days when it is south of Izapa.

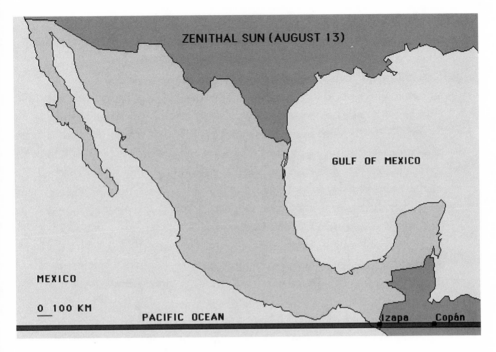

Figure 9.
The zenithal sun makes its southward passage over latitude 14°.8 N on August 13 and its northward passage over the same parallel 260 days later on April 30. Located along this line are both the Classic Maya site of Copán, hypothesized as the birthplace of the sacred almanac by Nuttall in 1928, and the Formative site of Izapa, first identified by the author as the hearth of the calendar in 1973.

fireworks which are virtually unequaled throughout the rest of the year, beginning usually on the night of August 11 but decidedly reaching their climax on the evening of August 12. The following day at noon, August 13, the sun passes through the zenith over Soconusco.

The signs were therefore unmistakable. First the heavens would give their notice. All night long the skygazer would watch as stars burst from behind the towering mountains to the northeast and flashed across the sky. And the following morning, as the sun arched higher and higher across the heavens, he would watch as the shadow it cast grew steadily shorter, until, as the sun reached its zenith, its shadow completely disappeared. This then, he decided, was the day for his count to begin.

On the other hand, our skygazer was faced with something of a philosophical dilemma. Counting days was an entirely new experience, because up to now if it had been necessary to enumerate anything, it may have been only such things as fish, or cacao beans, or quetzal feathers — all items which are discrete entities. Now that the day for starting the tally had arrived, the skygazer had to decide *when* in the day it actually became "Day 1." Certainly not at noon, because that was in the middle of a day that was still in progress. For someone accustomed to think in terms of entities rather than fractions, it was no more logical to conceptualize a part of a day than it was a part of a fish, a cacao bean, or a quetzal feather. It therefore must have seemed obvious that the day could not be counted until it was completed, that is, at sunset. In any event, this is the pattern of thought which Mesoamericans were to employ in all their subsequent mathematical computations. Like the odometer on an automobile recording the distance traveled, a unit of time measurement was not counted until it had been completed.

From clues in the internal structure of the Mesoamerican calendar, the event just described appears to have taken place about the middle of the fourteenth century B.C. (Confirmation of this date may be obtained by correlating the Maya calendar with our own using the Goodman-Martínez-Thompson value of 584,285. This reveals that the beginning day of the 260-day sacred almanac, 1 Imix, coincided with August 13 in the year 1359 B.C. Remember, too, that because historians do not recognize a "*year zero*," as astronomers do, when the designation "B.C." is employed it represents a date one year older than the minus value which the latter use. Thus, 1359 B.C. to a historian is −1358 to an astronomer.)

An interval of 260 days is, of course, divisible in many ways, and among the peoples of Mesoamerica two of the most common ways of grouping numbers were in "20's" and "13's." Both of these numbers can be thought of as global, or universal, "givens" known to virtually every people in the world. Obviously, the former module was the first to be discovered by humankind, for it represented a simple inventorying of an individual's own fingers and toes. The second module was much less obvious — at least, that is, until humankind began trying to measure time; then the importance of "13" quickly manifests itself, for this is the number of full moons within a "year." It is definitely possible that a lunar count of sorts was already in use in the Soconusco region, but if so, like all lunar counts it lacked the precision which our skygazer was hoping to achieve. In any case, the point that I am making is that it must have seemed quite logical for him to count in groups or "bundles" made up of either 13 or 20 days, and to assign each day in the "bundle" its own number and name.

Having started with the southward zenithal passage of the sun, the count was to continue until the sun once again passed overhead on its way northward. Depending where in Soconusco one was, that next shadowless passage took place about 260 days later—or as chance would have it, just as the skygazer was nearing the end of his 20-day count for the 13th time. (According to our modern calendar, this occurs on April 30.) Of course, the resolution of the 260-day cycle into these two key multiples may *not* have been totally a matter of chance. If, for example, our skygazer's initial count had been carried out at Chantuto—one of the coastal lagoons where some of the earliest population concentrations of Soconusco have been found—it may have produced an unwieldy interval such as 261 or 262 days between zenithal sun passages. In that event, he may have realized that a slight shift in geography would be repaid by a result which was mathematically far more harmonious. However, the temptation to move southward along the coast to find such a location was not great, because in that direction—once past Altamira—the protected lagoon environment was quickly replaced by long open beaches of wave-swept volcanic sand. By contrast the lush, well-watered slopes of the foothills must have seemed wonderfully attractive. Indeed, there is good evidence that the initial occupation of the area surrounding Izapa was already under way by 1500 B.C. (Ekholm, 1969, 19). It seems very likely, therefore, that if the felicitous 260-day interval had not been discovered quite by chance at a coastal site such as Altamira, a conscious decision must have been made to calibrate that interval at Izapa. And if that is true, then the choice of Izapa's location can well be cited as one of the first illustrations of applied astronomy and mathematics in the New World.

Having now "massaged" his count into workable modules, the skygazer had next to develop a system for identifying the individual days. (Because we do not know what the skygazer called the days of his count, we will use the terms that have come down to us from the Aztecs—who were his most recent heirs.) By assigning each day a number—never to exceed 13, but coupling it with one of 20 different names (signifying, for example, an animal, a plant, or a force of nature)—it would be possible to give it a unique identity within the 260-day count. Thus, beginning with "1 Alligator" and continuing with "2 Wind," "3 House," "4 Lizard," and so on, the count would run through its 13 numerical permutations of its 20 day-names and once again reach "1 Alligator" at the next zenithal passage.

So far so good. But as the skygazer continued his count, he may have been surprised to note that the third time he recorded a shadowless noon it was on a day he had labeled "1 Snake" instead of "1 Alligator." It is more likely, however, that he was well aware that the duration of the sun's journey to the north was considerably shorter than it was to the south, and perhaps he had already concluded that it was more realistic to measure time in "bundles" of 13 rather than of 20 days. The reason for thinking this is that, on this third passage of the zenithal sun, the elapsed time could not be evenly factored into any whole number of 20-day "bundles," but it could be conceived as 8 "bundles" each of 13 days duration. In any case, the cyclical regularity of such a pattern must have been reassuring: each interval of 20 13-day "bundles" in the south being followed by 8 13-day "bundles" in the north. Each time the zenithal sun passed overhead on its way south, a new 260-day cycle would begin on a day numbered "1" but with a different name. Thus, the skygazer watched as the beginning of each successive cycle shifted from "1 Alligator" to "1 Snake" to "1 Water" to "1 Reed" and then to "1 Earthquake." Only when the sun finally came back on its sixth round to "1 Alligator" again did he probably breathe a triumphal sigh of relief to think that he had mastered the secrets of its movements after all.

What the skygazer had discovered was that the cycle of the sun could be charted as 28 "bundles" of 13 days, with its zenithal passage alternating in groups of 20 and 8 "bundles" which repeated themselves every fifth time around. (With his discovery of the module of 28 "bundles," the Mesoamerican skygazer had unknowingly joined company with a small community of wise men searching the skies of India for similar clues to the cycles of the heavens. At about the same point in time and half a world away in distance, Vedic priests had also discovered the module of "28," only they used it in charting the motions of the moon rather than the sun. To them it appeared that the moon "rested" or "resided" for a period of 13 days in each of 28 "lunar mansions" as it moved across the sky during the course of a year.) Surely, anyone in Soconusco seeking to grasp the celestial rhythms could not fail to be impressed by the ingenious simplicity of the skygazer's formula. Here was a tool for alerting the farmer to the beginning of the rainy season that was easily understood by everyone: The rains would start on or about the time of the sun's northward passage (April 30), and the corn would be ready to harvest by the time of its southward passage (August 13). In short, it seemed that the skygazer had unlocked one of the most important secrets of the heavens.

That such an annual cycle must have had overwhelming significance to the early farmers of Soconusco is borne out by the seasonal rhythms that continue to dominate the lives of the local peasants in that region to this day. When Thomas Lee interviewed the native farmers in the vicinity of Izapa in 1964, he learned that they managed to obtain two corn crops a year without irrigation. The principal crop, the *temporada*, was planted in the last part of April or early May, just ahead of the beginning of the rainy season — and concurrent with the northward passage of the zenithal sun. Throughout the months of May, June, and July the rains would increase in intensity, and during this period of concentrated heat and humidity the farmer and his family were obliged to weed the corn every 20 days to keep down the competing vegetation. At the end of July the crop was ripe enough to break the stalk (a process called *doblada* or *dobla*), which terminated further growth in the plant and allowed the husk both to shed rainwater and to begin drying. The harvest of dry corn was begun in mid-August — at the time of the southward passage of the zenith sun — with the cobs being stored in an open bin.

The second crop, or *segunda*, was planted during the first three weeks of September (just before the autumnal equinox), the seeds being sown between the standing stalks of the *temporada*. Twenty days later the corn patch would be weeded and the stalks would be cut down. By December, just in time for the winter solstice, the *dobla* would take place, and during January the second crop would be harvested. On average, the yield of the *segunda* was about one-third less than that of the *temporada*, but field work was also less at this season. Though religious rituals marked each of these milestones of the agricultural year, Lee discovered that there were definitely more fiestas to be celebrated while the *segunda* was growing, because it demanded far less time and effort to produce. Thus, calendar, livelihood, and ritual all seem to have been closely interwoven from the very beginning (Lowe, Lee, and Martínez, 1982, 71–72).

If for no other reason than that the skygazer had (apparently) solved one of the fundamental riddles of their universe, he was hailed as a person of special insight, of uncommon intelligence, and one who enjoyed the favor of the gods because he had been allowed to share in the mysteries of the world. That he should have been exalted by the common people is scarcely any surprise. Although they may not have understood the significance of his discovery, they could not fail to be awed by its results. Knowledge was indeed power, and the skygazer would soon become an individual of respect and authority perhaps equal to or exceeding that of the "big man" or chieftain who exercised political control over the society—that is, if they were not already one and the same individual.

Whether any organized religion had existed before this time is difficult to know for sure. Certainly the invocation of magic to insure the success of the hunt or of the fish catch must always have been a part of the people's ritual life. In the same way, they must have worshiped or at least attempted to placate the forces of nature over which they had no control: the fiery eruption of volcanoes, the violent shaking of the earth, the cataclysmic waves which on occasion rolled in from the sea, the tempestuous storms which periodically lashed the coast, the frightening disappearance—however temporary—of the sun or moon during an eclipse, the fearsome strength and awesome beauty of the night-stalking jaguar, the "evil spirits" that caused people to sicken and often to die for no apparent reason. Even within their earthly paradise, there were numerous aspects of the people's surroundings which challenged their understanding. It was small wonder, then, that they so willingly entrusted the ministrations of these forces and spirits to that special elite of wise men in their midst who functioned as shamans or priests.

Again, ceramic evidence may shed some light on the nature of the Soconuscans' early religious beliefs. We have already spoken about the numerous representations of obese males, or man-animal figures which have been interpreted as supernatural or shamanistic symbols of authority. In contrast to these are the literally hundreds of clay figurines of voluptuous nude women which have been found (Clark et al., 1987, 11). In these, a naturalistic depiction of the female body has been accompanied with detailed attention to hairstyles and jewelry, giving them a vibrant, erotic quality. It is probable, therefore, that in the initial stages of Soconusco's cultural evolution the presence of a fertility cult may well have constituted one of the people's principal forms of religious expression.

What is certain is that once a method for reckoning time was developed it allowed for more formalization of religion to take place. Now the celebration of periodic rituals or ceremonies could be scheduled and/or orchestrated in advance. Special days could be set aside for religious observance, with different spirits or forces being accorded recognition at different times of the year. The very days themselves, with their identities distinguished by numbers and names, acquired "personalities" — some auspicious, some malevolent, and some neutral. It soon came to be believed that a person had his or her personality and fortune determined by date of birth. In short, possibly within the span of a single generation the calendar became an integral part of the people's spiritual and private lives, for almost all aspects of their existence seemed to be bound up with time and its cyclical patterns.

The ready adoption of the 260-day sacred almanac by the common people gave the practice of religion a new currency and centrality in their society — and the priestly caste a new stature and prominence. The importance of knowing how to maintain the day-count, when to schedule the proper rituals, and how to interpret the auguries of the different events that occurred could no longer remain the property of a single skygazer. To allow for the continuance and transmittal of this knowledge, it must be passed on to other and younger members of the society in an orderly fashion. Because theirs was a preliterate society, this was most likely done through the rote memorization of passages pregnant with meaning — perhaps in the form of rhyming verses to serve as mnemonic devices—a sort of poetry laced with scientific knowledge. Numerical records, on the other hand, could have been kept as tallies of ticks marked on a wooden board with a piece of charcoal, just as shamans in the mountains of Guatemala continue to do to this day.

But these "secrets" could not be shared with just anyone. If the priesthood was to maintain its own privileged position of power and authority, its fund of knowledge could only be imparted to individuals who could be entrusted to guard it as something exclusive and special—individuals whose attention and dedication to this knowledge must transcend all of their other earthly concerns. It seems clear that the solution which the priestly caste found to ensure such complete devotion on the part of its young novitiates was not unlike that practiced in other societies elsewhere in the world: remove the worldly distraction of carnal desires by insisting on celibacy and/or sexual abstinence. However, archaeological evidence (from the Olmecs, Zapotecs, and Maya) strongly suggests that verbal injunctions were not insurance enough, and that the price of admission to the priestly caste may well have come to involve castration if not total emasculation. (There are numerous indications in the art of these peoples that such a practice was not necessarily a fate reserved solely for conquered captives, but that it was also a ritual of a religious nature. Piña Chan, for one, makes reference to this in his final work on the Olmecs [1989, 191].)

On the one hand, our skygazing priest must have reveled in the power which his knowledge had given him. His "discovery" had not only brought him heightened respect and enhanced authority personally, but it had also laid the groundwork for the intensification of religious activity and the emergence of an entire social class whose very raison d'être was the calendar itself. On the other hand, it must have been terribly disquieting for him to realize that, after a few rounds of the calendar, it was not really working as he had first assumed it would. Yes, there were always 260 days between the time that the sun passed overhead on its way south and the time it passed overhead again on its way north. But the days on which these solar passages occurred did not continue to take place on "1 Snake," or "1 Water," or "1 Reed," anymore. Instead they began falling on later days, such as "2 Wind," "3 Deer," and "4 Monkey." Certainly there was nothing to be gained and everything to be lost by admitting that the calendar was defective. This privileged bit of information must surely not be shared with anyone but a member of the inner sanctum.

But more than that, should the calendar continue to deviate further and further from the observable realities of the meteor shower or the beginning of the rainy season, even the untutored masses would gradually become aware of its shortcomings. Where would the priest's credibility be then? For his own reputation's sake, let alone for reasons of intellectual honesty, he would have to pin down the cycle of the seasons more accurately than he had on this first attempt.

The 365-day secular calendar

Where the priest had erred, of course, was in concluding that the cycle of the sun could be measured in 28 "bundles" of 13 days. This meant that he had equated its annual migration through the heavens with an interval of 364 days, when in actuality it took about a day and a quarter longer than that. Thus, after only four years had elapsed his count was already off by 5 days. This might go unnoticed by the commoners at first, but certainly, as the error increased with each passing year, it wouldn't be long before "the cat was out of the bag."

But, if the sun couldn't be pinned down accurately enough by its zenithal passages, how might the priest fix the length of the year with yet greater precision? He knew, of course, that the sun moved across the heavens between two fixed points. At its southernmost extreme, however, the sun both rose out of and set into the unmarked sea, so there was no means of fixing its position there; but at its northernmost turning point, the sun both rose out of and set into the great wall of mountains which towered above Soconusco's inland approaches. By patient observation of the sun as it neared its northern extreme he reasoned that he could find a place from which its turning point could be calibrated against a permanent marker in the landscape — namely, a mountain.

Once this idea had occurred to our skygazing priest, he must have quickly set about searching for the vantage point from which this phenomenon could best be observed and against a landmark where it could best be calibrated. The mountains to the northwest were neither so lofty nor so sharply defined as those to the northeast, so the latter would definitely meet his needs better. The peaks on the northeastern horizon were, of course, the cones of a great row of volcanoes that began with them and stretched far to the southeast through what today are the countries of Guatemala, El Salvador, Nicaragua, and Costa Rica. One of these great volcanoes would lend itself splendidly for his purpose; indeed, it promised to add an element of theater to his endeavor because what the priest was preparing to do was to demonstrate that the annual cycle of the sun could be measured by the interval between successive risings of this fiery orb out of the crater of one of the great mountains of fire.

We can only imagine with what anticipation he approached the "moment of truth," knowing how awestruck his menial subjects would be as it transpired. But, not content with the forthcoming theatrics which would accompany his "discovery," he was also polishing up the details of his new calendar and the means of employing it so that his second attempt at mastering celestial mechanics would be far more successful than his first, less sophisticated effort.

As his principal modification, he now recognized that the year had 365 days and not 364. But, because he was hampered by a mind-set that failed to recognize fractions (after all, you either have a finger or a toe or you don't!), even if he had been aware that the year was almost a quarter day longer yet, he could not have conceptualized it. He therefore visualized the year as being composed of 18 "bundles" of 20 days each, leaving 5 extra days left over at the end of the year. Each of the 18 "bundles" he recognized as a unit (which we would term a "month," although it clearly had nothing to do with an interval defined by the moon).

Moreover, he had come up with another ingenious concept, again apparently stimulated by his inability to recognize fractions. Although he understood that his new time-count would begin with the rising of the sun, he was careful to note that the day it was initiating was not really a day until it had finished — in the same way that even though the zenithal sun passed overhead at noon, the day on which it occurred was not a day by the count until the sun had set. Thus, although there were 20 days in each of his 18 "bundles," he chose to number them 0 through 19. The concept of zero in itself was ingenious, because it didn't just symbolize "nothing"; it really meant "in progress," because until it was "com-

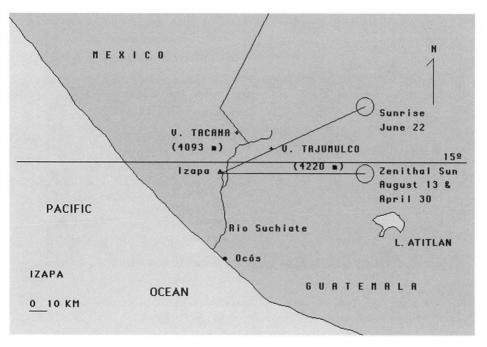

Figure 10.
The site of Izapa lies on the right bank of the Río Suchiate, which today forms part of the boundary between Mexico and Guatemala. In addition to its key latitudinal location with respect to the zenithal sun passages on August 13 and April 30, Izapa is also sited in such a fashion that the position of the rising sun at the summer solstice is marked on the northeastern horizon by the cone of Tajumulco, the highest mountain in all of Central America.

pleted," there was no place for 1. And not until day 19 was completed could one speak of the first "month" or "bundle" having been finished. The day literally did not have a discrete identity until it was a matter of history; or, to put it another way, it had not truly existed until it was over!

Although it may have been the skygazing priest's intent to replace his first attempt at a calendar with this second, more accurate version, he probably did not long entertain such a notion. Already accepted and "sanctified" by the use of the masses, the 260-day sacred almanac had assumed such a place in their lives that it could not easily be rescinded. (Its continued prominence in the agricultural and ritual cycle of Soconusco, as demonstrated earlier, is adequate proof of that.) Even if it did not

Figure 11.
The volcano Tajumulco looms up on the northeastern horizon as seen from Izapa. With an azimuth of 65°, its peak marks the sunrise at the summer solstice (June 22).

work to predict the coming of the rains, it had already become such a central feature of the people's ritual existence that to attempt to expunge it would have meant demolishing the very underpinnings of their religious beliefs.

As the summer solstice neared, it was clear that the priest had yet another momentous idea in the back of his mind. Already, at his direction, his scouts had narrowed down the ideal vantage point from which to observe the impending sunrise. So, when his retinue of followers trekked with him up into the foothills on the evening of June 21, it was to a site where the forthcoming "celestial spectacular" could not have gone unappreciated by even the most simple of peasant farmers. The following morning, the glowing disk of the sun rose out of the crater of the loftiest volcano in all of Central America—Tajumulco, in what is today southwestern Guatemala. And it was on this site—from where the 260-day sacred almanac and the new 365-day secular calendar could both be calibrated—that the priest decreed the building of the first great ceremo-

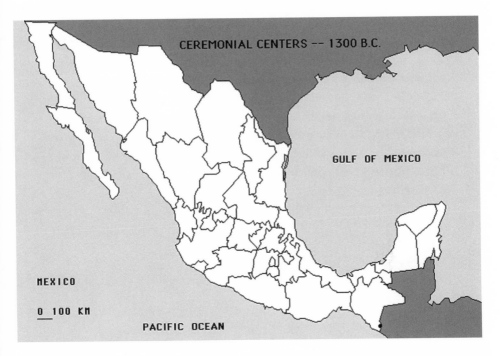

Figure 12.
Around 1300 B.C. Izapa was probably the only semiurbanized agglomeration in all of
Mesoamerica. It was the direct outgrowth of the appearance of ranked chiefdoms in the
Soconusco region, which first emerged some two to three centuries earlier. Through most of
its early history it probably functioned more as a religious retreat and pilgrimage site than as
a center of population and trade.

nial center in all of Mesoamerica, a place whose name has come down to
us as Izapa.

Again, by using the Goodman-Martínez-Thompson correlation
value of 584,285, it is possible to fix the date of this event according to
our own calendar with perfect accuracy. As I programmed my computer
to search for the beginning of the secular calendar, I could confidently
start with the correspondence between Maya and Julian dates which
Goodman provided us. But in addition, one further assumption was required: that the first day of the 365-day secular calendar — known to the
Maya as 0 Pop — must have coincided with the summer solstice. If we

accept that assumption, we find that 0 Pop did in fact fall on June 22 during the years 1324 to 1321 B.C. (i.e., the astronomical years −1323 to −1320). (Of course, were we to employ June 21 as the date of the summer solstice, this would advance the correlation by four years, i.e., 1328–1325 B.C. instead.) Thus, it is entirely conceivable that, as has been sketched out in the scenario above, both the 260-day sacred almanac and the 365-day secular calendar were the product of the same individual—a "New World Hipparchus," as Sylvanus Morley has termed him—for the beginning dates of both counts are separated by little more than 30–35 years!

Chapter 5

The Olmec Dawning

Momentous as the developments of the Ocós period had been within Soconusco, other regions of Pacific Mexico were also being brought increasingly into the orbit of the expanding civilizations of South America during this same time frame. In the alluvial lowlands of what today are the states of Colima, Jalisco, and Nayarit, the so-called Capacha ceramic complex had appeared about 1450 B.C. One of its hallmarks was a type of stirrup jar whose origins may be traced to the Machalilla culture, another variant of the Chorrera culture from Ecuador. From its toehold on the western coast of Mexico, the Capacha culture managed to penetrate into the interior of the country by following the valley of the Río Grande de Santiago, and sometime around 1300 B.C., distinctive chamber burials — again suggestive of South American design — were being cut into the volcanic ash as far inland as the upland site of El Opeño in Michoacán state.

Returning once more to Soconusco, we find that archaeologists working in that region have set off the century and a half between 1350 and 1200 B.C. as a distinct phase in the cultural evolution of the area — a

period which they have called the Cherla. The distinguishing characteristic of this period they have likewise identified as "Olmec influence."

The very mention of the Olmecs prompts us to question: Who were
these people, and where did they come from? Certainly, from the time of
the discovery of the very first "Colossal Head" in southern Veracruz state
in 1862 until well into the 1980's, most of the finds which corresponded
to an Olmec art style could be traced to what has been called by Ignacio
Bernal "the Olmec metropolitan area," located in the Gulf coastal plain
of Mexico. Naturally, this would imply that if the Olmecs originated in
the general area of Veracruz and Tabasco states, they would have had to
have moved *southward* across the Isthmus of Tehuantepec to have had
any appreciable influence on the cultural evolution of the Soconusco region. However, such a postulated movement, especially at the time of the
Cherla period, is totally unsupported by any archaeological evidence. On
the other hand, there are numerous indicators that a vigorous movement
in the opposite direction — toward the north — was going on at precisely this time, in which case the so-called Olmec influence must have
been a native-born development emanating from Soconusco itself.

One such indicator is the Ocós ceramic style (Clark prefers to call it
the "Locona"), which appears to have had a major northward diffusion at
this time. Another indicator, less exactly datable to be sure but falling
well within the time frame in question, is the degree of differentiation
which has taken place between two branches of the Mayan language —
the tongue that was spoken throughout the Gulf coast region of Mexico
as least as far back as 1500 B.C. Morris Swadesh, a renowned proponent
of glottochronology, or the dating of languages by their relative differentiation from each other, has argued that Huastec, which is now spoken in
the far north of Veracruz state, was separated from Yucatec, which is the
indigenous language spoken in the area of Campeche and the Yucatán
Peninsula, sometime during the thirteenth century B.C. Although he
does not suggest a mechanism for accomplishing such a "split," the most
likely possibility would have been the driving of a "wedge" into the Gulf
coast region by a non-Mayan-speaking group. Such a wedge, in turn,
would far more likely have been the result of a sustained overland movement from the south than an episodic seaborne invasion from the north.
The continued presence of peoples of Zoquean speech at the northern

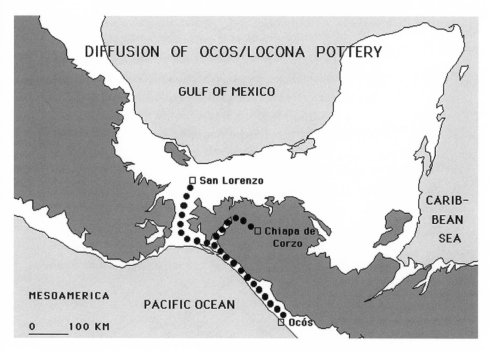

Figure 13.
The diffusion of Ocós/Locona pottery out of Soconusco was no doubt paralleled by a diffusion
of sculptural techniques as well. This contention is further strengthened by the realization that
the absence of any stone whatsoever in the alluvial plains of eastern Mexico means that a tradition
of stone carving can scarcely have arisen spontaneously there. When all such evidence is combined
with what we know about the origins of the calendar, it becomes apparent that the conventional
theories of Olmec diffusion outward from the Gulf coastal plain must be turned quite around.

end of the Tehuantepec Gap (the Popolucas in the eastern foothills of
the Tuxtla Mountains), in the Oaxaca highlands to the west of the Gap
(the Mixe), and in the Chiapas highlands to the east of the Gap (the
Zoque) — all of whom were linguistically related to the recently extinguished Tapachulteca dialect spoken in Soconusco — testifies to the existence of a language whose geographic distribution once bridged the Isthmus of Tehuantepec from the Pacific to the Gulf.

In the field season of 1983, I and a student assistant journeyed into
the backcountry of southern Mexico to visit and record the languages of
the three extant groups of Zoque-speakers. Using a 100-word diagnostic
glossary devised by Swadesh, we attempted to make at least a crude

statistical analysis of their degree of interrelationship. For whatever merit it may have, our analysis revealed that about two thirds of the words in the glossary were either shared by or very similar to one another in the Popoluca and Zoque languages, but that only about half of the words were recognizably similar between the Mixe and Zoque tongues. Of the three peoples, the Mixe were decidedly the most aloof and suspicious — traits that likewise correlated very well with their high degree of isolation.

However, at the time we made this journey into the backcountry of Mexico, I was unaware of the study made in 1976 by the linguists Campbell and Kaufman. They had concluded that the "Olmecs at least in part were Mixe-Zoque speakers" and that it made no difference to their hypothesis whether the Olmec origins were in the "Veracruz-Tabasco, Morelos, or northeastern Oaxaca" areas (Campbell and Kaufman, 1976, 89–99). They were able to trace about 450 loan words in adjacent tongues which clearly had come from Mixe-Zoque and which demonstrated that the donor people had had a fairly sophisticated culture already around 1500 B.C. Not only were there many basic cultigens on that list, but also included were suggestive terms implying a vigesimal counting system, a calendar, measurement, divination, human sacrifice, "some form of writing," and the names of creatures such as the alligator and iguana. Perhaps constrained by the conventional view that the Olmecs had emanated from the Gulf coastal plain (or some region adjacent to it), Campbell and Kaufman expressed surprise that such "distant" languages as Xinca and Lenca in Central America also showed a strong Mixe-Zoque influence; however, for anyone recognizing Soconusco as their original core area (as I have argued here), finding their influence among the adjacent peoples in El Salvador and Honduras comes as no surprise at all.

The evidence seems clear, therefore, that sometime in the Cherla period, an extensive movement of Zoque-speaking peoples spread out of Soconusco, across the Tehuantepec Gap and into the Gulf coastal plain of Mexico, bringing with them their characteristic Ocós-emulated pottery. Not only was this movement forceful enough to send the original Maya dwellers of the region scurrying for safety both to the north and to the east — the Huastecs and the Yucatecs, respectively — but its cultural

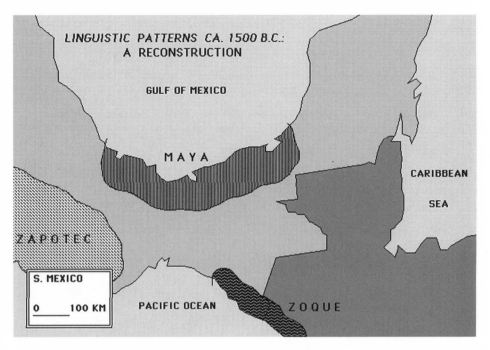

Figure 14.
To explain the pattern of distribution of native languages which existed in southern Mesoamerica at the time of the Spanish conquest, it is necessary to look back at the cultural geography of the region nearly three millennia earlier. At that time it appears that three distinct language families could be identified in the region: Along the entire Gulf coast, Mayan was spoken, whereas in the highlands of Oaxaca to the southwest, Zapotec was the principal tongue. In Soconusco the dominant language at the time appears to have been proto-Mixe-Zoque.

characteristics were so distinctive that for the first time in the panoply of Mesoamerica's evolution we can speak of the appearance of an Olmec art style. Coming so closely in the wake of the development of both the sacred almanac and the secular calendar, we can ask: What prompted this explosive northward expansion? Was it the result of some great natural disaster in Soconusco, such as a volcanic eruption, a cataclysmic earthquake, a devastating hurricane, or a monstrous tsunami? Or some terrible internecine conflict which forced thousands of refugees to flee for their lives into the sparsely inhabited jungles of the north? Perhaps the explanation is that even resource-rich Soconusco had been pushed to the limits of its "carrying capacity," and overpopulation had finally obliged

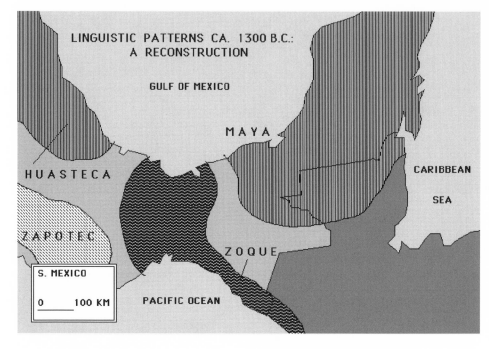

Figure 15.
According to Swadesh, about 3300 years ago the Mayan language family was split into two
groups — the Huastecs along the northern Gulf coast and the remainder of the Mayan-speaking
peoples to the south and east. The author hypothesizes that this was the result of an overland
invasion across the Tehuantepec Gap by Zoque-speakers, for this would have been at precisely
the same time that the sacred calendar was being diffused from Izapa to the so-called Olmec
centers of the Gulf coast. The diffusion of language was just one of several cultural traits which
appear to have taken place at the same time.

the Zoques to expand into the territories of their Maya neighbors to the
north. Or, might the recently acquired calendars, with their implicit
recognition of the importance of time and its fundamental role in religious life and ritual, have impelled them to launch a missionary "cru-
sade" into these outlying regions? Certainly, any of these scenarios is possible, though some are more probable than others. All that we can be
sure of is that the migration did in fact take place; what triggered it, we
will probably never know.

Although no archaeologist or linguist that I am aware of has ever
hypothesized such a migration as that which I have described here, the

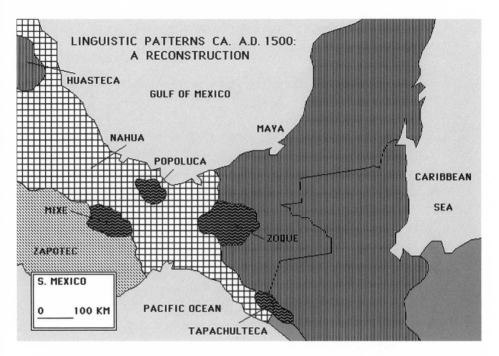

LINGUISTIC PATTERNS CA. A.D. 1500:
A RECONSTRUCTION

HUASTECA

GULF OF MEXICO

MAYA

NAHUA

POPOLUCA

CARIBBEAN

SEA

MIXE

ZAPOTEC

ZOQUE

S. MEXICO

0   100 KM

PACIFIC OCEAN

TAPACHULTECA

Figure 16.
The vigorous expansion of the Nahuatl-speaking Aztecs into southern Mesoamerica in the fifteenth
century A.D. reshuffled the linguistic patterns of the region considerably. As the Aztecs pushed
south to open trade routes to Soconusco, the Zoque-speaking peoples fled into the adjacent
mountain areas to take refuge. As a result, people identified today as Popolucas inhabit the eastern
foothills of the Tuxtlas, the Mixe withdrew into the highlands of Oaxaca, and the Zoque pulled
back into the uplands of Chiapas. The original Zoquean core of Soconusco was all but submerged
by Nahuatl-speakers, although the Tapachultecas managed to retain their own linguistic identity
in the mountains back of Izapa until the latter decades of the nineteenth century.

geographic realities of its having taken place are virtually indisputable.
No other single event or series of events can as logically explain (1) the
separation of the Huastecs from the rest of the Maya family, (2) the scattered, refugelike distribution of Mixe-Zoque speakers in the mountains
of southern Mexico, or (3) the presence of Mixe-Zoque influences
among the peoples of El Salvador and Honduras. While I defer entirely
to Swadesh as to its timing, I am happily reassured by how closely his
glottochronology accords with my own dating of calendrical diffusion.
By the same token, I am heartened that many respected archaeologists

have come to believe that the origins of Olmec high culture may ultimately be traced to the Soconusco region (Adams, 1991, 43).

ORIENTATIONS AND ALIGNMENTS: MARKING TIME IN SPACE

Formula 1: "The mountain where the sun turns"

The earliest known ceremonial center which has been credited to the Olmecs is San Lorenzo, dating to ca. 1350 B.C. — i.e., just at the break between the Ocós and Cherla phases of Soconuscan cultural development. San Lorenzo has intrigued archaeologists with its many sophisticated features: the artificial terrace some 50 m (160 ft) high on which it is built (which had been fashioned, some researchers claim, in the shape of a flying bird); its extensive stone-lined drainage system; and its numerous sculptures, many of them "Colossal Heads" which appear to have been toppled into adjacent ravines and ritually buried. To the geographer, though, its location is of special interest.

Location, of course, may be defined in several different ways. For example, it can be expressed *mathematically,* in terms of latitude and longitude, but in the context of the Olmecs, who were unfamiliar with such concepts, such a definition would be meaningless. Location can also be expressed in *relative* terms, that is, one place may be defined in relationship to another. Using such a definition, the location of San Lorenzo, relative to the Zoque homeland in Soconusco, is seen to be *adjacent*; in other words, if the region of Soconusco itself was *central* to the life of the Zoques, then San Lorenzo was the nearest major Olmec ceremonial center to that area. Thus, its geographic proximity to Soconusco, together with its being the oldest known Olmec center, strongly suggests that it was founded as part of the northward expansion of Zoque-speaking peoples in the fourteenth century B.C.

In speaking of urban settlements, of which San Lorenzo certainly was an incipient example, the geographer may employ two further definitions of location as well. One is *site* — the description of the actual plot of ground on which the settlement was founded — and the other is *situation* — the relationship of a place to its surroundings. The former definition, for example, involves defining a place in terms of being located on a river terrace, on an island, at the top of a hill, or in the midst of a swamp. Although the terms used may be generic, such as terrace, island, hill, and swamp, the actual site of any given place is specific and unique. Hanover, New Hampshire, for example, is located on a postglacial river terrace known as the Hanover Plain, situated on the left bank of the Connecticut River, just above the mouth of Mink Brook — a totally specific site, occupied by no other settlement. New York (or originally New Amsterdam) was located at the southern tip of Manhattan Island, where the Hudson River empties into New York Bay, whereas Venice, Italy, was founded in the marshes just to the north of the delta of the Po River on the coast of the Adriatic Sea.

Defining a place's *situation* is to spell out its relationship to its surroundings. For example, Hanover, New Hampshire, has one state highway traversing it north-south along the Connecticut Valley and a bridge linking it with Vermont across the river; consequently, it does not command or interact with a very large hinterland, and as a result has far fewer commercial and industrial establishments than does a population node just five miles away that serves as the intersection of two railroads, two interstate highways, two federal highways, and two state highways, and that furthermore boasts a regional airport. In contrast, to describe the situation of New York City is to define the largest, busiest, most populous and extensive hinterland of any metropolitan area in the United States. In a comparative sense, Venice, despite its poor site (which has resulted in the city's sinking into the marsh), had a premium situation during the Middle Ages when most of Europe north of the Alps formed part of its hinterland, thanks to the easy access provided by the Brenner Pass.

The comparison of Venice and New York makes another point, namely that the significance of places changes through time. When Venice was at the peak of its grandeur, there was no such place as New York. And there is nothing in the cards that says that New York will forever remain the most important urban agglomeration on the North American continent. By the same token, the decision of the Olmecs about 1350 B.C. to locate San Lorenzo precisely where they did was obviously colored by concerns which were important then but may be all but forgotten today.

However, before we examine the specifics of San Lorenzo's location we should address a more general question relating to the absence of Olmec settlements *between* Izapa and San Lorenzo: Why were there no ceremonial centers founded in the intervening areas of Soconusco and Tehuantepec? Perhaps the most striking reason for this relative void in settlement was the local geography. As one moves northward through Mexico along the coast of Soconusco, not only does the coastal plain grow narrower but it also becomes considerably drier. By the time one reaches the vicinity of Tonalá, the foothills pinch close to the lagoons, the rain forest degrades into scrub, and the rivers have shriveled from perennial watercourses into intermittent streams. There simply was no hinterland capable of supporting an urban center of any size, at least in terms of the technological levels of the Olmecs. By the time the Pacific coastal plain opened into the southern approaches of the Tehuantepec Gap, the countryside had degenerated into a hostile semiarid region of low, thorny trees. As a people native to the rain forest, they did not again encounter an environment in which they felt "at home" until they had crossed over the divide of the Tehuantepec Gap into the vast tropical lowland of Mexico's Gulf coast. There they found a region of huge, me-andering rivers winding their way through a canopy of lush green forest many times the size of their original home in Soconusco — a beckoning land with whose ecological challenges and possibilities they were already thoroughly familiar.

But how was it that they opted to build their first great ceremonial center at San Lorenzo? For one thing, the site which they chose was on the south bank of a branch of the Río Coatzacoalcos, the principal river draining the Gulf coast lowlands at the northern entrance to the Tehuantepec Gap. The lack of stone in the alluvial lowlands of eastern Mexico meant that the Olmecs had to quarry whatever building material they needed in the Tuxtla Mountains of southern Veracruz state where local volcanism had produced two or three stratovolcanoes and a profusion of cinder cones. (It is generally thought that the Olmec quarries were lo-cated near Punta Roca Partida on the north coast of the Tuxtlas.) From these seaside quarries, they would have had to freight the huge basal-tic blocks from which they carved the "Colossal Heads" about 100 km (60 mi) along the coast before entering the river and poling them 50 km

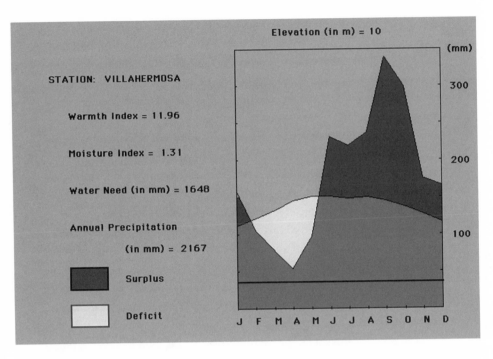

Figure 17.
The climatic station of Villahermosa is typical of the Gulf coastal plain of eastern Mexico, the region Bernal has termed the "Olmec metropolitan area." Its water need, or temperature curve, varies a little more than that in Soconusco, because the low-sun months are somewhat cooler than on the Pacific coast. This is due to the outbursts of cold air ("northers") that sweep down from Texas at this season, bringing some rain. As spring arrives and the northers cease, a dry season is experienced until May when the summer monsoonal rains begin. The peak precipitation in the Olmec region occurs in the early autumn when the passage of a hurricane or two can bring especially heavy rains to the Gulf coast. Again, the warmth and moisture indices reveal that this is a tropical humid region whose native vegetation was a dense forest cover. (Data from Secretaría de Recursos Hidráulicos.)

(30 mi) farther into the interior. Finally, they had to choose a location as close to the river bank as was practicable, for it was one thing to maneuver a 20- to 25-ton block of stone on a log raft but quite another to move it overland any distance.

What, then, was so special about the site of San Lorenzo that they felt obliged to freight the stone 50 km (30 mi) upstream? Would not a similar terrace, closer to the ocean, have sufficed just as well? Moreover, even though the water levels in the great rivers of eastern Mexico may rise and fall by as much as 10 m (35 ft) between the wet and dry seasons, was it really necessary to construct a terrace 50 m (160 ft) high on which to build their ceremonial center? Clearly, if ease of transportation and protection from the river at flood stage were their primary concerns, a lower site closer to the Gulf of Mexico should have fulfilled their needs just as adequately.

If the explanation for San Lorenzo's location cannot be found in its site, perhaps we should examine its situation instead. What is the relationship of this particular location to its surroundings? Just as Lucien Lefebvre pointed out that the primary motivations for early people to engage in travel were commercial, religious, and military in nature, so these same motives prompted them to found settlements. San Lorenzo's situation at the northern end of the Tehuantepec Gap certainly would have been a strategic one in terms of the exchange of goods — had a commercial economy existed at the time — but given what we know of the early Olmecs, that is highly unlikely. On the other hand, San Lorenzo could likewise have had a strategic importance in the military sense as well, for it did in effect control a major route of movement; its site, however, had surely not been chosen with any defensive considerations in mind, so such an explanation must also be dismissed. Essentially, we are left with a religious motive for its founding: But because its *site* had no special "sacredness" associated with it — as did, for example, the oracle of Delphi, or the Kaaba in Mecca — only its *situation* could have had a religious significance. What might this have been?

Looking back into the Olmec experience — as we understand it — for some association between place and religious significance, the only example we have is that afforded by the siting of Izapa in relationship to the summer solstice sunrise over the volcano Tajumulco. That example is instructive in itself, because it suggests the central importance of the calendar, and, in this case, even of the secular calendar, in the lives of the people. Surely, as the Olmecs began their northward expansion out of Soconusco, it would have been readily apparent to the priests that, even though the sun continues to make two zenithal passages across the Gulf coastal plain in a given year, it does so at a shorter interval than in their homeland. Therefore, the 260-day count was no longer valid, nor were such key dates as "1 Alligator" or "1 Snake." On the other hand, the sun continued to make two "turns" in the heavens — once in the north and again in the south, at opposite ends of its annual migration. Although the zenithal passages no longer took place on the same days as they did in Soconusco, the days when the sun "turned around" did remain the same. Only now, because the expansion of the Olmecs had taken them across the Tehuantepec Gap and into the Gulf coastal plain, there were no longer any topographic features on the northern horizon against which to calibrate its extreme position in that direction. The mountains all lay behind them to the south, and it was quite apparent that the highest peak which they passed on their northward trek — Zempoaltepec (3396 m, or 11,138 ft) — still could be seen on the southwestern horizon. If, then, they were to retain a working version of the calendar which had been developed in Izapa, it would have to be based not on the zenithal passage of the sun but on its turning point in the heavens. Furthermore, because the sun's northern turning point could not be calibrated due to an absence of mountains in that direction, it would have to be its southern turning point instead. Moreover, because the highest mountain within view lay to the southwest, it would have to be calibrated at sunset rather than at sunrise as it was in Izapa. In short, whether they realized it or not, they would be seeking an alignment which was just the opposite of that at Izapa — an orientation to a winter solstice sunset position rather than to a summer solstice sunrise.

(A word about solsticial alignments in Mesoamerica: Even though the region extends through 10 degrees of latitude — from about 13 to 23° N — because it lies so near the equator, sun angles scarcely differ by more than a degree across the entire region, in other words, less than could be distinguished by someone practicing naked-eye astronomy as these people did. For all intents and purposes, the azimuth of the summer solstice sunrise can be equated to 65° throughout the region, or 25° north of east. Similarly, the winter solstice sunrise can be equated to 115°, or 25° south of east. Sunset positions on each of these days may be marked against the corresponding positions along the western horizon — i.e., 295°, or 25° north of west for the summer solstice, and 245°, or 25° south of west for the winter solstice. Naturally, none of the Mesoamerican peoples reckoned in terms of angles or degrees, so although we express such measurements in these units, the alignments which they established were done solely through repeated observations in the field. It is, however, not inconceivable that, having once realized what the extreme points of the sun were, they made a graphic representation of its limits. If so, the resultant diagram would have approximated a recumbent cross — a so-called Saint Andrew's cross — which indeed has been recognized as one of the most frequently repeated artistic motifs used by the Olmecs.)

Having already had the experience of locating the site of Izapa by using solsticial orientation as a "principle," the Olmec priests were well prepared to do it again in the case of San Lorenzo. At Izapa the site that was chosen was the point where the alignment with Tajumulco (i.e., sunrise at the summer solstice, or an azimuth of 65°) intersected the Río Izapa, which served as a source of water for the ceremonial center. In the case of San Lorenzo, the site would be dictated by the point where the alignment with Zempoaltepec (sunset at the winter solstice, or an azimuth of 245°) intersected the Río Coatzacoalcos, not only for access to drinking water but also for expediting the transport of stone from the Tuxtlas. Naturally, pinpointing such a location may have taken more than one "field season," but even so, it was probably carried out by three or four "survey teams" rather than just one. The priest could initially have gotten a pretty good idea of the stretch of the river along which the proper vantage point for his planned ceremonial center would be found, and then, as the winter solstice neared, he would have posted his teams at intervals along the appropriate part of the waterway to observe the sunset over the distant mountain. The final choice of the site would be that of the team which reported the sunset directly behind the mountain.

That some version of the scenario just described must have taken place about the year 1200 B.C. seems quite certain, for large-scale maps reveal that the relationship between the site of San Lorenzo and the highest mountain within the range of its visibility, Zempoaltepec, is precisely that of the winter solstice sunset. Although there has been some debate over why the Olmecs had built their ceremonial center on an artificial terrace some 50 m (160 ft) above the river, it may well have been not only to protect their settlement from the high waters of the river in flood but also to improve their visibility of the mountain they had chosen as a calendrical marker. In any event, here we have exquisite evidence of a so-

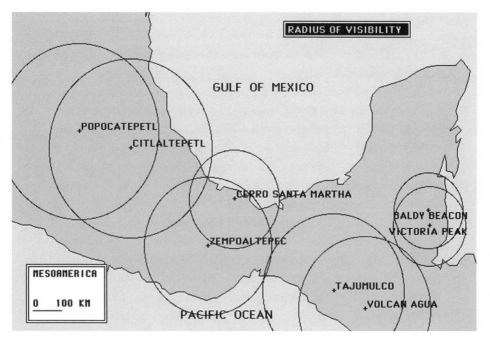

Figure 18.
On this computer-generated map, the theoretical radius of visibility of certain key topographic features as viewed from sea level is shown. However, there is no guarantee that any given place within the radius of visibility has a clear line of sight to the topographic feature in question. This must be determined from either observations in the field or measurements made on large-scale maps.

phisticated idea having served as the locational rationale for the earliest known ceremonial center of the Olmecs—a planned settlement whose location was a carefully chosen compromise between the need for drinking water, a navigable waterway, and the dictates of the sun-god!

Here was urban planning on a grand scale. Whether the Olmecs pressed local Maya into service in building the terrace on which San Lorenzo was to be located, or in quarrying and freighting the stone used for the sculptures of the "Colossal Heads," or in constructing the elaborate drainage system which served the ceremonial center is really beside the point. Here was a well-organized hierarchical command system at work, directed by priests who were thoroughly conversant with the calendar and its uses, who could allocate labor and resources to the most extensive manmade undertaking the region of Mesoamerica had yet seen, and all of it most probably in the name of religion. In a word, the Olmec civilization had been launched — and in a most spectacular and dramatic manner.

Yet, in the hindsight of history, something must have gone wrong at San Lorenzo, for by 900 B.C. it seems to have been abandoned. Perhaps internal dissension brought about a dissolution of its social structure. Perhaps what might have been a site pleasing to the sun-god was not especially conducive to meeting the daily needs of the common people; after all, the rainforests surrounding San Lorenzo lacked the richness and diversity of ecological resources found in Soconusco. Whatever it was, the great "Colossal Heads" which had been quarried, transported, and carved so laboriously were now rolled down into the ravines which dissected the edges of the terrace and carefully covered up, and within a generation or two, the jungle had totally reclaimed the site.

This, of course, was not the undoing of the Olmecs, for already before 1000 B.C. a second ceremonial center, known to the modern world as La Venta, had come into being to the northeast. This time a site had been chosen much closer to the sea, in fact barely 20 km (12 mi) inland from the Gulf. Again, it lay on the banks of a navigable river, this time the Río Tonalá, which today forms the boundary between the states of Veracruz and Tabasco. And this time it had a site rather similar to that of Venice, in that it lay in the midst of coastal marshes. In fact, Michael Coe has picturesquely called it "a sanctuary in the swamps." However, this description is probably a more accurate characterization of Venice than it is of La Venta, for the former's founding was the result of people fleeing before the invading Germanic tribes, seeking shelter in the marshes of the Po delta, while we have no evidence of a similar episode having been responsible for the rise of the latter. On the other hand, the limited size of the island and its relative isolation in the swamps suggests that the principal function of La Venta may have been as a religious pilgrimage site (Adams, 1991, 62).

Indeed, we have every reason to view with a certain degree of puzzlement just why the Olmecs chose this site for their second exercise in urban planning. Although it lies on the right bank of the Río Tonalá and is surrounded by marshes, its immediate setting is high and dry enough to

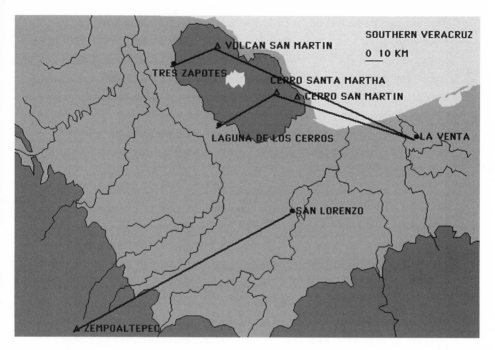

Figure 19.
Most of the principal Olmec ceremonial centers in the so-called metropolitan area of Mexico's
Gulf coastal plain demonstrate solsticial orientations to the highest mountain within sight. For
example, San Lorenzo is oriented to the winter solstice sunset over Zempoaltepec, Laguna de los
Cerros is oriented to the summer solstice sunrise over Cerro Santa Martha, and Tres Zapotes has
a similar orientation to Volcán San Martín. Interestingly, La Venta appears to be oriented both to
the summer solstice sunset over Volcán San Martín and to the August 13 sunset over Cerro Santa
Martha. As explained in the text, La Venta illustrates an evolution in locational principles that
probably took place sometime about 800 B.C.

have spared it from inundation by rainy-season floodwaters. (Whether its
site has been artificially built up in any way has never been commented
on in the archaeological literature; it is called simply an "island.") Certainly its commanding feature is a clay pyramid, or mound, some 30 m
(100 ft) in height. Otherwise, its outstanding characteristic is its carefully
planned symmetry around a central axis which is oriented 8° west of
north.

The latter feature has intrigued archaeologists but has never satisfactorily been explained by them. One attempt by Marian Hatch, arguing

for the site's orientation to the star Eta Draconis (magnitude 2.73), sought to invoke an astronomical connection, but ultimately not a very convincing one (Hatch, 1973). In the heyday of La Venta's existence, about the year 1000 B.C., Eta Draconis would have set just shy of an azimuth of 351°, but thereafter, due to precession, or the "wobble" of Earth on its axis, it would have set farther and farther away from this point. (Indeed, in the same year its declination was 69°, or 21° away from the north celestial pole, which is the closest it has been within the last 3000 years.)

On the other hand, anyone living in La Venta would have an absolutely unencumbered view of the entire northern horizon, having nothing but a featureless coastal plain merging with the sea in the distance. Surely, one of the first discoveries a skygazing priest would have made — if he was not already aware of it — was that the sky and/or its stars rotated. Here, at La Venta, he could see many of the constellations with which he had been familiar at Izapa, or perhaps even at San Lorenzo, make a complete circle in the heavens. Although he was already familiar with the fact that the same constellation had a different location in the sky at different times of the night, and for that matter, at different times of the year, once they disappeared over the western horizon and the sun had risen in the east, he had no idea where the stars had gone. Now he could see that they really went around in a circle.

There is no evidence that this discovery in any way helped the early Mesoamericans to stumble onto the recognition of Earth's sphericity or of its diurnal or annual movements. But what it did do was to cause the skygazing priest to zero in on that part of the sky which moved the *least*. In the year 1000 B.C., the star which came closest to being at the "center" of the sky was Kochab (magnitude 2.07), whose declination was 83°.5. Since Kochab is circumpolar at the latitude of La Venta, there would be no way that the skygazer could fix its position against the horizon; therefore, if he had oriented the site to what he presumed to be its farthest west position, he may well have misjudged the alignment of La Venta's central axis by about 1°.5. This is still an impressive approximation, given that he most likely had no instruments other than a pair of crossed sticks to aid him in making his observations.

As it turned out, the Olmec propensity for order and symmetry definitely worked to the archaeologists' advantage in excavating the site. After Matthew Stirling had discovered La Venta's axial arrangement aimed at an azimuth of 352° and uncovered a huge mosaic depicting a jaguar's face made out of carefully quarried blocks of green serpentine, Robert Heizer and Philip Drucker, who continued the site's excavation in the 1950's, correctly surmised that another such mosaic must lie buried on the opposite side of the axis. The twin mosaics, which had been ritually covered by layers of different-colored sands, were composed of some 1200 tons of stone which had been laboriously cut and hauled from Niltepec, some 180 km (110 mi) to the south across the Tehuantepec Gap. La Venta, often called "the capital of the Olmecs," was not only another triumph of the Mesoamerican intellect, but also a vivid illustration of the organizational skills of a young and dynamic civilization. It appears to have functioned as the most important center of the Olmecs at least until about 600 B.C.

Although the internal layout of the site itself can possibly be attributed to an orientation toward Kochab, the specific siting of La Venta has yet to be explained. Why was it located precisely where it was on the banks of the Río Tonalá? Certainly, the access to higher and drier land, drinking water, and a navigable river were imperative, because La Venta had to import its building stone from the Tuxtlas in the same way that San Lorenzo did. Was the 30-m- (100-ft-) high pyramid simply another manifestation of the triumph of political organization, or did it have a utilitarian function as well? Because La Venta clearly lacked any strategic advantages, either in a commercial or a military sense, the choice of its site must have been dictated even more strongly by a religio-astronomic motive.

If one climbs the pyramid on a relatively clear day, mountains are visible on the horizon to the southeast in Chiapas, to the southwest in Oaxaca, and to the northwest in Veracruz state. However, it is by far the latter — the Tuxtlas — which are the closest, and hence the most prominent of such features.

Three stratovolcanoes dominate the skyline of the Tuxtlas. The nearest to La Venta as the crow flies is Cerro San Martín at a distance of 76 km (47 mi). Almost directly behind it, as seen from La Venta, stands Cerro Santa Martha at a distance of some 88 km (55 mi), and back of that in turn rises Volcán San Martín at a distance of 132 km (82 mi). Although various map sources give differing elevations for these three peaks, the nearest one (Cerro San Martín) is the lowest (1250 m, or 4100 ft) but nevertheless the most visually prominent from La Venta. Judging from its configuration, it appears to have been considerably higher in the past, for the long gradual slopes of what once was its cone terminate abruptly on their inner sides, suggesting that the entire top of the mountain has been blown away. Whether a catastrophic eruption of such massive proportions occurred within the 3000 years since La Venta was founded, it is impossible to say at this time. (Evidence of a volcanic eruption of absolutely cataclysmic proportions has been demonstrated for Ilopango in El Salvador about the year A.D. 260, so such a possibility is not as "fanciful" as it might first appear.) On the other hand, Cerro Santa Martha is without question the highest of the existing peaks in the Tuxtlas. Depending on which map one consults, its elevation is given as 1787 m (5861 ft) or as 1879 m (6163 ft). It is clear from the most detailed Mexican map of the region (compiled from aerial photographs taken in 1976) that Cerro Santa Martha's crater has been extensively breached on its northeast side by vigorous stream erosion, but again, how much of this has occurred within the last three millennia is not easily determined. In any case, local informants note that Cerro Santa Martha has water in its crater (suggesting that it may have been dormant for some time) and contrast this with Cerro San Martín's crater, which they claim has sulfur in it. In any event, the azimuth measured between La Venta and the highest remaining lip of each of these craters is slightly over 285°, or a good 10° away from the sunset position on the summer solstice. On the other hand, the most distant of the three stratovolcanoes — Volcán San Martín, whose height is variously given as 1402 m (4600 ft) or 1773 m (5815 ft) — lies at an azimuth of ca. 295°, and therefore may well have served La Venta as a topographic marker for the summer solstice sunset (see figure 19).

A third major Olmec site has only more recently been discovered in the Gulf coastal lowlands of eastern Mexico, but as yet has not been systematically excavated. Known as Laguna de los Cerros, it is situated on the southern edge of the Tuxtlas in the valley of the Río San Juan, a tributary of the northwesterly flowing Río Papaloapan. It is thought to be

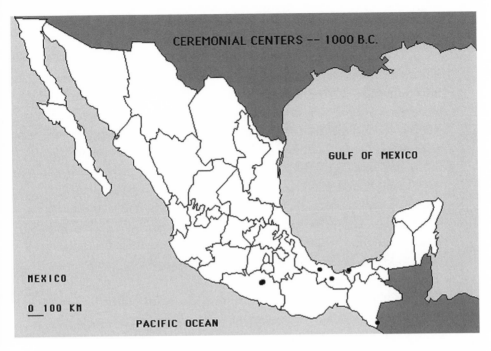

Figure 20.
By about 1000 B.C., knowledge of the calendars and the principle of solsticial orientation
had spread into the Olmec metropolitan area. San Lorenzo at the northern entrance to the
Tehuantepec Gap and La Venta and Laguna de los Cerros on the eastern and western approaches
of the Tuxtla Mountains, respectively, were thriving centers at the time. The Olmec fascination
for jade, which in Mexico is only found in the Balsas Depression of Guerrero state, may have
prompted the founding of Teopantecuanitlán by that date as well. Discovered only in 1985, the
site is currently being excavated by scientists from Mexico's Institute of Archaeology and History.

almost as old as San Lorenzo and possibly somewhat older than La
Venta, an assumption which accords perfectly with a postulated Olmec
diffusion spreading outward from the Tehuantepec Gap. Furthermore,
its location is again a compromise between a water-oriented site with access to a river, both for the water itself and for the transportation it affords, and a situation which is aligned to the summer solstice sunrise over
Cerro Santa Martha (see figure 19).

The diffusion of the Olmecs and their calendrically based religion
was not solely northwestward into the heartland of present-day Mexico,
however. There is also evidence of a very early spread of their cultural

influences south and eastward into modern Guatemala, El Salvador, and the borderlands of Honduras and Nicaragua. Farther eastward in Soconusco lies Abaj Takalik, where artifacts of Maya origin are found superimposed on Olmec foundations and at least two early Long Count inscriptions have also been uncovered. Not too surprisingly, the site likewise seems to have been chosen for its alignment to the volcano Santa María at the summer solstice sunrise. Here a navigable waterway was not a concern, however, because basaltic boulders for construction abound in the immediate vicinity.

About 80 km (50 mi) farther east yet is El Baúl with its rich assemblage of primitive sculpture (some of it magnetic), another very ancient Long Count inscription, and a strongly suggestive orientation to Volcán Agua at the summer solstice sunrise. We have already described nearby La Democracia as the center of the "Fat Boy" sculptures, with their intriguing magnetic properties.

Certainly the largest of the Guatemalan sites with Olmec-like carvings is Kaminaljuyú, on the western outskirts of the country's capital city. Once a sprawling site of more than 200 platforms and pyramids, it has been severely damaged by Guatemala City's urban growth and few of its original structures remain intact. Dated to at least 800 B.C., and possibly earlier, Kaminaljuyú occupied a similar geographic situation to that of San Lorenzo in the sense that it commanded a strategic pass across the Atlantic-Pacific divide. Ironically, the belated Spanish recognition of this place's "centrality" within Guatemala caused them to relocate the colonial capital to this location from Antigua Guatemala, following the latter's damage in a severe earthquake in 1773. Like other "Olmecoid" ceremonial centers, Kaminaljuyú also demonstrates a solsticial orientation — in this instance, to the Volcán Fuego at the winter solstice sunset (see figure 21).

Perhaps the southeasternmost of the Olmec-influenced ceremonial centers of Mesoamerica was Tazumal, situated in what is the northwestern corner of present-day El Salvador. Not only are Olmec influences clearly seen in its artwork, but the site appears to have been oriented to the winter solstice sunrise over what formerly was the great volcano of Ilopango, just to the east of San Salvador, the country's capital. The latter volcano — now a vast water-filled caldera — experienced a massive

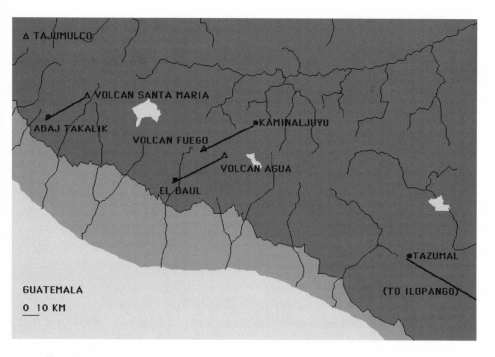

Figure 21.
Olmec diffusion southward and eastward into the Pacific coastal plain of Guatemalan Soconusco
and what is today the adjacent part of El Salvador saw the founding of several other early
ceremonial centers, many of which continued the tradition of solsticial orientation to the highest
mountain within sight.

eruption about A.D. 260, which devastated the adjacent settled areas and
gave rise to large-scale out-migrations of the local people (see figure 21).

Formula 2: "The fifty-second sunset"

Sometime during its six to eight centuries of existence, La Venta witnessed the construction of a new series of structures (the so-called Stirling Complex) near the southern end of its great plaza. Interestingly,
when these structures were first mapped, they were shown to have devi-
ated some 23°.5 from the site's axis, which, as we have explained, is
aimed 8° west of north. The fact that this angle corresponds to the incli-
nation of the earth's axis is probably strictly a coincidence, but in any

case, it means that the walls of the Stirling Complex are oriented 15°.5 off of the cardinal points. Thus, in a northerly direction it has an azimuth of 15°.5, in an easterly direction it faces 105°.5, to the south the azimuth reads 195°.5, and to the west, 285°.5. Only the latter of these azimuths is of any interest, because it marks the sunset position on August 13 — "the day that time began," according to the sacred almanac. Could this alignment be an architectural "reinforcement" of a topographic orientation toward Cerro San Martín and/or Cerro Santa Martha? If so, it could mean that by about 1000 B.C., priests at La Venta had come up with a formula for recording when the zenithal sun was passing overhead at Izapa!

(It should be noted that in a more recent survey of La Venta carried out by the National Institute for Archaeology and History [a copy of which is reproduced in Adams, 1991, 56–57], the structures of the Stirling Complex are shown to have the *same* axial alignment as the remainder of the site — i.e., 8° west of north. If the original survey was in error, naturally the arguments presented above are no longer valid. However, this does not invalidate the discussion which follows for how the "formula" itself was derived.)

In reality, the formula was as simple as it was ingenious. The problem at San Lorenzo had been that the priests had no way of knowing when it was August 13, because in their part of the world the zenithal passage of the sun did not occur on that date. Thus, they had settled on using one of the solstices instead, because the date of the sun's turning point was the same everywhere, they had discovered. Whereas at San Lorenzo they were obliged to use the winter solstice sunset to calibrate their calendar, when La Venta was founded it appears that they could once more think in terms of the summer solstice, as had originally been done in Izapa. Indeed, the only difference was that instead of marking the sunrise as they did at Izapa, they were obliged to use the sunset at La Venta.

Once back in the mental groove of using the summer solstice to calibrate the secular calendar, it would not have been long before some priest realized that the beginning date of the sacred almanac can itself be calibrated by reference to the summer solstice. In effect, he was recognizing that, if the solstice occurred on June 22 and the "beginning of time" occurred on August 13, there was a fixed interval of time between these two dates. Using our modern calendar to demonstrate his thought process, we would count 8 days to complete the month of June, add 31 more for the month of July, and then count 13 until the sunset of August 13, yielding a total of 52 days. (For anyone used to thinking in "bundles" of 20's and 13's, what a neat package this was — 4 rounds of 13 days = 52 days.) Thus, no matter where one wanted to build a ceremonial center, one could always find out when it was August 13. All that was required was to count 52 days from the time that the sun turns around in the north and mark the horizon at sunset!

In pinning down the time frame of the discovery of this second principle of orientation, we can say that it was probably *not* in use when La Venta was founded about 1000 B.C. — but only if Volcán San Martín had been the topographic feature against which the summer solstice sunset had been calibrated. If, however, the suggestive azimuth of either Cerro San Martín or Cerro Santa Martha had been employed in locating the site, then it would already have had to have been known at that date. In any event, it seems almost certain that it had been recognized by the time the site was abandoned about 600 B.C. If it were possible to date the founding of some other ceremonial site(s) that likewise had an August 13th alignment to within La Venta's span of existence — i.e., between roughly 1000 and 600 B.C. — then perhaps we could narrow down the timing of the discovery of this second principle more closely.

Tres Zapotes, another major Olmec center located farther west along the coastal plain of Veracruz, is generally believed to have been founded about 800 B.C. Its orientation is to Volcán San Martín in the Tuxtlas, but it uses the mountain to mark the summer solstice sunrise (see figure 19). A host of other ceremonial centers extending northward along the coast and westward onto the Mexican plateau likewise date to the general period between 1000 and 800 B.C. and invariably demonstrate solsticial alignments: The Totonac site of Remojadas, for example, is oriented to the summer solstice sunset over Nauhcampatépetl, or Cofre de Perote, as it came to be known to the Spanish. Similarly, Zempoala, farther north along the coast of Veracruz, is aligned to Citlaltépetl, or Orizaba, at the winter solstice sunset (see figure 22). In the highland basin of Puebla, the pyramid of Tepenapa at Cholula — the New World's largest

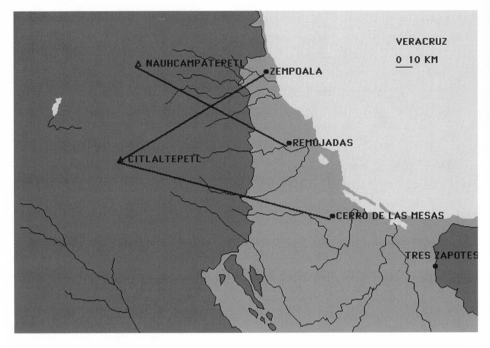

Figure 22.
Farther north along the Gulf coast, we find that the Olmec site of Cerro de las Mesas (founded ca. 800 B.C.) is oriented to Citlaltépetl (Orizaba), the highest mountain in Mexico, on the August 13th sunset. Lacking a solsticial orientation, it may therefore be the first ceremonial center in Mesoamerica where the August 13th orientation was used. Both Remojadas and Zempoala, on the other hand, demonstrate solsticial alignments: the former to the summer solstice sunset over Nauhcampatépetl (Cofre de Perote), and the latter to the winter solstice sunset over Citlaltépetl.

pre-Columbian structure—is oriented to Ixtaccíhuatl at the summer solstice sunset. In the Valley of Mexico, the two oldest known agricultural settlements—Zacatenco and El Arbolillo—both of local origin, clearly had no such alignments, whereas Tlatilco and Tlapacoya, the most ancient of the Olmec-inspired settlements in the basin, are clearly oriented to the winter solstice sunrise over Ixtaccíhuatl. And near the southern edge of the valley, the four-tiered round pyramid of Cuicuilco, probably the oldest true ceremonial center in the basin of Mexico, is unmistakably aligned to the cone of Popocatépetl at the winter solstice sunrise.

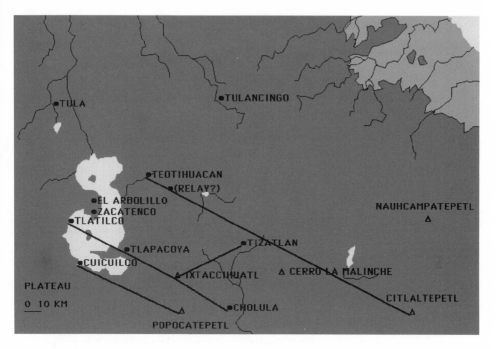

Figure 23.
On the Mexican plateau, all ceremonial centers where "Olmec" origins or influence are found demonstrate solsticial alignments. The twin volcanoes of Popocatépetl and Ixtaccíhuatl were used as winter solstice sunrise azimuths for Cuicuilco, Tlatilco, and Tlapacoya in the Valley of Mexico and as a summer solstice sunset azimuth by Cholula in the Puebla basin. Ixtaccíhuatl also served to mark the winter solstice sunset from Tizatlán. One of the most intriguing solsticial alignments is that of Teotihuacán, which lines up perfectly with the winter solstice sunrise over Citlaltépetl (Orizaba). Because a low ridge intervenes betwen them, the mountain is not visible from the city; however, in 1993 what may have served as a "relay station" between the two was investigated by the author. Later Toltec ceremonial centers such as Tulancingo and Tula pointedly demonstrate that the principle of solsticial orientation was either forgotten or had died out by the time they were founded.

However, the most innovative orientation along this northward prong of Olmec advance seems to have been that of Cerro de las Mesas (most likely founded ca. 800 B.C.), about 60 km (35 mi) southeast of Veracruz. Unless we are dealing with merely another suggestive "coincidence," this site aligns to Orizaba at sunset on August 13. Therefore, if the date of its founding is accurate, we probably have here the first illustration of the application of the "summer solstice + 52 days" formula anywhere in the Olmec world—at least outside of La Venta (see figure 22).

It should also be kept in mind that northward and westward beyond Cerro de las Mesas, the Olmec influence seems to have been limited to the activity of a small elite composed of "missionaries" or "soldiers" or both, rather than any massive in-migration as seems to have been the case in the southern Gulf coastal plain. The fact that this elite could have had such a strong impact on the peoples of these other regions would seem to testify to the strength of both their religious and their intellectual message.

Another prong of Olmec expansion—no doubt of the same elitist militaristic-missionary type—can be traced up the valley of the Río Tehuantepec into the highlands of Oaxaca where the principal "converts" were the Zapotecs. Their main ceremonial center, Monte Albán, dates back to at least 600 B.C., but differs from virtually all other such settlements in Mesoamerica in being located at the top of a mountain—a 500-m (1600-ft) eminence which overlooks the present-day city of Oaxaca. With a commanding view over the great Y-shaped valley formed by the Río Atoyac and its main tributary, Monte Albán has a spectacular site, but one which could not have been dictated by any solsticial alignment. It would have been sheer chance if the mountain on which it is located happened to line up with another mountain—and specifically the highest within view!—on any of the key dates of the year. (Indeed, as the Olmecs penetrated the mountain fastnesses of the Sierra Madre del Sur, they appear to have had to abandon their predilection for orienting sites to commanding topographic features, because in most instances the very ruggedness of the region precluded the establishment of long lines of sight.) This means, therefore, that if any calendrical orientation is to be sought at Monte Albán, it would most likely commemorate August 13, as the beginning of the sacred almanac, and hence would have employed the "summer solstice + 52 days" formula. If that had actually been the case in the initial layout of the ceremonial center, we will never know, because the great plaza at the top of the mountain underwent a drastic process of "urban renewal" about the third century B.C. when all the buildings save one—the so-called Mound J, an arrow-

Figure 24.
Among the earliest recognizable calendrical glyphs are these
discovered at Monte Albán and thought to date to the time
of the ceremonial center's founding (ca. 600 B.C.). However,
evidence uncovered by archaeologist David Peterson strongly
suggests that the calendar arrived in Monte Albán in fully
developed form, because the date August 13 played a
fundamental role in its annual cycle even though it had
no local astronomical significance whatsoever.

head-shaped structure near the south end of the plaza — had been reconstructed on an axis 5° east of north. On the other hand, on a slightly
lower ridge of the mountain to the northeast, a structure known as
Mound Y (also identified as Tomb 105) clearly reveals from the large,
irregular stones used in its construction that it had been one of the earliest buildings on the site, but due to its being located relatively off to

the side, it had escaped the later "urban renewal" process. Significantly, when its orientation was checked, it was found to look out at the western horizon at an azimuth of 285°.5 — the alignment of the setting sun on August 13. This discovery means that the Zapotecs were not only aware of the sacred almanac by at least 600 B.C., but that they had oriented at least one of their key structures to its beginning date, which indicates that the "summer solstice + 52 days" principle was already known at that time.

Because of the antiquity of the inscriptions at Monte Albán, Alfonso Caso, among others, believed that the Mesoamerican calendrical systems had their origins in the highlands of Oaxaca. However, the recent work of anthropologist David Peterson at Monte Albán has revealed that "the 260-day calendar definitely did not originate at Monte Albán," but "must have been developed elsewhere and been brought to Monte Albán in a fully developed state" (unpublished manuscript; personal communication). Interestingly, his evidence suggests that the original Zapotec version of the 260-day calendar had days with fixed numbers and names, beginning on August 14 and running through April 30. Thereafter, the first 105 day-numbers and -names are repeated in a second, shorter cycle which ran from May 1 to August 12. Peterson maintains that August 13 was a nameless, or "zero," date which was probably never recorded, and that every four years it was repeated and/or counted twice, allowing the Zapotec calendar to remain synchronized with the true length of the solar year. Peterson also notes that the side walls of one of the oldest structures at Monte Albán, Mound K, are oriented to the sunrise positions on March 9 and October 5, which he suggests reflects the Zapotecs' method of defining a 52-day interval before and after the zenithal sun passages at Izapa. Both of these ideas—a 365-day calendar with fixed day-names and divided into two separate cycles, one a longer 260-day cycle beginning on August 14 and the second a shorter 105-day cycle beginning on May 1; as well as a means of architecturally establishing a 52-day interval before and after these two critical dates—have, of course, special relevance to the discussion at hand.

Thus, if the "summer solstice + 52 days" formula had not already been discovered by the time of La Venta's founding, it certainly seems to have been in use when Cerro de las Mesas was founded a couple of hundred years later, and from there it appears to have diffused both back to La Venta, where it may have been incorporated into the alignment of the Stirling Complex (if one accepts the site plan produced in the initial survey), and also to Monte Albán, where it had dictated the layout of Mound Y around 600 B.C. However, the special twists given to the sacred calendar and the means of calibrating its beginning and ending dates are Zapotec innovations of which we have only recently become aware, thanks to Peterson's research.

Two other calendrical innovations also seem to be the product of the Zapotecs because there is no evidence that they occur anywhere outside their culture area. Peterson makes the point that Mound J, the arrowhead-shaped structure near the southern end of the main plaza, appears to have been constructed to commemorate the azimuth of the sunrise on the days of the zenithal sun passage over Monte Albán (May 8 and August 5), the alignment of its original front steps having been 72°. However, the "point" of the arrowhead is aimed at an azimuth of 252°—an orientation which he claims commemorates the sunset azimuth on the days when the sun is at its *antizenithal* position, or in other words, when it is overhead at the corresponding latitude in the Southern Hemisphere (November 10 and February 2). It is interesting to note that the only other Mesoamerican structure having the same kind of arrowhead configuration and demonstrating a similar (supposed) antizenithal orientation is the so-called Mound O at Caballito Blanco, about 30 km (20 mi) to the east of Oaxaca. Sometime around the year 275 B.C., when Monte Albán underwent a major urban renewal, a massive platform was added to the front of Mound J, with its new staircase being oriented to an azimuth of 48°. Anthony Aveni has demonstrated that in the years surrounding that date, the star Capella (magnitude 0.97) rose at this azimuth just before dawn on the day of the first zenithal sun passage, i.e., May 8; thus, from having been a structure whose orientation was totally dictated by solar azimuths, Mound J from 275 B.C. onward incorporated a stellar alignment into its newly reconstructed front façade.

For a people who were unfamiliar with the sphericity of the earth, or for that matter, with a heliocentric solar system, the notion of the antizenith seems to have been a quantum leap into the unknown. What possible significance such dates as November 10 and February 2 could have had for the residents of either Monte Albán or Caballito Blanco is difficult to imagine. To be sure, they bracket the winter solstice in the northern hemisphere by 89 days, just as May 8 and August 5 bracket the summer solstice by a similar interval, but aside from such temporal symmetry there is little else in common between these pairs of dates.

I would suggest, rather, that it was not the southwestern point, or "arrowhead," of Mound J that was important, but the alignment of its southern and western walls, which form a right angle oriented to the cardinal points. Thus, although all the other structures surrounding the great plaza of Monte Albán have walls oriented about 5° east of north, this is the only part of any structure at the site whose architecture preserves a true north-south, east-west alignment. When viewed from either end of the plaza, the west wall of Mound J's arrowhead could have served as a meridian, remaining in shadow from dawn until local noon and then basking in full sunlight until the sun set. That such a use might have been made of this feature is attested by a series of photographs taken by the author in January 1993 revealing how the vertical wall literally "flashed" into light at local noon, i.e., 12:27 P.M. The western wall could also have served as a meridian marker by anyone viewing the structure from the opposite end of the plaza, and thus may have been used to calibrate midnight as well.

Beyond the mountains to the northwest of Monte Albán lived a people who posed a constant threat to the Zapotecs and who ultimately moved in to conquer them. These were the Mixtecs, or so-called "people of the clouds," who, because of their geographic location, were not reached by Olmec missionaries and the innovation of the calendar until sometime after the Zapotecs. Indeed, archaeologists date their ceremonial center at Huamelulpan to ca. 300 B.C., and although not much remains of the main pyramid there, its massive foundation stones not only bear carvings of calendrical glyphs in virtually mint condition but they also are squarely oriented to the sunset position on August 13. Thus, both the calendar and the knowledge of how to calibrate it had reached into the mountain fastnesses of the Mixtecs by at least the third century before Christ.

Yet another prong of Olmec advance led south and westward out of the Puebla basin along the valley of the Río Atoyac into the Balsas

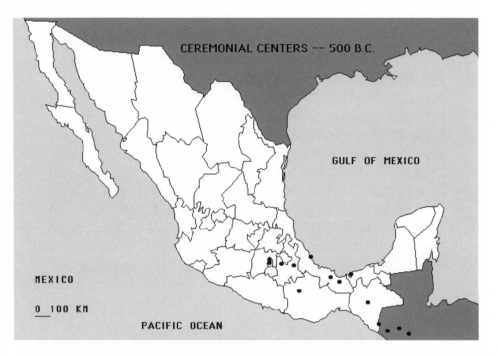

Figure 25.
By 500 B.C., Olmec influence had diffused the urbanization process both eastward along the Pacific piedmont of Guatemala and El Salvador and northwestward into the highlands of Oaxaca and onto the Mexican plateau. Although places like San Lorenzo had already been abandoned, an urban network of over a dozen ceremonial centers stretched for 1000 km (600 mi) through the heart of Mesoamerica.

Depression. The principal ceremonial center located near the Atoyac's headwaters was Las Bocas, not far from the present-day city of Izúcar de Matamoros. Its site appears to have been chosen to permit the calendar's calibration by observing the summer solstice sunrise over Citlaltépetl (Orizaba), located 135 km (84 mi) to the northeast. To the west of Izúcar, near the banks of the Río Amatzinac, lies the ceremonial center of Chalchatzingo whose site seems to have been chosen, in part at least, because of the spectacular volcanic plug on which much of its "monumental" art has been etched. However, there is the intriguing possibility that a calendrical concern may likewise have been involved in the choice of its location, for it is directly in line with the setting sun at the

Figure 26.
The main pyramid at the Mixtec site of Huamelulpan, Oaxaca, was constructed about 300 B.C. The massive stone blocks which underlie its southwestern corner not only demonstrate some well-preserved calendrical glyphs but also reveal an orientation of the front wall to the sunset position on August 13.

summer solstice over the volcano Nevado de Toluca (4624 m, 14,954 ft). The Olmec site at Gualupita, now swallowed up by the modern city of Cuernavaca, likewise seems to owe its location to its orientation to the summer solstice sunrise over Ixtaccíhuatl, 105 km (65 mi) to the northeast. But probably the principal ceremonial center along this southwestward prong of Olmec expansion was Teopantecuanitlán, or "the place of the temple of the jaguar," discovered in 1985 by Guadalupe Martínez Donjuán.

Strategically located in a broad valley at the confluence of the Balsas River and its largest right-bank tributary, the Amacuzac (also called the Río Grande), Teopantecuanitlán is built around a sunken court, two walls of which are surmounted by great jaguar-face monoliths. Although the site may have been occupied from about 1400 B.C. to 600 B.C., it appears that its principal structures date from ca. 1000 B.C. Here in the hot and arid Balsas Depression of northern Guerrero state, not far from where Covarrubias had argued that the Olmec hearth was to be found, the combination of the rivers with their life-giving water and the fertile alluvial soils made for an agricultural oasis of great productivity. It is also likely that one of the principal sources of Olmec jade lay somewhere nearby in the Balsas Valley of Guerrero (Adams, 1991, 73), hence the reason for their early penetration of this remote region. On the other hand, both the reported antiquity of the site (supposedly predating the origin of the sacred almanac) as well as the ruggedness of the local relief in the adjacent Sierra Madre del Sur region (precluding any long-distance lines of sight) essentially rule out a calendrical motivation for the choice of Teopantecuanitlán's location.

Perhaps the most triumphal breakthrough of the calendar and the religious ideology that embodied it came in the Valley of Mexico, due primarily to a natural catastrophe which occurred there about 200 B.C. The volcano Xitle, located a short distance to the southwest of the ceremonial center of Cuicuilco, began an ominous eruption, sending streams of lava cascading down toward the ancient settlement. The priests and the people had plenty of warning, so there was nothing to do but evacuate, and this they did by rounding the shores of the great Lake of the Moon to the northeast, thereby putting that body of water between themselves and the fiery volcano. From the relative safety of their refuge on the northeast side of the lake they could watch as the glowing rock flowed down over their city, covering everything but the main pyramid — a circular, four-tiered structure surmounted by a broad ramp. When the eruption was over and the lava had finally cooled, the only evidence that a vibrant, thriving ceremonial center had ever occupied the site was the deserted pyramid now locked in a ring of solid stone. (Were it not for this pyramid projecting up through the lavafield, it would have been doubtful that anyone would ever have known that a city lay buried there. Unlike most other sites that are excavated a spadeful of earth at a time, Cuicuilco had to be dynamited to reveal the secrets of its past) (see figure 23).

Already the heirs of several centuries of history, the survivors of Cuicuilco were not about to surrender to fate just because they had lost their city. Almost immediately they set about laying out an even grander metropolis, conceived and constructed on an immense scale in the relative safety of a broad plain bordering on the Lake of the Moon and commanding a low pass out of the Valley of Mexico toward the lowlands of the Gulf coast. Not only did it occupy a strategic location for trade, but it also controlled an immensely valuable resource which it could exchange for products from other regions — namely obsidian, or volcanic glass, highly prized for making tools and weapons because of the razorlike edges it yielded.

We know the city only by the name the Aztecs called it: Teotihuacán, or "place of the gods." They gave it this name because of the colossal size of its pyramids, despite the ruined condition in which they found them many centuries later. Even today the Pyramid of the Sun and the Pyramid of the Moon loom out of the plain like miniature mountains. Thinking these pyramids to be the resting places of gigantic deities, the Aztecs called the broad avenue running down the middle of the site the "Street of the Dead." What the Aztecs did not know, and what remained for the archaeologists to discover when the site was photographed and surveyed from the air in the 1960's, was that the "Street of the Dead" was merely the principal axis of an urban settlement that sprawled over hundreds of acres. Meticulously oriented to a grid that was offset from the cardinal points by 15°.5, the city had impressed its pattern on the entire countryside, even, it appears, influencing the layout of the *chinampas*, or "floating gardens," at the far southern end of the Lake of the Moon. Of course, once this pattern was mapped, an explanation had to be sought for its orientation, and in the course of time several hypotheses have been advanced. The explanation that is given visitors to the site in the little local museum is that it defines the sun's setting position on the day that the zenithal sun passes over. For Teotihuacán, located at latitude 19°.5 N, that occurs on both May 18 and July 26. Using a fairly simple trigonometric equation in which we insert 19.5 in the formula for both the declination (latitude) of the sun and the latitude of the place in question, we obtain a sunset azimuth of 290°.7 — a full 5°.2 off of the alignment which the excavators of Teotihuacán themselves have measured.

Several other attempts had been made to explain the layout of Teotihuacán by means of astronomy, including that of archaeologist James Dow, in 1967, who thought it had to do with either the setting of the Pleiades or the rising of Sirius. In 1973, astronomer Anthony Aveni settled on the hypothesis that the site had been oriented as it had because it marked the setting position of the Pleiades about the year A.D. 150, the date when he assumed the city had been laid out. However, he concedes that if his dating is off by even so much as 50 years, the alignment would be 0°.5 in error due to the effects of precession. (Of course, the same kinds of difficulties would be involved in any argument based on star positions.) To account for the host of other ceremonial centers which share what he has generalized as the "17° offset" of Teotihuacán, Aveni further assumes they were simply copied from the original, because by the time they were built—many of them in the period after A.D. 1100—the Pleiades idea would be off by as large an error as the zenithal sun-passage idea had yielded. Ironically, he essentially demolishes his own thesis a little farther along in his paper by admitting that the Pleiades are so faint as they near the horizon that they can hardly be seen when they are setting anyway (Aveni, 1973). (Despite this inconsistency, when *National Geographic* published a feature article on Teotihuacán in its December 1995 issue, they once again cited Aveni's hypothesis as the explanation for the city's grid pattern.)

A couple of years after Aveni's explanation had been advanced, two new solutions to Teotihuacán's orientation were put forward. One was the result of excavations at the site which revealed that beneath the Pyramid of the Sun lay a lava cave which opened to the northwest. Conclusion: It had been the aperture of this cave which provided the alignment upon which the entire city was plotted with such care (Heyden, 1975). However, no archaeologist has ever explained how such a finely measured orientation could ever be derived from the jagged walls of a basaltic tube—and they probably never will, because it can't really be done. Ironically, Millon and his disciples use the astronomical orientation of the cave as their raison d'etre for the city's layout, while at the same time appropriating the notion that the cave defined "the place where time began" (Berrin and Pasztory, 1993, 17–19). Of course, in the process they overlook the fact that the Mesoamerican "celebration" of both the August 13th sunset and the solstices had been going on for well over a millennium before Teotihuacán was even founded.

It remained for me and a group of my students to rediscover the principle which had motivated the city planners of Teotihuacán some 20 centuries earlier. Sitting atop the Pyramid of the Sun one January morning in 1975, I asked my students to look out over the site and consider the layout of the city below us. If the structure on which we were sitting was correctly named—and most prehistoric places or structures are not, as for example, Teotihuacán itself—what was it oriented toward, I asked. Because we had just climbed up the steps which surmount the pyramid on the side facing the "Street of the Dead" (i.e., the west-north-west), they immediately answered, "To the sunset." I congratulated them on their perspicacity and then asked them, "On which day?" Of course, most of them had seen the explanation provided in the local museum, so the answer came back, "The days that the sun passes directly overhead." This time I chided them for having "cheated" by recalling what was said in the museum, and then I asked them to confirm this figure by making their own calculations. A few minutes later the group of disgruntled students turned to me and reported that "it doesn't work; those are *not* the days." "All right then," I continued, "on what days *does* the sun set directly opposite the Pyramid of the Sun?"

Out came the calculators again, because now the formula had to be transposed. The latitude of the site was known (19°.5), and the azimuth of the sunset was known (285°.5); what they had to solve for was the declination of the sun (in other words, its latitude) to yield the days on which such an event occurred. A few more moments went by and a series of hands went up. The answer: "The sun would be overhead at latitude 14°.8 North." I smiled and asked if that meant anything to anybody, and all the students shook their heads. I then suggested that they check the copy of the solar ephemeris we had taken along to see on which days the sun was overhead at that latitude. A brief examination of the ephemeris revealed that the sun passed through the latitude of 14°.8 N on April 30 on its way northward and again on August 13 on its way southward. "Does either of those dates mean anything to you?" I asked, and again I drew a total blank from the students. "That happens to be the latitude of Izapa, in southernmost Mexico," I explained, "and August 13 happens to be the date that the Maya believed the world began—and here we find that date commemorated in the layout of the largest pre-Columbian city ever to be constructed in the New World, a thousand kilometers and a thousand years away from where it all began." What greater proof or sweeter vindication could any hypothesis ever receive? That day I felt as

Figure 27.
A view of Teotihuacán, the greatest metropolis of pre-Columbian Mesoamerica, looking southward from the Pyramid of the Moon toward the Pyramid of the Sun and the "Street of the Dead." Although a variety of reasons have been advanced for the city having been sited exactly where it is — that is, in a somewhat offside valley about 15 km (9 mi) away from the former shoreline of the Lake of the Moon — one intriguing clue may be that it lies directly in line with the winter solstice sunrise over Citlaltépetl (Orizaba), the highest mountain in all of Mesoamerica.

though I had been admitted to the inner sanctum of the Olmec priest-hood, for I was privy to something which they knew and I knew, but no one had known for 2000 years in between.

(This discovery was first published in 1978 and reconfirmed by two physicists at M.I.T. in 1980. At the time it was made, many of the details described in the preceding pages had yet to be filled in, so the entire story did not unfold as painlessly as might be surmised from the account given here. It is likewise interesting that nowhere in the literature is mention made of the fact that the positioning of the Pyramid of the Moon relative to the Pyramid of the Sun was carried out with such exactitude that for an observer standing on the former, the latter serves to mark the merid-ian — i.e., a true north-south line. Thus, not only can the precise time of local noon be calibrated by the passage of the sun over the Pyramid of

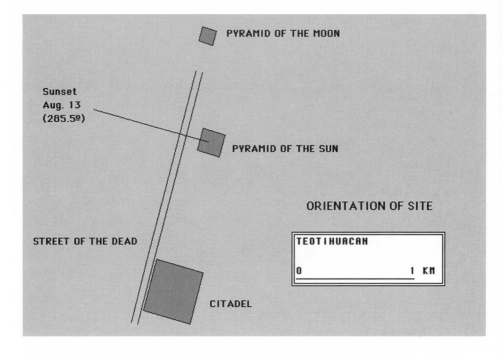

Figure 28.
The largest metropolis of the pre-Columbian New World, Teotihuacán numbered in its heyday perhaps as many as 200,000 inhabitants. It is meticulously laid out on a grid which is offset 15°.5 from the cardinal points. Thus, its main avenue, the "Street of the Dead," runs from 15°.5 east of north to 15°.5 west of south, while its most impressive structure, the Pyramid of the Sun, is directly oriented to a point 15°.5 north of west—the position at which the sun sets on August 13. The siting of the Pyramid of the Moon at the far end of the avenue was likewise done with such care that a sight-line directly over the top of the Pyramid of the Sun marks the meridian, thus allowing the priests of the city to fix the times of noon and midnight with complete accuracy.

the Sun, but the zenithal positions of the moon and stars can easily be defined as well.)

In the same 1978 article I made an almost heretical suggestion: I enclosed two maps of Mesoamerica which showed how more than two dozen key ceremonial centers in the region had been solstically oriented toward the highest mountain within view, in some cases to sunrises, in others to sunsets, and in some instances to the winter solstice while in others to the summer solstice. On the map showing the Valley of Mexico and Teotihuacán I projected a line between the largest metropolis ever built in pre-Columbian Mesoamerica and the region's highest mountain, the 5700-m (18,700-ft) volcano, Orizaba, or Citlaltépetl ("the mountain of the star"), as it was known to the Aztecs. I had discovered this relationship — a sunrise orientation at the winter solstice — from my study of large-scale maps of the region, but was perfectly aware that Orizaba was not visible from Teotihuacán because of an intervening mountain ridge. Because the alignment hardly seemed to be a chance one, I hypothesized that there may have been some kind of "relay station" on the intervening ridge from which the priests, or their agents, might have been able to calibrate the winter solstice sunrise for the benefit of the residents of Teotihuacán, and I hoped at some time to be able to check out this theory in the field. From bearings taken from the Pyramid of the Sun and from computer maps supplied by CIMMYT, the Center for the Improvement of Maize and Wheat at Texcoco, and with the aid of a Geographical Positioning System receiver provided by the Trimble Navigation Corporation, I was able to locate the supposed site of this "relay station" with pinpoint accuracy during the field season of 1993. Interestingly, I found that a boundary or triangulation marker had been recently erected there (it had a date of 1991, apparently scratched into the cement while it was still wet) — either to define a property line, a municipal limit, or a survey point — and that it was surrounded by several irregular piles of stones, seemingly collected from the adjacent mountain top. Strewn around the crest of the hill, but heavily concentrated on the western side facing Teotihuacán, were numerous pottery shards representing many different types and styles of ceramic vessels, as well as several obsidian blades, most of which appear to have been used to line the edge of wooden swords (*macana*). Although these artifacts all date to Aztec times, the fact that many of them represent parts of braziers and bowls strongly suggests that the site was used as a religious shrine (Deborah Nichols, personal communication). While the evidence is circumstantial at best that the site may have functioned as the author had originally proposed some 15 years earlier, its religious significance seems not to have gone unappreciated by Mesoamerica's last civilization (see figure 23).

Though Teotihuacán ultimately became the largest urban metropolis in Mesoamerica, it did not constitute the ultimate outlier of civilization on the edge of the great northern desert, or "la gran Chichimeca," as the Spanish later came to call it. At the time of the city's founding, the climate appears to have been moister over the Mexican plateau than it is today, and the frontier of Mesoamerican religion, commerce, and urbanism extended farther out into the basins and foothills of northern and western Mexico than it would have under the conditions which have prevailed over those regions in the last thousand years. Indeed, what surely must have been Mesoamerica's most forward outpost of urban settlement during this favored period of more adequate rainfall was the site now known as La Quemada, or Chicomostoc, in the central part of the state of Zacatecas.

Strategically located near the headwaters of the Río Juchipila, the major northern tributary of the Río Grande de Santiago, Chicomostoc appears to date to the first centuries of the Christian era. Located on the top and flank of a commanding hill with a wide view over the northern approaches to the Juchipila Valley, it was clearly a fortified point erected as an advance outpost of central Mexican civilization against the nomad warriors of the north. The hill itself is of geologic interest, because it consists of a lava flow which has overridden an area of limestone. The latter stone breaks easily into tabular blocks, and it is these which were used to erect the great wall that circles the perimeter of the hill; the site's single, steep-sided pyramid; the imposing ball court which stretches out beneath it; and, most impressively, the great enclosed courtyard or palace with its huge, unmortared columns — the so-called "Hall of Columns." The doorway of this structure, interestingly enough, looks out toward the western horizon at the sunset on August 13. Although the site's founding would appear to have closely followed that of Teotihuacán, its architecture seems to owe little inspiration to the great metropolis; in fact, it may well have been, in part at least, rebuilt by the later Toltecs, for multiple columns were one of their stocks in trade. Punctuating the limestone formation along the western and northern base of the hill are a series of caves which gave the site its indigenous name (*Chicomostoc* means "seven caves" in Nahuatl) and which also figure prominently in the legendary origins of the Aztecs.

Interestingly, about a 1000 km (600 mi) away to the east a similar expansion of settlement was taking place about the same time. Sometime during the second century B.C. civilization was beginning its advance

Figure 29.
At Edzná the commanding structure known as Cinco Pisos has a view out across the flat expanses
of the Yucatán Peninsula for 20–30 km (12–20 mi). At the base of the stairway leading up its
western front stands an ingenious gnomon consisting of a tapered shaft of stone surmounted by
a stone disc whose diameter is the same as the base of the shaft. At noon on the days of the sun's
zenithal passage, the entire shaft is darkened by the shadow of the disc above it.

into the Yucatán region, carried by a people whom the archaeologists
have called the "Pioneers." Surely, people of Mayan tongue had inhabited the region for many centuries in the past, but now for the first time
the rise of a more advanced culture could be detected in the development of ceremonial centers with monumental structures. Although the
Yucatán was a difficult environment in which to nurture an urban settlement, due to the lack of surface water, the undependable rainfall, and the
stony character of the soils, the first major agglomeration in the region
seems to have arisen in what has to have been the most favorably endowed area of the entire peninsula. At the risk of appearing to be a geographic determinist, it could be said that the Mayas had located the best
place first!

This was Edzná, in the interior of Campeche state about 50 km
(30 mi) to the southeast of the port city of Campeche. It is located on the
edge of what is the largest *aguada*, or alluvial basin, in all of the Yucatán,

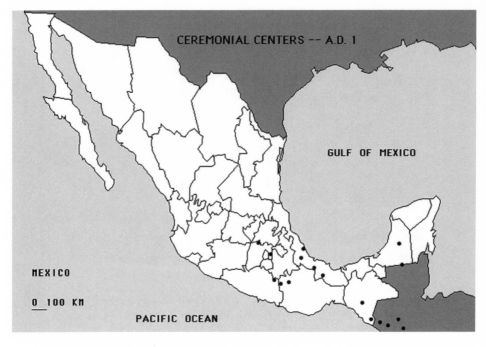

Figure 30.
By the beginning of the Christian era, additional ceremonial centers had appeared in the highlands of Oaxaca and on the Mexican plateau. Among the Maya the earliest urban places had only recently been founded at Edzná and El Mirador.

and consequently had one of the most extensive agricultural hinterlands of any settlement on the peninsula as well as one of the more dependable water supplies. Excavations undertaken by Dr. Ray Matheny of Brigham Young University in the late 1970's revealed not only that Edzná was the earliest major Maya urban center, dating to about 150 B.C., but that at its peak it probably numbered some 20,000 inhabitants. Centered on a five-story pyramid which the archaeologists have termed simply "Cinco Pisos" (Spanish for "five stories"), the site is laced by a series of great radial canals, first seen by Matheny in 1973 as he flew over the area near the end of the rainy season. Fully as impressive as the pyramids at Teotihuacán in terms of the man-days required for their construction, these canals were originally thought by Matheny to have some kind of astronomical orientation, but an astronomer he called in for assistance came up with nothing of consequence. When I first visited the site in 1978, it was with a different question in mind — not why was the ceremonial center where it was, because that was already apparent from its siting on the edge of the *aguada*, but rather what orientations, if any, might the place reveal in terms of its internal structure. Cinco Pisos, I found, looked westward out across a large plaza which was bounded on its far side by a long ridgelike structure with a notch in its middle; and rising up behind the notch, was the top of a second, smaller pyramid. From the doorway of Cinco Piso's courtyard, through the notch, to the top of the small pyramid seemed to offer as carefully constructed a line of sight as could possibly be imagined, and when I measured its azimuth, I found that it was 285°.5 — once again the sunset position on August 13! Indeed, checking the map of the site's layout as a whole, it was perfectly obvious that this orientation represented the guiding principle for all of Edzná, just as it had at Teotihuacán. Thus, in the Yucatán where the very flatness of the terrain all but precluded solsticial orientation to a mountain, the "summer solstice + 52 days" formula was already in use from the time of the first appearance of urban agglomerations in the landscape.

Chapter 6

The Long Count: Astronomical Precision

FIXING THE DAY THE WORLD BEGAN

*F*ollowing the development of the sacred and secular calendars in Izapa in the fourteenth century B.C., their diffusion continued throughout the length and breadth of Mesoamerica during the following two millennia, having most likely reached the Maya highlands of what is now western Honduras by about the fifth century A.D. Although many different peoples of Mesoamerica had by then come under the influence of the two time-counts, including the Zapotecs, Mixtecs, Teotihuacanos, and Maya, it is probably safe to say that the diffusion process itself can largely be attributed to the migrations, military exploits, and "missionary" activities of the Olmecs. Certainly, central to their role as the "mother culture" of Mesoamerican civilization was their preoccupation with time, the elaborate set of religious rituals which they had created to celebrate it, and the distinctive numerical and glyphic systems which they had devised to record it. And common to all of the cultures which had come under the calendars' influence had been the rise of ceremonial centers and urban places whose very locations had been fixed by marking in space certain key points in time, such as the solstices and the sunset on August 13. As yet, of course, the calendars' impact on the Nahua peoples had not even begun, for their arrival in the Valley of Mexico was still at least a century away.

So, too, had the peoples and cultures of western Mexico remained innocent of the Olmecs and their advances (Adams, 1991, 113), largely, it would seem, owing to the relative isolation of the region caused by its topographic ruggedness. (Kent Flannery's argument [1968] that the region was ignored because the Olmecs tended to deal only with societies of equal sophistication is scarcely credible, because the Olmec were everywhere the dominant cultural and commercial actors at the time; hence, they would have had *no one* with whom to interact if that had been the case.) Although some traces of contacts with the plateau are to be found at El Opeño as early as 1300 B.C., it was not until well into the Christian era that Mesoamerican high cultures began to penetrate the mountain fastnesses of the Mexican west (Adams, 1991, 113).

As a result, the coastal regions of Colima, Jalisco, and Nayarit continued to enjoy closer cultural bonds with South America through this period than with the Mesoamerican heartland. In Middle Formative times (800–500 B.C.), the lower reaches of the Balsas River (in what is now Michoacán state) were the site of the so-called Infiernillo phase burials, once more associated with a distinctive type of pottery. By 250 B.C. a new funerary custom, the so-called shaft tomb, was spreading rapidly through the alluvial lowlands of Colima, Jalisco, and Nayarit and subsequently into the interior up along the Santiago corridor. A cultural trait whose origins can be traced back to Peru, Ecuador, and western Colombia, it ultimately penetrated as far inland as the Lake Chapala region. The northern Michoacán site of Chupicuaro, now covered by an irrigation reservoir, appears to have been the main contact point between the the cultures of the highlands and the west during the centuries bracketing the beginning of the Christian era (Adams, 1991, 121).

About the same time that Chupicuaro was reaching its peak as an interactive border post between the two culture worlds, another advance in intellectual sophistication was unfolding in the Mesoamerican heartland. It was perhaps inevitable that, with the passage of time, new and more exacting demands would be made of the calendars, giving rise to innovations in their use that were totally unforeseen at the time of their creation. For example, even though the 365-day secular calendar had attained an improved margin of accuracy over the 260-day sacred almanac, it still missed calibrating the true length of the solar year by about a quarter of a day per year. But for a people who could not comprehend the concept of fractions, there was no obvious way that this matter could ever be reconciled—at least in other than the manner they chose, which was to ignore it.

Nevertheless, because the two calendars ran concurrently, certain realities of their operation must gradually have became apparent to the priests who were responsible for using them. For one thing, they would have realized that the lowest common denominator of the two time-counts amounted to 18,980 days. This is because the sacred almanac of 260 days would require 73 rounds to bring it back into phase with the secular calendar of 365 days, which during the same period would have completed 52 rounds. In other words, $260 \times 73 = 18,980$, whereas 365×52 yields the same result. Thus, all Mesoamerican societies came to believe that "history repeats itself" every 52 years—for if, for example, the beginning day of the sacred almanac, 1 Imix, had fallen on the beginning day of the secular calendar, O Pop, in a given year, then it would take 52 years before the same two day-names and -numbers would again coincide.

For most of the peoples to whom the Olmecs bequeathed the calendars, no further sophistication seemed necessary. After all, the average longevity of a typical person in those days was probably not much more than 30 years, so it would have been the rare individual indeed who would have lived to see the same day-names and -numbers recur within his or her lifetime. In fact, in many of the cultures the 52-year period was itself equated with a "lifetime," whereas a double-period of 104 years was referred to as the lifetime of "a very old person." As a result, in most of the cultures, important events, such as the births and deaths and accessions to power of key members of the society, were seldom specified more closely than to the 52-year period in which they occurred. Thus, when we find glyphs telling of a personage by the name of "8 Deer," we know that the given individual was born on a day with that number and name, but we can't pinpoint the calendar year in which the event occurred unless we know the specific 52-year cycle during which it took place. This custom of citing dates only in terms of a given 52-year cycle has been called the "Short Count," especially by researchers working with the Maya.

However, the association of the Short Count with the Maya is only accurate of their final period of decadence and decline, for through most of their brief but illustrious history, the Maya employed a different, very precise calendrical notation which has come to be known as the Long Count. To credit them with the development of the Long Count would be to misread the facts of the calendars' evolution; this, too, seems clearly to have been an Olmec creation — and indeed, both a brilliant and precocious one at that.

We can only guess at what prompted its development. Perhaps it was simply the dissatisfaction with a time-reckoning system that had so little concern for history that it couldn't define the great events of a society closer than to a given 52-year period. Or perhaps it was an attempt to "squeeze" more precision out of the two time-counts, neither of which recorded the celestial cycles with convincing accuracy. Or was it intended to facilitate more sophisticated computations, such as those involved in the prediction of eclipses? Or perhaps it was just some priest's means of "guesstimating" when the world had begun? After all, these kinds of questions have likewise prompted the various dabblings which have occurred from time to time in Western civilization, not alone with our own present Gregorian calendrical system but with the previous Julian system as well.

The first clue as to when the Long Count was devised is found in the coefficient established by the Goodman-Martínez-Thompson correlation. Each of these researchers realized that the Mayan calendrical glyphs always had reference to a day called 4 Ahau 8 Cumku as the beginning date of their count. This means that the Maya believed that the present epoch of the world began on a day numbered 4 which coincided with the last name (Ahau) of a 20-day "bundle" of the sacred almanac and which coincided with a day numbered 8 which fell in the last 20-day "month" (Cumku) of the secular calendar. (All Mesoamerican cultures believed that the world had existed in four earlier epochs, each of which had been terminated by a different kind of cataclysm. For example, the Aztecs believed that the first world, or "sun," began on a day named "4 Water," and that it came to an end on a day with a similar name as a result of great floods. The second "sun" began on "4 Ocelot," and was terminated on a day of the same name when tigers devoured the world. The third "sun" was called "4 Rain" and was destroyed by a deluge of fire and brimstone on another day of that name. The fourth "sun" was called "4 Wind" and was ultimately ended by a tempest on a day of that name. Our present world, "4 Movement," began on a day with that name and will end with great earthquakes on some occasion when the calendar reaches that day-name again [Krickeberg, 1980, 23].)

Thus, if we were to restate the Maya description of the beginning of the present world in terms of our own calendar, it would be like saying that it had begun on a day numbered 4 which was a Saturday about the middle of December. What had happened during the earlier three days, or in the week before Saturday, or in the course of all the months before December, didn't seem to bother the Maya. Whereas someone growing up in the Western cultural tradition would probably have believed that "beginnings should be beginnings" and that it would "make more sense" if the world had begun on a day like Sunday which fell on the first of January, this was surely not the thought process of the Maya.

In fact, it is just because the Maya date for the world's creation is so "strange" that most researchers recognize it as a hypothetical reconstruction made well after the calendar was in everyday use. Indeed, it was a case not unlike the Romans tracing the mythological founding of their city to Romulus and Remus in 759 B.C., or Bishop Usher fixing the creation of the earth at 10 A.M. on October 23, 4004 B.C. by using the Bible as his authority. But what remained to be established was the correspondence between the Maya date of 4 Ahau 8 Cumku and a date in our own calendar, and this is what Goodman, Martínez, and Thompson each independently set out to do. (Of course, well over a score of other researchers have sought to do the same thing, but none of these other correlations have proven to be as convincing as that of these three scholars.)

Joseph Goodman was a newspaper editor in Virginia City, Nevada, back at the turn of the century. A friend of Mark Twain, he was also a "puzzle buff," and in his readings he came across mention of the strange Maya date and the question as to what it might correlate with in our own calendar. In 1905 he published a short article in which he put forth the results of his computations, namely, that the Maya date could be equated with August 11, 3114 B.C.

Of course, there were no bona fide archaeologists in Goodman's day, so little or no professional notice was taken of his deductions. A couple of decades went by before a Mexican astronomer independently tried his hand at the problem. In 1926, Juan Martínez Hernández came up with a date which placed the beginning of the Maya calendar one day later, on August 12, 3114 B.C. This time, however, the result was not ignored, having been advanced by a professionally trained academic. Of course, that did not necessarily make it correct, so British archaeologist John Eric Sydney Thompson put his mind to the problem and a year later, in 1927, published his findings. Based on his examination of Maya eclipse tables, the correlation of 4 Ahau 8 Cumku should be one day later still, he said, placing it at August 13, 3114 B.C. (It is because all three of these researchers came to virtually the same solution that this correlation has come to be called by all of their names.)

As it turned out, if Thompson had left well enough alone, a subsequent generation of archaeologists, astronomers, and other aficionados of prehistory would have found life a lot easier. But, in 1935, Thompson had "second thoughts," deciding not only that Goodman had been correct in the first place but also that the Maya really weren't astronomers after all, but only "astrologers." This meant that the correct date was indeed August 11, 3114 B.C., and that later researchers would be ill-advised to look for astronomical meanings behind Maya dates, because if they found them, they could only be "coincidences." The dean of Mesoamerican archaeologists having spoken, the matter was finally settled — or so they thought.

When I published my hypothesis of the origin of the 260-day Mesoamerican sacred calendar in *Science* in September 1973, one of the first responses I received was from Sir John Eric Sydney Thompson, recently knighted by Queen Elizabeth II for his substantial professional contributions to the discipline of archaeology. Short and terse, Thompson's note chided me for "overlooking" his book from 1950 in which he claimed to have effectively disposed of any astronomical arguments for the calendar's creation, even going so far as to cite the specific pages I had missed. I dutifully reread the passages he alluded to, and after considerable thought and some trepidation — I had never before written to a knight of the British Empire — I wrote, "I had read the pages you cited, but I thought you were wrong then and I still think you are wrong." Needless to say, that was the end of our correspondence — but certainly not of the controversy which surrounds the so-called Maya calendar. (Indeed, as the reader will already have discovered, this is largely what the present volume is all about.)

Thompson's understanding of how the 260-day almanac arose came down to one of two possibilities: Either it represented a permutation of the numbers 13 and 20, both of which had a special significance to the Maya, or it represented an approximation of the human gestation period. In any case, he argued that it had nothing to do with astronomy. When it had been pointed out to him by Merrill in 1945 that the zenithal passage of the sun over Copán — the major Maya astronomical center in the mountains of western Honduras, located at precisely the same latitude as Izapa — occurred on August 13, the day that his own correlation originally indicated the Maya had believed was the "beginning of the world," he had dismissed it as a "coincidence." Of course, when Thompson "revised" his date for the origin of the Long Count to August 11, that automatically put all subsequent attempts by astronomers to reconcile the Maya calendar with our own off by two days — making the argument of "coincidence" seem all the more credible. On the other hand, neither Thompson nor any of his disciples has ever explained *when* the permutation of 13 and 20 actually was carried out to put the Long Count in motion, or *whose* gestation period was so significant as to base the starting point of an entire calendrical system on it. Indeed, while birth makes it perfectly clear when a gestation period has ended, what recorded act specifically defines when it began? Or, for that matter, how do we know that it actually took 260 days to complete? If modern science is at pains to define the moment of conception, how in the world could the early Mesoamericans have decided that the length of the gestation period was precisely 260 days?

Ironically, in the same vein, some writers on the subject of the Mesoamerican calendar have taken me to task because my explanation of the 260-day almanac's origin is 2 days at variance with Thompson's revised formula. Had it ever occurred to them that Thompson might have been right the first time, perhaps they wouldn't persist in such specious arguments.

It seems extremely unlikely that the "New World Hipparchus" who was responsible for the development of the 260-day sacred almanac and the 365-day secular calendar had any other intent in mind than to devise a means of recording time or, even more specifically, of predicting the advent of the rainy season. Certainly, there could be no notion whatsoever that either calendar—especially one that he himself had been instrumental in developing—should attempt to define "when the world began"; after all, he himself had been around before the calendar was, and the world, in turn, was obviously a lot older than he. Such an idea would probably have been as preposterous to him as the notion of fractions! Indeed, perhaps he would have been hard-pressed to think in any longer spans of time than from one rainy season to another, because that, after all, was what the calendar was all about—at least to him.

Any notions of "history" or ideas of time as an ongoing continuum must have been the product of a mind or minds that could have contemplated the whole question from the vantage point of a considerable hindsight. After all, as the initial Olmec priest himself recognized, a day has not really existed until it is over. By the same token, a person's lifetime, or a 52-year cycle, has not really existed until it has been completed. Only after several generations have passed is the notion of "history" even possible. And when it becomes desirable or useful to characterize the span of history, it is necessary to do so in units of time and in a context that has meaning to the society for which the history is being devised. Thus, Christians calibrate history according to the birth of Christ, Muslims according to the Hegira of Muhammad, etc.; and no doubt because we are accustomed to using a decimal system, we find it convenient to speak in terms of "decades" and "centuries"—though on a human scale such measures as the latter are rather meaningless.

In a culture which employed a vigesimal system and for which the number 13 had a special, if not magical, importance, it is not surprising that the most meaningful units would have been some multiples of these values. The most basic unit was the day, known as a *kin*, or "sun," in Mayan. The second-order unit was a "bundle" of 20 days, which we have called a *uinal,* or literally a "moon." The third-order unit we have called a *tun,* and it represents the one deviation from the vigesimal system which the Maya permitted themselves. Composed of 18 "bundles" of 20 days, rather than the full complement of 20 "bundles," it was in recognition of the fact that 360 days is a much closer approximation to a length of a year than 400 days was. (For all measures other than time, however, the strict vigesimal system was employed.) The fourth-order unit consisted of a "bundle" of 20 *tuns,* or what we have called a *katun.* Because each *tun* was five days shorter than an actual year, each *katun* equated to a time span of 19 years and 260 days, for a total of 7200 days in all. Because these were the most "human-scaled" units of the Maya calendar, Thompson contended that *katuns* were the most important "building blocks" of their timekeeping system. (More about this later.)

The fifth-order unit is the so-called *baktun,* which consists of a "bundle" of 20 *katuns,* or a total of 144,000 days (i.e., 20 × 7200). Equated to a measure which is somewhat more meaningful to us, a *baktun* represents a span of time 394 years and 95 days in length. Yet another interval of time as the Maya conceived it was what we call a "grand cycle," composed of 13 *baktuns,* which can likewise be translated as "a world." If the present world began on August 13, 3114 B.C., then it is due to end on December 23, A.D. 2012, according to the Maya, because that is when the 13th *baktun* will be complete.

But where, and by whom, was this "master plan" of Maya world history devised? Again, one must look to the internal structure of the so-called Maya calendar to see what clues it affords us. If *katuns* were the most significant "building blocks" in the Maya time-count, as Thompson has argued they were, then I would suggest that the manner in which to begin is to find out how many times a *katun* has ended on 8 Cumku. This was the date in the secular calendar, it will be remembered, that our unknown history-minded priest had decided that the world had begun, most likely because he was looking for a time to assign to the zenithal sun's passage. (Whether or not he knew *where* the zenithal sun had passed overhead on that special day, he was certainly aware that that passage had been the mechanism for starting the calendar, as we shall clarify later.)

By designing a computer program which used as its beginning date the correlation between Maya and Gregorian calendars worked out by

Goodman—namely, that 13 Ahau 8 Xul equaled November 4, A.D. 1539—I proceeded to run the program backward, having instructed the computer to indicate each time that a *katun* ended on 8 Cumku. The first time that the computer stopped was on 8 Ahau 8 Cumku, which equated to the date of September 23, A.D. 1204. This, of course, was well after the Classic Period of the Maya had come to a close and their civilization was in decline, so this result could quickly be discarded. The next time the computer stopped was on 11 Ahau 8 Cumku, which equated to a date of September 18, 236 B.C. (This seemed like a feasible date, but I was not prepared to make any judgment until all the evidence was in. Naturally, because there was a full 1440-year interval between the first computer result and the second, it was already apparent that if the same interval occurred before the next result was in—which was more than likely—then the final result would be far too old.) Sure enough, the only other time that a *katun* had ended on 8 Cumku was on September 13, 1675 B.C., when 1 Ahau corresponded with that date. I therefore was led to conclude that whoever had projected the time-count back into history had done so in the year 236 B.C., because this was the only time frame that would have been consistent with what we know of Maya history. This meant that the day on which this projection had been made was identified in the Long Count—which was now being used to record dates for the first time—as 7.6.0.0.0. In other words, the creator-priest of these newly meshed time-counts had decided that seven *baktuns* and six *katuns* had elapsed since the theoretical "beginning of the world."

It should be noted that a Maya Long Count inscription must contain a minimum of nine terms to define it. First, there are the five numerals describing the number of *baktuns*, *katuns*, *tuns*, *uinals*, and *kins*, respectively, which have elapsed since "the beginning of time." These are followed by the number and day-name of the date in the sacred almanac and then by the number and day-name in the secular calendar. As a result, the date that was recorded was absolutely unique. Even so, at some later time, other glyphs were added to the inscription to make it astronomically yet more precise, as for example, by enumerating how many days had elapsed since the last new moon.

The result which had been produced by my computer program was entirely consistent with what we knew of Maya inscriptions, because none had ever been found which predated the seventh *baktun*—a period of time that ran from 353 B.C. to A.D. 41. On the other hand, what the 236 B.C. date did show rather conclusively was that the so-called Maya Long Count was not a product of the Maya at all, but rather the creation of their predecessors, the Olmecs, for civilization (in the sense of ceremonial centers and monumental structures) had not even reached the Maya at this juncture in their history.

Unknown to me at the time I had launched my computer investigation of the Maya calendar was the fact that in 1930 a mathematician by the name of John Teeple had come to exactly the same conclusion, but had done so by approaching the question of the Long Count's origin from quite another direction than I had taken. Having recognized how the recurrence of the 73 cycles of the 260-day sacred almanac coincided with the 52 years of the secular calendar, Teeple had suggested that what the Maya had done was to use a multiple of 73 *katuns* to arrive at their hypothetical "beginning of time." Of course, he was unaware that the designer of the Long Count was impelled to establish an August 13 starting date for the count, regardless of how many *katuns* were thought to have intervened. As a result, Teeple's formula was to employ two cycles of 73 *katuns*, or 146 *katuns* in all, to reach the point in time when he believed the Maya priests had chosen to initiate the Long Count. One hundred forty-six *katuns*, of course, can be broken down into seven *baktuns* plus six *katuns*; thus, the Maya date on which Teeple concluded the Long Count had been commenced was 7.6.0.0.0 (Teeple, 1930).

When I carried out my computer analysis of the Maya calendar, I was also unaware that Thompson had likewise taken note of Teeple's computation. However, while lauding him as "a brilliant mathematician," he had dismissed his result as unlikely and unconvincing, thereby effectively consigning Teeple's conclusion to the trash-heap of oblivion—at least until I inadvertently reinforced it with my own finding. Ironically, the realization that I had been "anticipated" by Teeple was reassuring to me, because even though we had approached the problem from very different vantage points, we had arrived at the same conclusion. On the other hand, even though I now found myself in the company of "a brilliant mathematician," I was even further at odds with the dean of Maya archaeologists!

MATHEMATICS WITHOUT TEARS

Perhaps the initial motive for devising the Long Count was an attempt to give the Olmecs some perspective of history, and in that, it was singularly successful. Time could now be appreciated as a continuum, and its expanse was infinite. When the Olmecs spoke of the "beginning of the world" or "the beginning of time," it may have been only the "present world" they had in mind. On the other hand, there is good reason to believe that they conceived the current "grand cycle" of 13 *baktuns* in which they existed as but one more reincarnation of worlds that have existed in the past and but one more step on the way toward future worlds. In any event, common to all later Mesoamerican cultures was the notion that four previous worlds had already come and gone.

But while there was something philosophically reassuring about the view of time which the Long Count afforded them, the Olmecs also found that it was an eminently practical device as well. Now they had a means of defining every day that passed as being absolutely unique — at least within a time span of one "grand cycle," or 5125 years. And the position of every day within that round of 13 *baktuns*, or 1,872,000 days, was numbered consecutively from "the beginning." The imprecision of the Short Count, or defining a day within a given 52-year period, was gone. Human life spans lost their meaning when compared to the "life spans" of the sun, moon, and stars, and of the celestial rhythms which governed their movements. The Long Count had opened a whole new vista, not only in history but also in mathematics.

The principles of zero and place notation had already been worked out by our "New World Hipparchus" when the secular calendar had been set in motion; the Long Count now just put those principles into use as never before. Many of the secrets of the heavens remained to be deciphered, and certainly one of the most pressing — primarily because it was so frightening — was the seemingly random disappearance of the sun or moon. Was there a cycle between such happenings, they asked? Was there a way that they could keep careful enough records so that they would eventually know when such a happening was going to take place? For that matter, what really was the cycle between two full moons, or two new moons? And surely one of the most problematical of celestial bodies — the third-brightest object in the heavens after the sun and moon — had to be Venus. Its importance could not be doubted, but its erratic behavior — first as morning star, then disappearing, next as evening star, and then disappearing again — seemed to defy explanation. After all, in a culture where fractions did not exist, the counts could become long and involved before any celestial cycle such as that of the moon or Venus would emerge with a number of whole days. At least, when all the days were reduced to numbers, counting them was far simpler, especially the longer it took to define such a cycle.

A case in point was the determination of a lunation — that is, the time between one full moon and another, which modern atomic clocks record as just less than 29.5306 days. The closest approximation the Maya ever made to this interval was by counting full moons for 12 *tuns* and 80 *kins*, by which time 149 lunations had taken place in exactly 4400 days. At this point, they were only about 0.0004 off the value we use today. Thus, even though they were handicapped by their inability to conceive of fractions, the Maya, through long and patient counting, were able to achieve a level of precision in their astronomical studies which few other early peoples in the world ever matched.

It is interesting that amid the renaissance of European science the same idea of assigning each and every day its own distinctive number — also to facilitate the calculation of astronomical intervals — surfaced once again. This time it was a French-born Italian by the name of Joseph Justus Scaliger who devised the count and the year was 1582. A true Renaissance man, Joseph Scaliger was the son of a classical philologist and medical doctor who had lived and worked in France and made his primary reputation as a poetry critic. Joseph himself became a professor at the University of Leiden in the Netherlands in 1593 and made significant contributions to such fields as numismatics, epigraphy, and literary analysis, in addition to chronology.

Scaliger, like his Mesoamerican predecessor eighteen centuries earlier, was a product of his own culture and was constrained not only by a starting date that was fixed by the calendar with which he was familiar but also by one that had a special astronomical significance. Indeed, a further constraint under which he operated, which most probably had not been a concern of his Mesoamerican counterpart, was his own appreciation of history. Scaliger lived at a time when the true antiquity of the Egyptian and Near Eastern civilizations was just beginning to be appreciated, so his time-count would have to accommodate events that may have happened at least as far back as 4000 B.C. In other words, if Scaliger did not choose his starting date carefully enough, computations involving very ancient observations from places like Egypt would necessarily involve negative numbers and this would have served more to complicate his case rather than to expedite it.

Not too surprisingly, Joseph Scaliger chose January 1 as the beginning day of his count, but of course it had to be a very special January 1 that had occurred before 4000 B.C. By searching the astronomical records and making his own computations, he discovered that in the year 4713 B.C., the 28-year solar cycle, the 19-year lunar cycle, and the 15-year indiction cycle would all have coincided. (The latter, interestingly enough, was a concept widely used in medieval chronological studies but had nothing to do with astronomy. Rather, it was related to the tax reassessment system used in the Roman Empire, and probably had been originally adopted from Egypt.) Inasmuch as the least common multiple of the three cycles was 7980 years (i.e., 28 × 19 × 15), any day could be identified within that span of time with absolute specificity. Both the 7980-year period and the day-count within it he named for his father, Julius Caesar Scaliger, and thereby added two new concepts to the tool kit of Western science: the Julian Period and the Julian Day number. Needless to say, although the former is now regarded as "quaint" and anachronistic, we continue to use it because there has been no compelling reason to start counting over from some other date. In other words, January 1, 4713 B.C., continues to serve the Western world as well today as the date August 13, 3114 B.C., appears to have served the Mesoamerican world for well over a millennium.

Before we leave this matter of the Long Count and its belated European counterpart, let us pause a moment to consider the relationship between them. This, after all, is what the correlation of the two calendrical systems is all about. To establish the Julian Day number of the date on which the "New World Hipparchus" began his count of the 260-day sacred almanac, we first must subtract the number of years between the time that the Julian Period began and when the Olmec time-count was set in motion. Keep in mind that the term "Before Christ," or "B.C.," is a historical denomination rather than an astronomical one, because historians recognize no "year zero," whereas astronomers do. Thus, 4713 B.C. in historical parlance is the equivalent of −4712 in astronomical usage. As long as the two dates in question both lie on the same side of Christ's "birth," there is no problem, but when one of the dates is "B.C." and the other is "A.D.," it should be remembered to subtract one year between them. One other thing to remember is that when Scaliger set up his Julian Day numbers in 1582, he was using the so-called Julian calendar (named not for his father but for Julius Caesar). By that time, however, the Julian calendar had gotten so far out of phase with the realities of the solar year that Pope Gregory XIII decreed the adoption of a new and more accurate calendar in October of that very year. This is the so-called Gregorian calendar which the Western world uses today.

Returning to our computation, we find that there were 1599 years which elapsed between 4713 B.C. and 3114 B.C., for a rounded total of 584,035 days according to the Julian calendar (which used 365.25 days as the length of the solar year). Of course, this represented the number of days between January 1 in both years, so we have to add a further 225 days to reach August 13. This means, then, that a total of 584,260 days had elapsed between the two dates using the formula supplied by the Julian calendar.

However, the reason that the Julian calendar had finally to be abandoned was that it was using a value for the length of the solar year which was 0.0078 days too long, because the actual length of the solar year (as determined by modern science) is not 365.25 days but 365.2422 days. As a result, the Julian calendar gained a day every 128 years, so that by the year 1582, when Pope Gregory finally tackled the problem of calendar reform, the vernal equinox had slipped from March 21 to March 11. (Even though the ecclesiastical council which met at Nicaea in 325 had decided that the vernal equinox should always fall on March 21 — as it did in the period from the year 200 to 325 — in order to expedite the fixing of the date of Easter, they had done nothing to rectify the calendar to insure that this would happen.)

To understand how a date in the Gregorian calendar would vary from one in the Julian calendar, it is necessary to subtract 325 from any year following the year 325, or to add 200 to any year preceding the year 200. Thus, in 1582 the number of years which had elapsed between the time that the Julian calendar was in phase with reality — as measured by the vernal equinox occurring on March 21 — and the time that the Gregorian calendar supplanted it was 1257, namely 1582 − 325 = 1257. Dividing this in turn by 128 reveals that the slippage of the Julian calendar within that time period was 9.8 (or 10) days.

By the same token, if we wished to calculate how great the disparity would have been between the Julian calendar and the Gregorian calendar in recording a date such as 3114 B.C., we add 200 to 3114 to obtain the number of years which elapsed between them (200 + 3114 = 3314) and then divide this by 128. The result in this case is 25 days, which must be added to the total of 584,260 which had elapsed between the beginning of the Julian Period and the theoretical date of the Maya's "beginning of time." Thus, the Julian Day number for August 13, 3114 B.C. is 584,285 — the value used by the (initial) Goodman-Martínez-Thompson correlation to calibrate the Maya calendar with the Gregorian.

THE GEOGRAPHIC DISTRIBUTION OF EARLY LONG COUNT INSCRIPTIONS

In establishing the geographic birthplace of the Long Count, the spatial distribution of the earliest known inscriptions may be of some assistance. Admittedly, the sample is small, for there are only eight known inscriptions which date from the first *baktun* of the Long Count's existence.

The oldest of these is Stela 2 found at Chiapa de Corzo, in the heart of Mexico's southernmost state, Chiapas. Although it had been broken at the top such that the *baktun* numeral is missing, Gareth Lowe, who discovered the monument in 1962, transcribes its date (7.16.3.2.13 6 Acatl) as December 10, 36 B.C. In doing so, he followed a line of reasoning which was first employed when a similarly broken stela had been unearthed in the Gulf coastal plain more than 20 years earlier. In the process, what had been the oldest known Long Count inscription was "bumped" into second place.

The second oldest Long Count inscription which has been found up until the present time occurs on a stela from Tres Zapotes, near the northern edge of the Tuxtla Mountains in the state of Veracruz. Known as Stela C ever since it was uncovered by Matthew Stirling during his excavation there in 1939, it early became a bone of contention between "Mayanistas" and "Olmequistas" (Ochoa and Lee, 1983, 181). The fact that its *baktun* number was missing, the stela having been broken at that point, only fueled a controversy that had long been brewing. If the missing *baktun* numeral had been a seven, Stela C would have been the oldest known example of a monument bearing a Maya Long Count date. But because its geography was all wrong, having been discovered in a classic Olmec area, "Mayanistas" such as Thompson and Morley argued that either the *baktun* numeral had been an 8, meaning that the Long Count had diffused into the Olmec area long after the Maya had devised it, or it was a "copy" of the Maya Long Count date which simply used a different (and by implication, later) starting date. Protagonists of the Olmec school, on the other hand, argued that the only calendrical inscriptions found outside of the Maya area until that time had all been of *baktun* 7 origin, so why should it be supposed that this was any different? In any case, by sheer good fortune, the missing piece of the stela was found in 1969 and the *baktun* value was indeed a seven! Its complete rendering in the Long Count is 7.16.6.16.18 6 Eznab, which equates to September 5, 32 B.C.

The third example of an early Long Count date comes from Guatemalan Soconusco, where a stela was uncovered at the site of El Baúl in 1923 by T. T. Waterman. His reading of what has come to be called Stela 1 was "corrected" by the German archaeologist Lehman in 1926, and refined further by Michael Coe in 1957. The latter reads it as 7.19.15.7.12 12 Eb, which equates to March 6, A.D. 37. John Graham, however, proposed in 1978 that it should be read as 7.18.9.7.12, which makes its equivalent date July 21, A.D. 11, instead. At the nearby site of Abaj Takalik, two additional early Long Count dates were discovered on a monument labeled Stela 5 in 1978. The first of these Graham reads as 8.3.2.10.15, which is equivalent to May 22, A.D. 103, and the second as 8.4.5.17.11, which equates to June 6, A.D. 126. Graham also believes that the inscription on Monument 2, which was found at Abaj Takalik in 1925, is calendrical as well; however, in the reproduction of this inscription which appears in Adams (1991, 94) the only clear-cut bar-and-dot numeral to be seen is a single numeral 11 at its far left. Graham's interpretation raises the entire issue of how Olmec numerals were originally written: Were they always necessarily dots and bars? I find this question of special interest, because in the first volume published on the monuments of Izapa (Norman, 1973), no mention was made of any calendrical inscriptions having been found at that site — perhaps the more accurate term should be "recognized." As Norman's second volume was nearing completion, he realized that "most of the monuments, whether carved or plain, have a calendrical function" (1976, 4), although my paper suggesting this possibility is not cited in his otherwise extensive review of the literature. When a third publication on Izapan monuments by Lowe, Lee, and Martínez appeared in 1982 (following by almost a decade the publication of my article in *Science* pinpointing Izapa as the birthplace of the calendar), it is conceded that the site's "sculptural inventory . . . make it likely that this center's participation was important in the formation of Mesoamerican religion and the ritual calendar" (299). (Interestingly, this time my work was cited in the bibliography but not without making the point that I was "anticipated" in my hypothesis "much earlier" by, among others, Rafael Girard [336]. Yet, when one consults the reference to Girard in the same bibliography, it is conceded that he made no mention of Izapa [330]. Girard, a Guatemalan, seems to have preferred to trace the birthplace of the calendar to a site in his own country, perhaps for reasons of nationalism.) However, none of the numerous "calendrical" monuments which Lowe illustrates and describes use the conventional bar-and-dot notation for numerals. If he is correct, then the obvious implication is that, while the calendars may well have been devised at Izapa, the numerical system used for recording them must have been the later invention of some priest elsewhere.

Early in this century a strange little statuette looking rather like a duck-billed platypus, but with an unmistakable Maya Long Count date on one side, was found in the Tuxtla Mountains. Bearing a date of 8.6.2.4.17 8 Caban 15 Kankin, the so-called "Tuxtla Statuette" posed one of the first "shocks" to the "Mayanistas" because its date — equated to March 15, A.D. 162 — was a full 130 years older than any Long Count date found within the Classic Maya area itself. However, because it was scarcely more than 20 cm (8 in.) tall, it was immediately classed as "*art mobilier*" by the "Mayanistas," implying, of course, that it could still have been Maya in origin even if it had been found in a distinctly non-Maya geographical area.

The most recent find containing Long Count dates was made in 1986 when a 2.5-m (8-ft) stone was fished out of the Río Acula in central Veracruz state. Now known as the La Mojarra stela in commemoration of the little fishing village where it was brought ashore, its two Long Count dates have been transcribed as 8.5.3.3.5, which equates to May 22, A.D. 143, and as 8.5.16.9.7, which is equivalent to July 14, A.D. 156.

According to the decipherment by Kaufman and Justeson, the inscription purports to describe the accession to power of a chieftain called "Harvest Mountain Lord" on the first date and his successful quashing of a rebellion led by his brother-in-law on the second date. Of special interest from a calendrical point of view is the fact that the two dates found on the La Mojarra stela begin with the day-number and day-name in the sacred almanac and end with the day-number and day-name in the secular calendar, unlike later Maya practice which placed the day-numbers and day-names of both the secular and sacred counts at the conclusion of the inscription. Thus, in the first of the two dates the glyph for 13 Kayab precedes the Long Count notation of 8.5.3.3.5, which in turn is followed by the glyph for 3 Chicchan; in each instance the numerals are shown to the *right* of their respective name-glyphs. In the second date the glyph for 15 Pop precedes the Long Count notation of 8.5.16.9.7, but here the numeral appears to the *left* of the name-glyph. Following this Long Count notation is the day-name glyph for Manik, but because the stone has been effaced to the left of it, what should have been the number five (i.e., a bar), in keeping with the pattern described above, is missing.

To summarize the eight early, recognizably Long Count inscriptions, then, we find that one occurred on an artifact which was "movable" and hence can probably be expected to shed little light on the geographic origins of the Long Count. The remaining seven inscriptions are all found on relatively massive stone stelae which are unlikely to have been moved far from where they were carved, and therefore must be taken into ac-

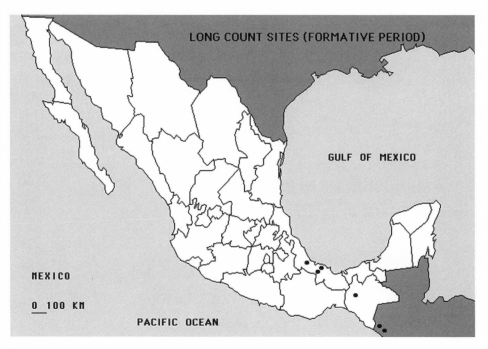

Figure 31.
The development and use of the Long Count marks a quantum leap forward in mathematical sophistication among the peoples of Mesoamerica. It was developed in 236 B.C. by the Olmecs, and during the Formative Period its use was restricted to a belt running from Soconusco through the Chiapas highlands into the Gulf coastal plain of Mexico.

count. Because two dates are found on each of two different stelae, the sample consists of six carved monuments in all. Of these, two were found in Guatemalan Soconusco and three were found in the Olmec area of central Veracruz, with the remaining one coming from the Grijalva Depression about halfway in between. Because of this distribution, it would be difficult to make a case for the Long Count having originated at either end of this Olmec axis, but it is clear even from the small sample at hand that a lively interchange of ideas was moving back and forth across the Tehuantepec Gap as early as the second century B.C.

Chapter 7

Calendar Reform and Eclipses: The Place of Edzná

HIGH NOON AMONG THE MAYA

*A*lthough both the 260-day sacred almanac and the 365-day secular calendar predated the Maya by well over a millennium, and the "principle" of using key calendar dates to define urban locations and the Long Count itself had likewise been developed by the Olmecs several centuries before the Maya emerged as a civilized society, it was the latter who seized upon these intellectual tools and honed them to the highest level of sophistication of any of the native peoples of Mesoamerica. Ironically, they did so in one of the most difficult environments in the entire region; yet, this same environment may ultimately have been responsible for their failure to survive as an advanced and vigorous culture until the arrival of the Europeans.

Having largely been displaced from their initial homeland in the Gulf coastal plain of Mexico by the migration of the Zoques in the thirteenth century B.C., most of the Mayan-speaking peoples ended up moving toward the east. (It will be remembered that only one group of Maya moved northward as a result of the Zoque advance, becoming in the

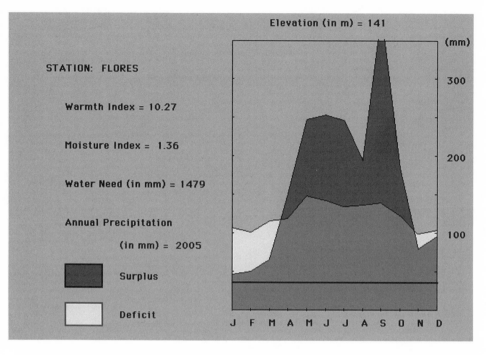

Figure 32.
The climatic station of Flores is located in the heart of the region of Petén, now a part of northern Guatemala. It is representative of Tikal and the core area of the so-called Old Empire of the Maya. Although its water need (i.e., temperature) curve is somewhat more variable than those of Soconusco or the Olmec region, its precipitation curve demonstrates both a monsoonal peak during the warmest months of the year and a very marked hurricane peak in early autumn. Its warmth and moisture indices insure its classification as a tropical humid climate, which supports a native vegetation of heavy rain forest.

process the Huastecs.) The area into which the Maya moved can be subdivided into three rather distinct geographic regions. The first of these was the Petén region of northern Guatemala and southern Yucatán: an area of relatively heavy precipitation mantled in dense tropical rain forest, developed on a deeply weathered base of flat-lying limestone, pocked with solution valleys — many of which contain lakes of some size — and laced by numerous rivers. The second region was the Yucatán Peninsula itself: an area of drier climate developed on a low and almost featureless limestone plateau with no surface drainage and supporting a vegetation cover of short, deciduous, tropical scrub forest. And the third region

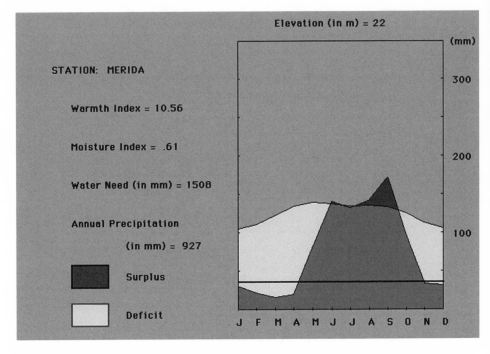

Figure 33.
Mérida, the capital and largest city of Yucatán, is located in the northwestern quadrant of the peninsula, away from the trade winds which blow in constantly from the Caribbean Sea. Its water budget diagram is typical of the region which constituted the so-called New Empire of the Maya, represented by such sites as Uxmal, Mayapán, and Chichén Itzá. Its relatively uniform water need (i.e., temperature) curve is unfortunately not matched by its precipitation curve, so much of the year the area experiences a moisture deficit. Monsoonal rains in the high-sun period seasonally provide enough moisture for a corn harvest, and a small surplus is usually recorded with the passage of an autumn hurricane. While the station's warmth index indicates that it is clearly tropical, the fact that Mérida only receives about 60 percent of the moisture it actually needs means that the native vegetation of the northern Yucatán is scrub forest. (Data from Secretaría de Recursos Hidráulicos.)

comprised the highlands of Guatemala: an area of subtropical to temperate mixed forest developed on a base of folded limestone ridges in the north that give way to lofty volcanic peaks in the south.

As was pointed out earlier, the Maya seem to have founded their earliest major ceremonial center in what has to have been the most favored geographic setting in all of the Yucatán — on the edge on the largest *aguada,* or alluvial depression, in the entire peninsula. Located in what

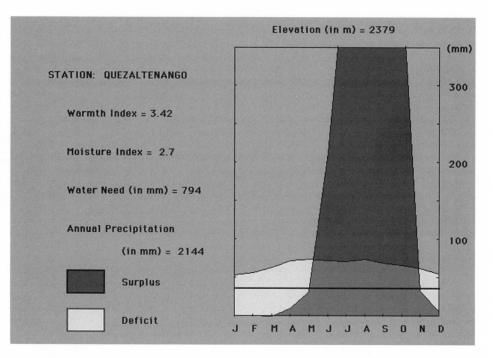

Figure 34.
The climatic station of Quezaltenango is located in the western highlands of Guatemala, just over the Sierra Madre from Soconusco. Its low latitude and high elevation combine to produce a very even water need curve which in no month exceeds 75 mm (3 in.). Although the station enjoys a 12-month growing season (delimited by the straight line near the bottom of the graph), an occasional frost can pose a risk to crops. Its extreme precipitation curve, with a low-sun deficit and a high-sun surplus, exemplifies a typical monsoonal climate. However, with a warmth index of less than 4.0, it qualifies as a warm-temperate humid climate which supports a native vegetation of mixed broadleaf and coniferous forest.

today is the interior of Campeche state, this vast soil-filled depression provided the agricultural support system for the incipient "city" we now know as Edzná. Dating to about 150 B.C., Edzná was a bustling urban node for more than 20,000 persons at the peak of its existence in the early centuries of the Christian era.

Although the layout of Edzná mimicked that of Teotihuacán, its contemporary on the Mexican plateau, by being oriented to the setting sun on the "day the world began," the Maya priests were no doubt quick to realize that August 13 was a date that had no real meaning to the peasant farmers of the Yucatán. The priests were certainly aware of the practice of using the zenithal passage of the sun to herald the beginning of a new year, but at Edzná the sun passed overhead at noon no less than 18 days earlier than the date that the Olmecs had established as "the beginning of time." Obviously, while the Maya couldn't change the facts of history, they could amend the calendar to accord more closely with the realities of their own physical setting.

Not only did the priests of Edzná appreciate the need for such a calendar reform, but their reckoning also told them that an auspicious time for such a change was drawing nigh. The Long Count was nearing the completion of *baktun* 7, and *baktun* 8 was soon about to begin. What more appropriate a time could they have contemplated for "turning over a new leaf"?

Yet, as *baktun* 8 neared and the zenithal sun passed overhead, it was as if the Maya's own auguries obliged them to postpone the calendar reform. Forty-five days before the dawn of *baktun* 8, they recorded the passage of the zenithal sun, which fell in that year (A.D. 41) on the Maya date 3 Men 3 Uayeb. It was the latter aspect of this date which must have given them pause, because the "month" of Uayeb was the five-day unlucky period at the end of the Maya year. During these five inauspicious days, the people were wont to keep as low a profile as possible, engaging in only a minimum of activities, as if hoping thereby to escape the wrath of the gods. Certainly, not until the zenithal sun had cleared Uayeb could the calendar reform be instituted safely and prudently. But because their calendar did not take into account the extra quarter day in the length of the solar year, this meant that a full 20 years were required to advance the calendar by five days. Since the coincidence of the zenithal sun with the "month" of Uayeb had begun in the equivalent of the year A.D. 28 — i.e., 13 years earlier — there were still 7 years to go before its passage would occur on 0 Pop, the first day of the secular year. Thus, the very first time that the zenithal sun passed overhead in the Maya area on 0 Pop occurred in the year A.D. 48 — an event which would have been recorded in the Long Count as 8.0.6.17.12 12 Eb 0 Pop.

In order to calibrate the zenithal sun passage, the Maya priests had erected at the base of the Cinco Pisos pyramid in Edzná an absolutely ingenious gnomon. (Remember that a gnomon can be any upright pillar or post; its function is to *not* cast a shadow on the days the sun is directly overhead.) The Edzná gnomon was a tapered shaft of stone about half a meter (20 in.) in height surmounted by a disk of stone which had the same diameter as the base of the shaft (see figure 29). Thus, on the days that the sun stood directly overhead, the disk at the top of the shaft would envelop the entire shaft in its own shadow, whereas on any other day a stripe of sunlight would fall across the shaft. Hence, there was no question as to what day would begin the new year.

There were also a couple of other things which the Maya priests may have realized at the invocation of their reformed calendar of which they may have been unaware earlier. They were well aware, of course, that every time one of their "Vague Years" of 365 days was completed, the date in the 260-day sacred almanac had advanced by another 105 days. But, because the least common divisor between the two counts was 5 and there were 20 day-names in the sacred almanac, there would only be 4 day-names that would repeatedly coincide with the beginning of the 365-day year. Thus, because their calendar reform was initiated on a day called 12 Eb in the sacred almanac, in the following year the Maya new year fell on 13 Caban (105 days later in the sacred almanac). However, in the year after that — because the sacred almanac used only 13 numerals — the new year fell on 1 Ik (another advance of 105 days). And in the fourth year, the Maya new year's day was celebrated on 2 Manik (105 days farther along in the almanac). By the beginning of the fifth year, the cycle of 20 day-names started over, so that the following four years began on 3 Eb, 4 Caban, 5 Ik, and 6 Manik, respectively — each year being identified with the next higher numeral but always with one of the same 4 day-names.

From this realization, the Maya developed the notion that these four days of the sacred almanac — Eb, Caban, Ik, and Manik — were "the bearers of the years"; that is, they "carried" the year along until it was passed on to the next "bearer," much as athletes run a relay race. This idea of "year bearers" gives us an insight into how the Maya envisioned time; each day was a "burden" to be carried by the deity who presided over it until his leg of the relay was complete, at which time he transferred it to the next deity, and so it went.

Reassuring as the notion of regular "year bearers" must have been to the Maya, they were still troubled by the fact that the beginning of their new year soon failed to coincide with the zenithal passage of the vertical sun. Naturally, this was because their "Vague Year" was 365 days long, rather than 365 days plus a fraction, so that in four years their secular calendar slipped a full day. Thus, when the zenithal sun passed over Edzná for the fifth time, it did so on 1 Pop rather than 0 Pop; by the ninth time, new year's day fell on 2 Pop; by the thirteenth time, its passage took place on 3 Pop, and so forth. Ironically, by measuring the passage of the zenithal sun over Edzná so precisely, the Maya priests came to realize as never before how imprecise their time-count really was. (In this same connection, it is interesting to note that Bishop Landa records that the Maya had, by the sixteenth century, shifted over to using the days Kan, Muluc, Ix, and Cauac as their year bearers.)

On the other hand, the decision by the priests of Edzná to make the beginning of their year accord with the zenithal passage of the sun over their city — an event which occurs on July 26 in our own calendar — left a lasting mark on Maya timekeeping. As it turned out, the parallel of 19°.5 N latitude on which Edzná is located neatly bisects the Yucatán Peninsula, which means that throughout the Maya heartland the zenithal passage of the sun was an event that had meaning and relevance to everyone. It appears, therefore, that Edzná, through the combined "accidents" of geography and history came to serve as the "Greenwich of the Maya," for nowhere else within the region they occupied could the July 26 zenithal passage be calibrated except there. In other words, no other ceremonial center within the Maya area is situated at precisely this latitude, so only at Edzná could the new year's date be pinpointed. In fact, writing about Edzná, Thompson observes that its priests seem to have exercised something akin to a "veto power" in calendrical matters, for he mentions a possible one-day correction to the calendar having been made there in the year 671, after which all the other Maya ceremonial centers appear to have fallen into line (Thompson, 1950).

Some researchers have assumed that each Maya ceremonial center had its own calendar, but the observation by Thompson cited above suggests otherwise. So, too, does the historical record, because Bishop Diego de Landa, the third Spanish prelate of the Yucatán, specifically records

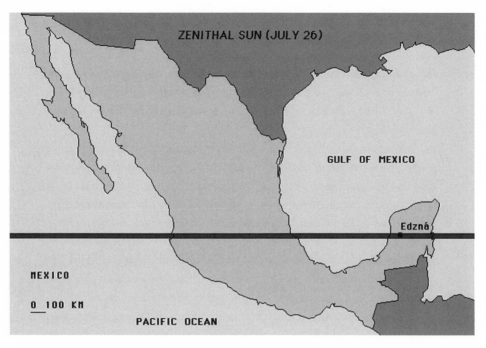

Figure 35.
One of the early Spanish prelates of the Yucatán, Bishop Landa, reported that the Maya marked
the beginning of their new year with the zenithal passage of the sun on the equivalent of July 26
in our calendar. Such an event takes place along the parallel of 19°.5 N, a line which neatly bisects
the peninsula but intersects only one major site in doing so — Edzná. Because the first day of the
Maya new year, O Pop, initially coincided with July 26 around the year A.D. 48, this would appear
to mark the beginning of their "reformed" calendar.

that the Maya began their new year with the passage of the zenithal sun,
and that the day this occurred was the equivalent of July 26 in the Gregorian calendar. It is of further interest to note that in the interval between the time the Maya priests undertook the calendar reform in the
year A.D. 48 and the time that Landa wrote, one entire Sothic cycle of
1460 years had passed, and astronomical events which were in phase in
the year 48 were again in phase in the year 1508. (The word *Sothic*
comes from the Egyptian name for the star Sirius. Because the ancient
Egyptian calendar also had 365 days, rather than 365.25 days, the rising
of Sirius, which marked the Egyptian new year, was likewise found to get

out of phase with the movements of the sun. However, by careful measurement the Egyptians found that after 1460 full solar years had passed — the equivalent of 1461 of their "imperfect" years — the sun and the stars would once more be back in harmony with each other.) Thus, the zenithal sun passage once again coincided with the day 0 Pop in the Maya secular calendar in that year and during the three following years.

All attempts to understand Maya civilization have been made immensely more difficult because Bishop Landa, in his religious zeal, managed to consign all but a handful of the Maya's books and records to his bonfires. The rather straightforward description of the astronomical importance of Edzná which I have sketched out above was by no means as direct and uncomplicated as it might sound. But it did begin with the two clues which Landa bequeathed to us — namely, that the Maya new year coincided with the passage of the zenithal sun and that this event occurred on the equivalent of July 26 in our present calendar.

Working from these clues, I reasoned that, if Landa's information was correct, I should be able to zero in on the geographic location where the Maya had devised their version of the calendar. A solar ephemeris revealed that on July 26 the noonday sun passes overhead at 19°.5 N latitude, so armed with this knowledge, I next turned to a detailed map of archaeological sites in the Yucatán (*National Geographic's* "Archaeological Map of Middle America," published in 1968). The latter showed only one ceremonial center of any significance at this latitude, its name being rendered as "Etzná"; to one side, there was a vignette describing it as a "Late Classic site [having a] temple atop a pyramid faced with four stories of rooms." A subsequent search of the literature turned up only a couple of references to Edzná, including the one attributed to Thompson which I cited above. Therefore, all I really knew about the place was that its construction had been dated to the period A.D. 600–900 and that it seemed to have had some "clout" when it came to resolving calendrical issues.

In the winter of 1976 as I was devising my computer program to run the "Maya" calendars back to the dates on which they had been initiated, I put in a "flag" to have the program alert me as to when the Maya day 0 Pop coincided with our day July 26. Employing Goodman's correlation as my starting point—namely, that the Long Count date of 11.16.0.0.0 13 Ahau 8 Xul = November 4, 1539, I set the program in motion and only seconds later I was informed that the coincidence I was looking for had occurred most recently during the years 1508–1511. Thereafter, the computer churned away until an entire Sothic cycle had passed and we were back in the period A.D. 48–51.

In view of the antiquity of this date as opposed to the relative "lateness" of Edzná's supposed founding, in my 1978 article reporting the findings of my computer study I decided to make no mention of the "Maya calendar reform" which I had hypothesized had taken place there. (The deductions which had led me to Izapa had embroiled me in enough conflict with the archaeologists, I felt.) Ironically, as my article was going to press in the winter of 1978, I chanced to meet Prof. Matheny, who had recently excavated Edzná, in the field. When I cautiously mentioned to him how my deductions had suggested a calendar reform having taken place there "about 600 years before the place was founded," he laughed and replied, "Well, Cinco Pisos may have been a Late Classic construction but our radiocarbon data show us that Edzná itself was a thriving concern already about 150 B.C." Encouraged by both my computer findings and Prof. Matheny, I then went on to Edzná to make the further discoveries reported in these pages.

MAKING SENSE OF THE MOON

Pinning down the movement of the sun, irregular as it was with respect to the Long Count, was like child's play for the Maya compared to their struggle to understand the movements of the moon. Once again their failure to recognize the concept of fractions obliged them to undertake lengthy counts of cycles in the hope of eventually finding two periods which coincided in nice, whole integers. A case in point is the length of a lunation, the period of time between two successive new moons. The Maya obviously realized that it was not 29 days, but it also was not 30 days. Attempting to describe a time period which was actually 29 days, 12 hours, 44 minutes, and 2.8 seconds in length was for them a philosophical impossibility. Yet, after they had counted 149 "moons" in a row they realized that exactly 12 *tuns* and 4 *uinals* had elapsed, or a total of

4400 days; they were then confident that the cycle would begin over again, with the moon occupying the same position it had had relative to the sun when the cycle began. That they could do so with reasonable assurance is demonstrated by the fact that 4400 days divided by 149 lunations yields an average of 29.5302 days per lunation — a value less than 0.0004 at variance with that used by modern astronomers!

More difficult yet, however, was trying to find some regular pattern in the moon's seemingly erratic bouncing around the sky. Unlike the sun, which moves progressively farther north or south each day until it finally reaches its "stopping place" and then turns around, the moon rises and sets at such different times of the day or night in such widely differing places along the horizon that it might seem "illogical," "crazy," or "drunken" in its behavior. Indeed, if it were not for the fact that on occasion the moon suddenly became dark, or, even worse, that the sun itself was sometimes "devoured" by darkness without warning, perhaps there would have been no real reason to try to make sense out of the moon's motions. Initially, the priests may have shared the layman's terror of the disappearing sun or moon, but not too many eclipses would have occurred before they may have suspected some functional relationship between the orderly path of the sun and the seemingly disorderly path of the moon. Yet, not until the "crazy" ricocheting of the latter could be understood would they be able to predict the occurrence of eclipses, and only after they had mastered that skill would they be in a position to exercise the full power of that knowledge over their untutored subjects.

The preoccupation of the early Mesoamericans with this matter of eclipses can probably be detected in one of the oldest Long Count inscriptions yet discovered, namely, Stela C from Tres Zapotes found by Matthew Stirling in 1939. Although the controversy over whether its missing *baktun* value was a "7" or an "8" was conclusively settled with the discovery of the detached fragment in 1969, no real attempt has been made to ascertain what its date actually recorded. Its inscription reads "7.16.6.16.18" in the Long Count, which may be transcribed into the Julian date of September 5, −31, or 32 B.C., if we use the Goodman-Martínez-Thompson correlation value of 584,285. (Of course, if we were to employ Thompson's "revised" value of 584,283 from 1935, the date would equate to September 3 instead.)

Figure 36.
Stela C from Tres Zapotes now reposes in the National
Museum of Anthropology and History in Mexico City. The
missing *baktun* value of its Long Count inscription was found
in 1969, confirming the carving's 32 B.C. date. The lower
edge of the stela is ruptured through the middle of the glyphs
that give the number and name of the day in the sacred
calendar.

In an earlier paper (Malmström, 1992a), I advanced the notion
that, although Stela C was only discovered in 1939, the meaning of its
inscription may well be found in a monumental work of European science first published in 1877. Known as *Canon der Finsternisse,* or "Table
of Eclipses," the volume is the work of Theodor von Oppolzer, an Aus-
trian count, and a team of his assistants, and constitutes a catalog of over

8000 solar and 5200 lunar eclipses ranging in date from 1208 B.C. to A.D. 2161. Although his 376 pages of calculations and 160 maps charting the central paths of the solar eclipses were all carried out by hand, their accuracy has only recently been reconfirmed by modern researchers using computers (Meeus and Mucke, 1979).

Listed as event no. 2803 in Oppolzer's list of solar eclipses is one whose path of centrality passed right over the Olmec ceremonial center of Tres Zapotes at dawn on the morning of August 31, 32 B.C. A more frightening celestial event can scarcely be imagined, for the sun rose out of the Gulf of Mexico totally black except for a ring of light around its outer edges. Oppolzer described it as an annular, or ringlike, eclipse, and subsequent calculations at the U.S. Naval Observatory have revealed that the disk of the sun was 93 percent obscured (personal communication). Surely, a "day without a sunrise" is not likely to have gone unrecorded by the Olmecs!

But, if this eclipse really is the same event as that described by Oppolzer, why does its date not coincide with that which he records? A number of possible explanations suggest themselves: (1) perhaps the Olmecs waited either three or five days to record it, depending on which correlation value of Thompson's one uses; (2) perhaps the stone carver who engraved the stela made an error of either three or five days in inscribing the date; or (3) perhaps the Goodman-Martínez-Thompson correlation value is incorrect by three to five days. Of course, there is also a fourth possibility — namely, that it had nothing whatsoever to do with the eclipse recorded by Oppolzer, and that it was merely a strikingly close coincidence of both geography and history.

The first hypothesis has no merit whatsoever, for if the Olmecs consciously chose to put off recording the date, they would certainly have no means for measuring eclipse cycles with any precision. Any basis they might have had for maintaining accurate records would thus largely have been vitiated.

The second hypothesis is credible; after all, "to err is human." If this is the case, the inscription on Stela C is more likely the result of an illiterate stone carver's mistake, however, than of a priest's miscalculation. But, if so, which is the "easier" mistake to make: to carve an extra three dots in the final, or *kin*, position — equivalent to a three-day error — or to carve an extra bar in the *kin* position — equivalent to a five-day error? Clearly, the mistaken addition of one symbol — the bar — would have been more likely than the mistaken addition of three symbols, so the discrepancy between Oppolzer and the Olmecs would appear to have been a matter of five days rather than three.

The third hypothesis — that the GMT itself may be off by three to five days — is hardly likely, but the merits of the second hypothesis are now reflected in the accuracy of the original Thompson correlation value of 584,285. If that value is used, then the five-day discrepancy between Oppolzer and the Olmecs is substantiated; if, on the other hand, we use Thompson's "revised" value of 584,283, then the lack of a correspondence between the two dates can no longer be explained as an error, and we would probably have to abandon any thought that the Olmecs were recording the eclipse after all. That, in turn, would mean discarding both the close historical "coincidence" between the two dates and the geographic "coincidence" of the passing of the eclipse's central path directly over Tres Zapotes. In effect, therefore, the inscription of Stela C, erroneous though it seems to be, appears to confirm the accuracy of the original Thompson correlation value between the Olmec calendar and our own.

In all fairness, however, it should be noted that there is one further complication in this interpretation of Stela C's date. The bottom edge of the inscription is broken just at the point where the number and name of the day in the sacred almanac is recorded. If the Long Count inscription itself is accurate, the day-number and -name should be 6 Eznab, and this is the way the fragmentary glyph at the bottom of the inscription is translated by most scholars. If the numeral is indeed rendered by a dot and a bar, then there is no question of its being a "6," but in keeping with my hypothesis that a second bar had been mistakenly added to the inscription. Obviously, my argument is not destroyed by such a reading but it is substantially weakened, for to be consistent with my hypothesis, the day-number should have been a "1" instead.

Of course, if the inscription is accurate as it stands, it would then reopen the whole issue of what it was that the Olmecs were actually recording on that intriguing occasion. If the blackened sun at dawn was not noteworthy enough to take cognizance of, what other event could have been so much more spectacular or important to them that they took notice of it instead? Was it the occultation of Mars by the sun that coincided very closely with the eclipse? Or might it have been the occultation of the bright star Regulus (magnitude 1.35) by the planet Venus that occurred during the following couple of nights? Neither of these seem very likely, for surely both of these astronomical events literally pale into insignificance when compared to a total solar eclipse. Thus, we are left with the very real possibility that *nothing* of note astronomically had prompted the carving of the inscription of Stela C but that something even more earthshaking had taken place in and around Tres Zapotes shortly after the ominous eclipse had occurred. Thanks to its location in the foothills of a volcanic region like the Tuxtlas, the most obvious possibilities become either a monstrous earthquake or a devastating eruption.

The point of this digression has been simply to illustrate that, about the time that Edzná was coming into being, the Mesoamericans appear to have begun recording eclipse data on their stelae, possibly in the hope that through accurate timekeeping they would eventually solve the puzzle of when these fearsome events would recur. In the intellectual community of the Maya, therefore, this problem must have been near the top of the agenda as Edzná was being founded.

In the flat and featureless landscape of Yucatán, it had been a rather simple matter to lay out a new city oriented to the sunset on "the day the world began" because the "summer solstice + 52 days" formula had already been developed. Nonetheless, in a region where the local topography presented no opportunities for calibration against a natural landmark, the "gun-sight" alignment from the courtyard of Cinco Pisos through the notch in the artificial horizon to the top of the small pyramid constituted an ingenious solution to the problem of the city's orientation. In the same way, the erection of the tapered shaft surmounted by the stone disk had been an ingenious solution to calibrating the passage of the zenithal sun. The problem now at hand required some means of marking the moon's rising and setting position along the circumference of the monotonously uniform horizon that stretched out from Edzná in all directions.

Figure 37.
View of the western horizon as seen from the top of Cinco Pisos at Edzná. The elongated mound across the plaza served as an artificial horizon for a priest standing in the doorway of the courtyard, allowing him to sight through the notch in the middle of the mound to the summit of the pyramid immediately behind it to calibrate the sunset on August 13—an azimuth of 285°.5. The pyramid which intersects the true horizon farther to the right, or northwest, is "La Vieja," whose azimuth marks the northernmost stillstand of the moon (i.e., 300°).

No doubt the first task was to provide the priests with a vantage point which allowed them a complete and unencumbered view of the entire 360° circuit of the horizon—hence the need to erect what was perhaps the highest pyramid yet constructed in Mesoamerica. When completed, the aptly named Cinco Pisos ("Five Stories") towered more than 40 m (130 ft) above the rocky platform on which it was sited, becoming in the process a true landmark visible from 40–50 km (20–30 mi) away. Although Cinco Pisos is a Late Classic structure (i.e., built between A.D. 600 and 900), its situation at a focal point for the ceremonial center's canal system (which dates to the Late Preclassic period—300 B.C. to A.D. 300) makes it seem likely that an earlier structure previously occupied this critical position. In fact, Matheny suggests that "perhaps the remains of the Late Preclassic structure still exist within

Cinco Pisos" (1983, 81). In any case, from the top of this key structure one could look out in any direction in a clear sight-line to the far horizon.

The real problem was to keep track of the places along the horizon where the moon either rose or set. That Cinco Pisos faced slightly to the northwest to begin with — having been oriented along with the rest of Edzná to an azimuth of 285°.5 — meant that the moon's *setting* position was the one the priests chose to calibrate. But with a horizon so distant and so featureless, one is tempted to conclude that most of the initial record keeping may have been done by marking lines in the appropriate directions on the top platform of Cinco Pisos itself. Only after the observations had narrowed in on a distinct enough point to erect some structure against the horizon at the required azimuth would that have been done.

Conceptually, the Maya already had the model of the sun's behavior on which to predicate their observations. Its northernmost stopping point marked the summer solstice, which in turn established the beginning date for the 52-day count which fixed "the day the world began" — i.e., August 13. If they could locate a similar position for the moon — its northernmost setting point — perhaps that would allow them to begin the count which would eventually reveal the secrets of the eclipse cycle.

Deciding what the northernmost setting point of the moon really was must have been a tedious and frequently altered judgment in itself. Each time the moon reached what appeared to be an even more extreme setting position, the count for the eclipse cycle would have to be started again. One can well imagine that sometimes years of patient counting and record keeping might have gone on before the moon unexpectedly pushed its setting position even farther north along the horizon and literally wiped out the whole exhaustive tally in one fell swoop.

When this process actually began and how long it took to yield any kind of meaningful results has to be pure conjecture. It is probably safe to say that the idea for launching the count may already have been formulated shortly after Edzná was founded, and may well have been under way when the calendar reform fixing the new new year's day was adopted. What we do know for certain is that the first time that mention is made of the phase of the moon corresponding to a given Long Count date is in an inscription dating from A.D. 357 (Coe, 1980, 159). This does not mean, of course, that the problem had been solved by then, but only that from that time forward this seemingly important fact was now to be regularly recorded along with the date itself. Indeed, this may be evidence that the lunar cycle had *not* yet been worked out, and that the priests felt the additional bit of information regarding the phase of the moon might actually be useful in finally establishing the cycle—once they could examine the records in retrospect.

This is not to say that the eclipse cycle could not have been worked out within the first half century that the quest was initiated. What the Maya were ultimately to learn was that the cycle required a full 6797 days, or 18.61 years, to complete, so if they had actually recognized the moon's northernmost stillstand on one occasion, they would have had to count that long to find the moon once more back at the same setting position. Of course, to confirm the accuracy of their count would require the completion of at least one more full cycle, so by this time more than 37 years would have elapsed. Thus, to postulate even the minimum time span necessary for such an achievement makes one appreciate the care and continuity which the Maya priests exercised in keeping a constant, running tally over the equivalent of more than an entire generation.

Although less than a half dozen of the original Maya manuscripts appear to have escaped the flames of the fanatic Spaniards, one of those that did survive is the so-called Dresden Codex, which has subsequently been recognized as an elaborate eclipse warning table. Thompson, among other scholars, assigns a twelfth-century origin to it, but concedes that its three base dates go back to the middle of the eighth century. (My suggestion that the Stela C inscription may have involved a five-day error owing to a stone carver's failure to understand the date he was carving finds an ironic parallel in the Dresden Codex. Thompson's study of the manuscript revealed that no fewer than 92 errors of transcription have been made in recording its dates [1972, 115–116], but no one, least of all Thompson, has ever suggested discounting the validity of the tables on that account.)

The three base dates of the Dresden Codex occur in the latter part of the year 755 and define two 15-day intervals. For this reason, Maud Makemson suggested, in 1943, that they most likely represent two solar eclipses bracketing a lunar eclipse (Makemson, 1943). While not disputing such an interpretation, Floyd Lounsbury, writing in 1978, argues that if this is correct, then these dates must have been arrived at by calculation rather than through observation, because no such celestial events took place in Yucatán in that year (Lounsbury, 1978, 816).

The three dates in question would equate to November 8, November 23, and December 8, 755, if the original correlation value of Thompson (namely, 584,285) is employed. (Naturally, if his "revised" version is used, it would put each of these dates two days earlier.) When the first of these dates was checked against a planetarium programmed to duplicate celestial events as seen from Edzná on that day, it was found that the sun and moon did in fact rise just eight minutes apart on that morning over the Yucatán, with an angular separation of less than 2°.5. In other words, there had been a "near miss" to a solar eclipse visible in the Maya area on that date.

For the second date, we once again employ the calculations of Oppolzer (1887). Fifteen days after the near solar eclipse over the Yucatán — i.e., on November 23 — he records a total lunar eclipse as having taken place, but ironically, his data demonstrate that it was visible only in the half of the world centered on the Indian subcontinent. On the third date, again using Oppolzer as our source, we find that a partial solar eclipse did indeed take place on December 8, 755, but its central path lay over the ocean between South Africa and Antarctica, where probably not a single human being witnessed it.

From this data we can draw two very important conclusions. First, by the year 755 the Maya had apparently worked out the motions of the moon with such precision that they knew when an eclipse *should* occur, but they still could not be sure if it actually *would* occur, in the sense of being visible to them. Second, the original Thompson correlation value of 584,285 is clearly the correct one, for an acknowledged eclipse warning table such as the Dresden Codex could certainly not have been based upon a foundation two days out of phase with the realities of the celestial sphere.

Although we cannot be certain when the Maya finally succeeded in working out the lunar eclipse cycle, it would seem that most of the basic "research" on the problem was carried out at Edzná. Located some

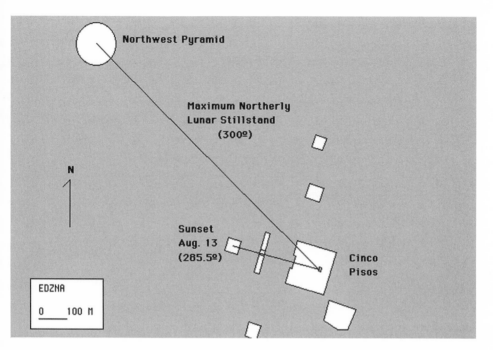

Figure 38.
In this map view of Edzná, we see the features shown photographically in Figure 37. The astronomical importance of Edzná may be gauged from these facts: (1) only at its specific latitude could the beginning of the Maya new year be calibrated, here with the assistance of a remarkable gnomon; (2) the "day the world began" was commemorated in the "gun-sight" orientation between the doorway of Cinco Pisos and the small pyramid across the plaza; and (3) lunar cycles were measured by using the line of sight between Cinco Pisos and "La Vieja" on the northwestern horizon.

300 m (1000 ft) to the northwest of Cinco Pisos is the ruin of a lofty pyramid which Matheny has termed "La Vieja," or the "Old One." The "La Vieja" complex appears to date to the Late Classic period as well, but has not experienced the "urban renewal" from which Cinco Pisos subsequently benefited (Matheny, 1983, 109). Even in its dilapidated condition it is still high enough to intersect the horizon as seen from the top of Cinco Pisos; indeed, it is the only manmade construction which does so. This fact immediately prompted me to measure its azimuth as seen from Edzná's commanding edifice, and the value I obtained was 300°. This means that the summit of the pyramid lies exactly 5° beyond the

sun's northernmost setting position at the summer solstice. Because the moon's orbit is just a hair over 5° off that of the sun, it seems very likely that the Northwest Pyramid, or "La Vieja," had been erected as a horizon marker to commemorate the moon's northernmost stillstand. Not only is "La Vieja" an eloquent testimonial to the patience and accuracy of Maya "science," but because of its specialized function, it is also probably worthy of being designated as the oldest lunar observatory in the New World. (Indeed, if Matheny's dating of "La Vieja" is accurate, then it is apparent that the Maya had succeeded in measuring the interval between lunar stillstand maxima at least by A.D. 300.)

Chapter 8

The Golden Age

THE RISE OF MAYA CIVILIZATION

A s the wave of urbanization swept over the peninsula of Yucatán in the centuries following the founding of Edzná, the flat and featureless landscape of the low, limestone plateau afforded the Maya with few opportunities to orient their incipient cities to topographic features of any significance. At El Mirador, in northernmost Guatemala, for example, evidence is just now coming to light regarding its impressive proportions, its age, and its configuration. Dating to just about the beginning of the Christian era, this site appears to have followed the pattern of Edzná in its layout, for its dominating structure — a lofty pyramid called by its excavators *Danta* ("tapir") — is squarely oriented toward the setting sun on August 13 over the *Tigre* pyramid, some 2 km (1.25 mi) to the west (Matheny, 1987, 334–335). This does not mean, however, that the principle of solsticial orientation had been either forgotten or totally abandoned, because that was definitely not the case. Where the topography permitted — and among the lowland Maya, this was in very few instances indeed — locating a ceremonial center with respect to a solsticial sunrise or sunset was still most probably the preferred principle to employ. Thus, when the ceremonial center of Uaxactún in the Petén region of northern Guatemala was founded — most likely about the first or second century A.D. — its site represented the point on the watershed between the Gulf of Mexico and the Caribbean from which the winter solstice sunrise could be calibrated over Baldy Beacon (1020 m, 3346 ft) in the Maya Mountains of Belize. (However, this did not prevent the local priests from "reinforcing" the azimuths of both the summer and winter solstices architecturally, for one of the earliest illustrations of archaeo-astronomic alignments ever reported — by Frans Blom in 1924 — was the relationship of the structures in Group E at Uaxactún. He noted that sight-lines from Building VII to the northern corner of Building I and to the southern corner of Building III mark the sunrise positions on the summer and winter solstices, respectively, while a sight-line through the middle of Building II commemorates the equinoctial sunrise [Rojas, 1983, 25, 28].)

Ironically, when the so-called Maya capital of Tikal was founded just 25 km (16 mi) to the south of Uaxactún about a century later, along the same height of land between the Caribbean and the Gulf of Mexico, its site marked the point where the winter solstice sunrise could be seen over Victoria Peak, which is the highest peak in the Maya Mountains (1122 m, 3681 ft). Indeed, one is tempted to speculate that the Maya may initially have thought that the culminating peak of that range was Baldy Beacon, but upon discovering some years later that this was not true, they felt obliged to build a second and larger ceremonial center to commemorate the critical calendrical event over the higher mountain. Otherwise, there is certainly little reason for having located two major ceremonial centers so close to one another — a matter which, it may be pointed out, has long puzzled most archaeologists (see figure 39).

Because the oldest Long Count inscription found at Tikal traces back to A.D. 292, archaeologists have chosen this general time frame as the commencement point of the so-called Classic Period. Thus, depending on the source consulted, the Classic Period of Mesoamerica's cultural evolution is usually considered to have begun in A.D. 250 or 300.

During the following two to three centuries, civilization spread through the jungles of Petén like a tidal wave. In what has to have been

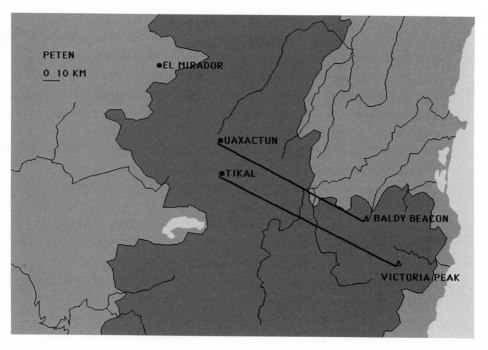

Figure 39.
Solsticial alignment to mountains was, of course, impossible in regions like the Yucatán, so
El Mirador built its orientation into its architectural monuments as Edzná had done earlier. Both
Uaxactún and Tikal, on the other hand, were close enough for the peaks of the Maya Mountains
to be utilized as winter solstice sunrise azimuths, but priests at both ceremonial centers likewise
reinforced their calendrical alignments by incorporating them into the layout of their buildings
as well.

the greatest crescendo of land clearing and city building that the Mesoamerican world had ever witnessed, the Maya peoples rose to unparal-
leled heights of political organization, economic prosperity, and social
sophistication. Although several writers have labeled this the "Old Empire" period of the Maya, Frans Blom more accurately defined it as the
"Petén period," for most of this feverish expansion was geographically
concentrated in the rain forests of what is today northern Guatemala, Belize, and the southern Yucatán. Only in later Classic times (after 600 A.D.)
did a similar wave of development occur farther north, giving rise to
what the same writers called the "New Empire" of the Maya, but which
Blom has characterized as the "Yucatán period" (Blom, 1983, 309–310).

The preferability of Blom's terminology derives not only from his insistence on the difference in geographic focus, but also because the Maya seem never to have developed anything like a unified empire. Indeed, most likely because of the environment in which they lived, their most extensive political unit did not evolve beyond the level of the city-state. The most unfortunate consequence of this fact, in turn, was an ongoing rivalry between adjacent political dynasties which manifested itself in an almost endemic state of warfare. A strikingly frequent subject of both Maya art and inscriptions are dynastic struggles and slave raids, whereas fortifications were an integral part of many of their early urban centers, such as Edzná, Tikal, and Becán.

Throughout the Classic Period, literally scores of major ceremonial centers were erected, and each of these in turn probably served as the "central place" for a cluster of as many as a dozen other subsidiary settlements. In each instance, the location of the ceremonial centers was dictated by the presence of water, in the form of either a *cenote* (Spanish for "sinkhole," derived from the Mayan word *tzonot*) or an *aguada* such as that which gave rise to Edzná. As populations grew, however, additional measures were undertaken to impound or store water during the rainy season, including the construction of *chultunes,* or underground reservoirs, cut out of the limestone bedrock and plastered with clay. Nevertheless, to suggest that the resultant settlement pattern of the Maya approximated that which would have theoretically developed on an isotropic (or homogeneous) plain, as some writers have done, is to ignore totally the fact that the availability of water was *neither* ubiquitous nor uniform throughout the region.

On the other hand, it is probably safe to say that during the entire Classic Period not a single major Maya ceremonial center was erected without preserving in at least one of its key structures an alignment either to a solstice or to the sunset on August 13. Denied the option of using a topographic feature for such a purpose, the Maya incorporated these sacred precepts into the very façades of their buildings. The palaces at Sayil and Labná, the Codz Pop at Kabáh, the Temple of the Inscriptions at Palenque, the Temple of the Magician at Uxmal, El Castillo at Chichén Itzá, and the main pyramid at Toniná are but a few examples of such alignments. All Maya ceremonial centers likewise employed the Long Count in the dating of their monuments.

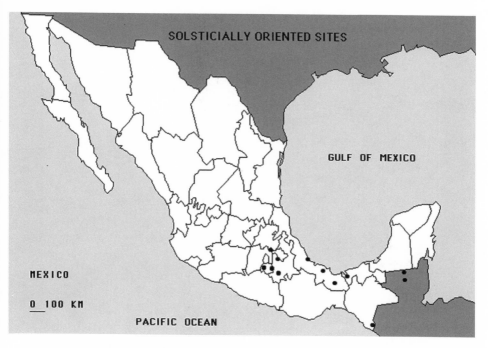

Figure 40.
The principle of solsticial orientation was developed as early as the fourteenth century B.C. and diffused as widely as was practicable in terms of local topography. Its heyday was definitely limited to Formative times.

IN QUEST OF ORIGINS

If there ever was such a period as a golden age among the peoples of Mesoamerica, it occurred during the late fifth and early sixth centuries A.D. By that time a relatively homogeneous cultural landscape extended from the southern margins of the region in El Salvador and Guatemala through Soconusco and the Gulf coastal lowland of Mexico as far westward and northward as the uplands of Oaxaca and the high basins of the plateau and as far eastward as the jungles of Petén and the outer reaches of the Yucatán Peninsula. Here was a culture region characterized by organized political entities with hierarchical social and economic systems dominated by priestly castes; great ceremonial centers laid out according to carefully executed plans and adorned with imposing structures of

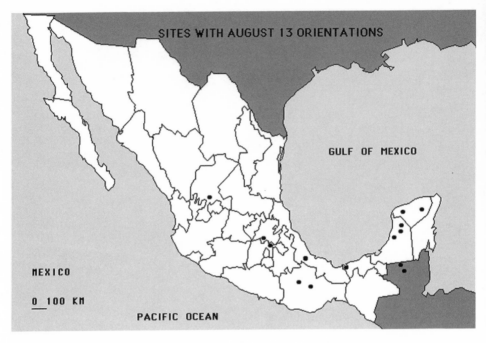

Figure 41.
The principle of orientation to the August 13th sunset was probably first utilized about 800 B.C. and continued well into Classic times. Its use implies an enhanced level of sophistication over and above the basic principle of solsticial orientation. The extent of its geographic diffusion is a good approximation of the limits of the Mesoamerican cultural realm as it existed at the peak of Teotihuacán's influence.

monumental architecture; an elaborate and extensive trading network which linked its every corner and penetrated even the adjacent areas of present-day Central America and the southeastern United States; and an essentially uniform religious philosophy. Although the names of the deities differed from one language area to another, it is clear from the manner in which they were artistically depicted that the rain-god, for example, be he known as Tlaloc, Chac, Cocijo, or Pije, was really one and the same. Moreover, the calendars with which the different peoples of the region recorded their history and scheduled their rituals were likewise but variations on a common theme. Indeed, by this time the cultural influences which had given "Mesoamerica" its regional distinctiveness had been diffused to all but the farthest reaches of its geographic frontiers.

Figure 42.
"El Caracol" at Chichén Itzá has long been recognized as an astronomical observatory whose
foundations are Maya and whose subsequent embellishments are Toltec. Perhaps the most
significant alignments of this structure are those of its front door and its principal window,
located just above it, both of which look out at the western horizon toward the sunset position
on August 13.

It was during this relatively peaceful and harmonious period that a
couple of what appear to have been Mesoamerica's most intriguing intellectual quests were undertaken. And because it was at precisely this juncture that the great metropolis of Teotihuacán had its greatest influence
over the region as a whole — as witnessed both in artistic motifs and architectural innovations — there can be little doubt that the impetus for
these quests stemmed from the priests who lived and worked in this
bustling highland city.

We have already seen how their "obedience" to the sun-god seems to
have led to the founding of a "relay station" on the ridge that visually
separated Orizaba from the Valley of Mexico and how they had laid
out their city in the valley to align both with the winter solstice sunrise
over Mexico's highest mountain and with the sunset on August 13 (see
figure 23). Somewhat later, their preoccupation with the movements of
Venus had prompted them to establish an astronomical observatory in
the northeastern hills at Xihuingo to mark the planet's extreme rising and

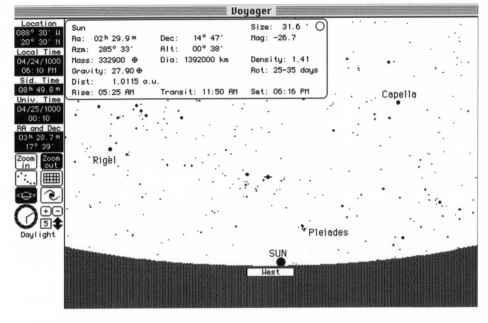

Figure 43.
This screen display produced by the VOYAGER computer program recreates the sky at sunset in late April in the year A.D. 1000, as it would have appeared through the main window of "El Caracol" at Chichén Itzá in the Yucatán. From the information inset at the top of the display, it will be noted that the sun is directly overhead at the latitude of Izapa (declination 14°.47) and that it is setting at an azimuth of 285°.5 — which would have been precisely in the middle of the observatory window. Although the Pleiades set within minutes of the sun — at the right-hand edge of the window — they were not visible in the bright afterglow of the sun. Such a reconstruction proves with dramatic eloquence the author's thesis that the sunset on August 13 — the only other day of the year that the sun is vertically overhead at the latitude of Izapa — constituted one of the key astronomical events in ancient Mesoamerican timekeeping. (The VOYAGER program is a product of Carina Software, San Leandro, CA 94577.)

setting positions (Wallrath and Ruiz, 1991, 297). Therefore, it was probably only a question of time before their curiosity would send them off on a couple of more distant expeditions to answer two of the most fundamental questions posed by their cultural heritage.

The first question had to do with the 260-day sacred almanac. Inasmuch as it had begun with the southward passage of the zenithal sun, it must be possible, they reasoned, to find a place *where* such an interval could be measured. Naively enough, they probably assumed that if they

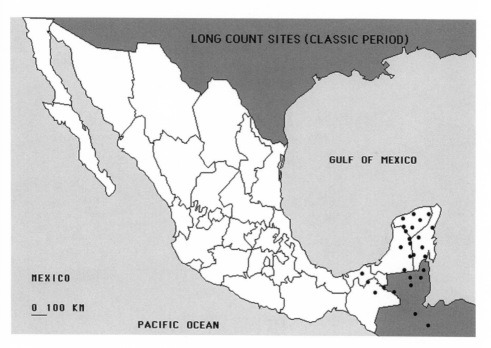

Figure 44.
For some inexplicable reason, the Long Count either never diffused into the highlands of Oaxaca or onto the Mexican plateau, or if it did, it was never appreciated and adopted by the peoples of these regions. As a result, its use was restricted to the Maya, for whom it became a tool of inestimable value in furthering their knowledge of complex astronomical cycles, such as those of Venus and of solar and lunar eclipses.

could locate that place, then they would have discovered the birthplace of their cultural forefathers.

The second question was related to the 365-day secular calendar. Its count was initiated when the sun reached its farthest northerly point in the sky. Every year the priests watched as the sun made its annual "pilgrimage" from far to the south — over Orizaba — to far to the north — somewhere in the northern desert. Would it be possible, they wondered, to find out where "the sun stands still"? (Expressed in terms of Western geography, they were asking where the Tropic of Cancer was located.) And, perhaps if they discovered *where* this happened, maybe they would even find out *why* it happened.

These, of course, were two very sound geographic questions and to

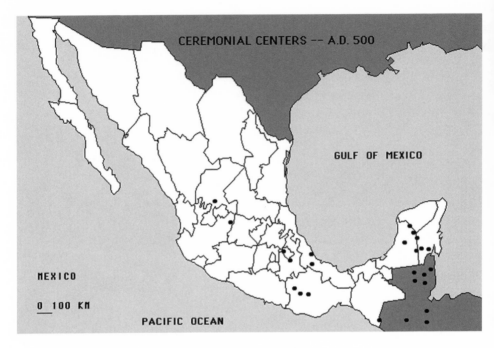

Figure 45.
The golden age of Mesoamerica came about A.D. 500 when the Maya wave of urbanization was spreading rapidly through the Petén, Yucatán, and into the highlands of western Honduras. The Zapotecs and Mixtecs constituted a localized pocket of urbanization in the valleys of Oaxaca, while on the Mexican plateau the metropolis of Teotihuacán was a flourishing city of some 200,000 inhabitants.

answer them fieldwork would be required. Expeditions would have to be sent out to determine physically where the sun passed vertically overhead on the equivalent of August 13 and where the sun "stood still" on the equivalent of June 22. In the first instance they realized that the quest would take them southward, no doubt to the fabled paradise of Tamoanchan. (According to the legends of Teotihuacán, their forebears had come from a lush, green forested region so named, replete with exotic birds and butterflies, far to the south.) Much as they may have been tempted to undertake this journey themselves — and who knows, perhaps one or more priests from Teotihuacán formed part of the expedition's personnel — this was a task best left to someone nearer at hand, so this assignment they allocated to their Maya subordinates in Tikal. The mandate was clear: keep going southward until a place was found where a 260-day interval exists between zenithal sun positions.

For carrying out the second expedition, the Teotihuacanos themselves were the best situated of any people in Mesoamerica, for the vast expanses of the northern desert began almost within sight of their own city. This was not to be an easy mission, however, for it would take the explorers directly out into the barbarous, unforgiving country of the "Chichimecs"—the nomadic hunters and gatherers who somehow scavenged a living from the meager resources of this desolate region. But again, the goal was not in doubt: keep going northward until a place was found beyond which the sun does not venture (beyond the zenith).

For an expedition starting southward out of Tikal, the choice of routes was a relatively clear-cut one. Even before the journey had started, the rainforest had closed in on every side. If their course veered too far to the southeast they would find themselves encumbered in the granite ridges of the Maya Mountains, whereas if it turned too far to the southwest they would soon get mired down in the swampy lowlands in the headwaters of the Usumacinta drainage system. To avoid these obstacles, they found it best to follow the height of land on which Tikal was situated (i.e., the drainage divide between the Caribbean Sea and the Gulf of Mexico) almost due south, at least until the final ridges of the Maya Mountains were passed. By that time, however, the folded ranges of the Cuchumatanes were looming up on the southern horizon, arcing into ever higher crests toward the southwest. Now they opted to swing east around the end of Lake Izabal, then across the Río Dulce, and over the low eastern spurs of the Sierra de las Minas into the broad fault-valley of the Motagua River.

By this time they had put more than 150 km (90 mi) of forest trail behind them, but the priests who were leading the expedition knew that many more days of travel still lay ahead. Back in Tikal the zenithal sun passed overhead on the equivalent of August 5 and did not again cross the zenith until May 8. Although the former date was only 8 days before the "day that time began," the sun was also 8 days too late in its second passage over Tikal, resulting in an interval of 276 days between the two zenithal passages. Now, as they entered the Motagua Valley, the priests checked the interval between vertical suns again, and found that it had narrowed to about 265 days. Its southward passage took place on the equivalent of August 10 and its northward transit occurred on May 2. There was no option now but to follow the Motagua upstream until the correct interval could be located.

As the expedition moved up along the river, it found a place where two tributaries joined the Motagua, one from each side of the valley. There, in this nexus of valleys, they also discovered that the bedrock changed dramatically from the white limestone with which they were so familiar in the Petén to a fine-grained rosy beige sandstone. It may well have been that the priests thought that their quest was over, because they erected here a ceremonial center which has become known to us as Quiriguá. Certainly, its location was a strategic one, for it ultimately came to dominate the trade routes which led from the Caribbean into the Guatemalan highlands. But if they thought they had found the "birthplace of time," they were wrong, because the closest interval they could measure between zenithal sun passages was 262 days. The sun was still moving southward a day too early and returning northward a day too late!

No doubt heartened by the fact that they must be drawing near to their goal, the priests probably sent scouts ahead to assess what results their continued journey up the Motagua Valley would produce. The report that came back may have been somewhat disappointing, for the scouts would have noted that the countryside quickly began to deteriorate into an environment the Maya had never experienced before. The forest thinned out and disappeared, becoming first an area of low scrub trees bristling with thorns, and finally, where not even these would grow, patches of cactus took over. Here, in the middle of the Motagua Valley, the Maya had stumbled into Guatemala's only region of semidesert, ensconced in the rain-shadow of the Sierra de las Minas—surely not the earthly paradise described in the creation myths.

Another bit of information which the scouts brought back must have unsettled the priests equally as much, for they reported that upstream, beyond this uninviting pocket of desert, the Motagua Valley curved to the west. Therefore, it would no longer provide a convenient corridor to "the birthplace of time," which still lay about one day of "sun travel" to the south. (At the time of year the zenithal sun passes over this region in its apparent north-to-south "migration" it is moving about 16 km [10 mi] per day.) The only reassuring news with which they returned was that, in the desert-pocket itself, a tributary river joined the Motagua from the south. Perhaps by following that to its headwaters a "green oasis" might be found where the sacred 260-day interval could be measured.

Thus, in the heart of the cactus-covered valley of the Motagua the Maya turned up the tributary valley of the Río Copán, following it first southward and then eastward into the mountains whence it came. As they climbed higher into the mountains, they watched as the desert browns were exchanged with forest greens as the scrub-thorn trees disappeared and stands of pine and oak took their place. Finally, where the valley widened out and the river slowed its pace in a series of sweeping meanders, the priests jubilantly announced that "this is the place!" The zenithal sun passed overhead on the equivalent of August 13, and 260 days later it passed over again on its way northward. It was not the tropical paradise that most of them had probably visualized when the expedition began, but it did meet the criteria of the "place where time began." In a sense, for the Maya it represented a "homecoming" in an otherwise alien land, for they had discovered a place where the sacred almanac — the very essence of their preoccupation with time — could be calibrated as it had "in the beginning" but in an environment with which they were quite unfamiliar. Copán, the ceremonial center which they founded here, was to become not only the southernmost major center of the lowland Maya civilization, but ultimately one of its most important astronomical centers as well. Its earliest Long Count stela dates to the year A.D. 426.

About the same time that the Maya priests were beginning their southward probe for the "birthplace of time," the priests of Teotihuacán were setting off into the northern desert to determine where the sun stopped on its annual migration. Like the Maya expedition, they were confronted with a choice of three possible routes. The first led out onto the plateau along the inner side of the Sierra Madre Oriental, the great eastern wall of the Mexican *meseta*. Shaped by the westward thrust of the North American plate, the Sierra Madre Oriental was made up of a jumble of contorted limestone ridges. By staying in the foothills, the

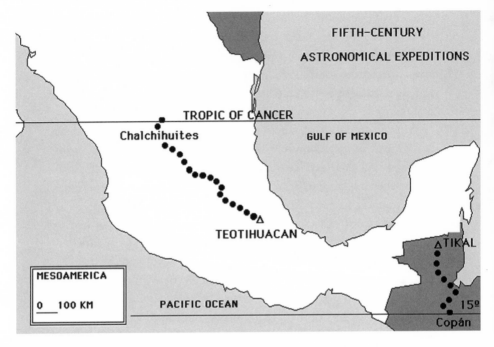

Figure 46.
About the first half of the fifth century A.D., it appears that the priests of Teotihuacán dispatched an expedition into the northern desert to determine the place where "the sun stood still" — in other words, the Tropic of Cancer. The astronomical site which the expedition founded was Chalchihuites, where sight-lines marking the summer solstice sunrise were perpetuated as trenches in the earth. About the same time, and perhaps under the influence of Teotihuacán, the priests at Tikal may have sent off an expedition to locate the parallel of latitude at which the 260-day sacred almanac could be calibrated — the astronomical site of Copán.

explorers could avoid the rugged terrain of the folded mountain crests, but along the backslopes of this range they would forever be in the rain-shadow of the moisture-bearing winds from the Gulf of Mexico; hence, water would be almost impossible to find.

A second possibility would be to strike out through the middle of the plateau, though along this route water would likewise be at a premium. Furthermore, out of sight of the principal mountain chains, even finding recognizable landmarks by which to mark their trail would be difficult, for amid the "swells" of this desert sea it was very easy to lose one's way. The third possibility lay along the foothills of the Sierra Madre

Occidental, the massive basaltic barrier which formed the western edge of the Mexican plateau. The result of extensive outpourings of lava during earlier movements of the North American plate, the Sierra Madre Occidental rose in many places to even higher elevations than its counterpart range on the east of the plateau. As a result, its crests intercepted whatever moisture escaped being squeezed out on the windward side of the Sierra Madre Oriental, and therefore they supported extensive forests of pine. Indeed, these cooler, damper uplands gave rise to several rivers of considerable size which descended to the floor of the plateau and in some instances even managed to snake their way for a distance out into the desert basins before disappearing into the sand or evaporating in a temporary salt lake. Surely, of the three alternatives this latter route was the most promising, because along it the occurrence of water would definitely be the most dependable.

When the expedition left Teotihuacán, the priests were probably under no illusion that they would find their goal quickly or easily, because in the sky above the pyramids of their home city the sun consumed no less than 69 days between its zenithal passages. Their journey would continue until they found a place either where the sun moved no farther north at all or where it stood still for a day or two and then turned southward once more.

It is, of course, conceivable that the expedition itself was timed to coincide with the sun's journey, for the sun's daily northward movement as it passed over Teotihuacán averaged only about 11–12 km (7–8 mi). Keeping pace with its migration would have been no real problem in a latitudinal sense, but finding a suitable route in terms of terrain and access to water posed more of a challenge — perhaps doubling the actual distance covered in a given day.

In any event, whether the journey was accomplished in one season or in many, it resulted in the founding of a ceremonial center at what is now known as either Alta Vista or Chalchihuites in the state of Zacatecas. Located at an elevation of 2200 m (7200 ft) in the eastern foothills of the Sierra Madre Occidental, it has access to a stream just below it and a sweeping view over the mountains to the east. Situated within 2 km (1.25 mi) of the Tropic of Cancer (Aveni, 1977, 5), it is aligned with Cerro Picacho, a notably sharp peak on the northeastern horizon, at the

Figure 47.
The ceremonial center of Chalchihuites, or Alta Vista, Zacatecas, appears to have been founded early in the fifth century A.D. by an expedition sent out from Teotihuacán to mark the northernmost limit of the vertical sun. From this place, located a short distance south of the Tropic of Cancer, the summer solstice sunrise could be calibrated over Cerro Picacho, the sharp peak in the middle background.

summer solstice sunrise. To reinforce this alignment the builders of the site dug trenches about 2.5–3.0 m (7–10 ft) into the hillside and plastered them with adobe. Nearby, a temple with 28 irregular columns apparently replicates the changing size of the moon as it advances from one phase to another, and on an adjacent hilltop, two pecked crosses of unmistakable Teotihuacáno vintage have been found (Aveni, 1977, 5). Dating to the late fifth or early sixth century A.D., Chalchihuites provides clear-cut evidence of the active astronomical concerns of the priestly elite of the great Mesoamerican metropolis at the apogee of its economic, political, and cultural existence.

THE TRIUMPH OF TIKAL: THE ASTRONOMICAL MATRIX

Although it is difficult to visualize Tikal without its five soaring skyscraper pyramids, archaeologists tell us that they were a relatively late embellishment to the Maya capital. Indeed, in the first centuries of its existence it was under strong influence from Teotihuacán, and following a war in A.D. 562 it was eclipsed by the rival city-state of Caracol to which it remained subject for over a hundred years. Not until it was freed from such foreign domination did Tikal blossom into the grandiose center that its spectacular ruins reveal today. Radiocarbon samples from the lintels of the doorways of the five skyscraper pyramids prove that all of them date to about the middle of the eighth century, plus or minus 50 years. This fact alone suggests that their construction was part of an integrated plan, no doubt conceived and directed by a single priest or group of priests.

But was this monumental effort simply a vainglorious attempt to enhance the impressiveness of the city—a dramatic example of the urban renewal of a ceremonial center which had already flourished, albeit in much less spectacular form, for over four centuries? Or was it just another grandiose public-works project that served to reinforce the authority of the priestly caste, while at the same time testing the patience of the laboring masses?

Unfortunately, the discovery that one or more of the pyramids contain the tombs of nobles and/or their consorts has tended to confuse some scholars who have been reluctant to lift their gaze out of the holes they have excavated in the ground and look skyward instead. As the loftiest creations of the Maya, the five pyramids of Tikal represent an earthly fixation with a celestial concern, for in 1979 I discovered that they had been constructed as an astronomical matrix whose purpose it was to calibrate the most important dates in the Maya year.

While it may be of interest to know that some of the pyramids also served as the final resting place of members of the Mayan elite, their primary function was to serve as observation platforms for priests working with the calendar. When first attempting to explain why it was necessary to construct pyramids that were the equivalent height of a modern 20-story building, I argued that it took a structure at least some 60 m (200 ft) in elevation to get above the canopy of the surrounding rain forest, which averages from 45–50 m (150–180 ft) in height in the area of Tikal. To this argument the reply was made that at the time Tikal was at its peak, the rain forest had all but been cut down and the city was surrounded instead by rolling fields of maize. Naturally, this may well have been the case, but it leaves us, then, still asking why it was necessary to build such high structures.

The true explanation most probably lies in a microclimatic condition which I first observed during field studies near Tikal, but about which one never finds mention in a standard physical geography textbook. It works as follows: in a rain forest region such as that which blankets the Petén of northern Guatemala, both the temperature and humidity are high during the day. After sunset, as the temperature begins to fall, even the drop of a few degrees results in the moisture in the air beginning to condense, and during the night the wisps of ground fog become thicker and thicker. Not until an hour or two after sunrise, as the temperature once more begins to rise, is the moisture reabsorbed into the air and the ground fog dissipates. Indeed, it is this condition which prompts Aviateca, the national airline of Guatemala, to radio Tikal each morning to inquire if the ground fog has lifted enough to allow the scheduled tourist flights from Guatemala City to land. It may very well have been this same condition which prompted the Maya priests to elevate their observation platforms to the point where the sky always remained visible to them.

The erection of five great pyramids, all of them more than 60 m (200 ft) in height and all of them constructed without benefit of the wheel or crane, has to be one of the most impressive accomplishments of any early people in any part of the world. The spectacular grandeur of Tikal is in large part a result of this remarkable engineering triumph. But what makes this accomplishment even more impressive is that all five of these pyramids were conceived and built with such exacting precision that they continue to function as a giant astronomical matrix to this day!

Whereas we have already described how the siting of Tikal caused the ceremonial center to be built on the height of land between the Caribbean Sea and the Gulf of Mexico drainage systems at precisely that point where the winter solstice sunrise could be calibrated over the highest point in the Maya Mountains, the internal spatial arrangement of the city itself is our concern now. It would appear that while all five of the pyramids were conceived as a functional unit, the sequence of their construction was of fundamental importance to the final layout of Tikal.

Figure 48.
The western horizon at Tikal as seen from Temple I. The low, squat structure in the middle foreground is Temple II, which serves not only as an architectural counterweight to Temple I as seen across the plaza of Tikal but also as a horizon marker for the enigmatic "8° west of north" orientation when viewed from Temple V. The latter orientation was present at La Venta about 1000 B.C., but also shows up at the Maya capital about A.D. 800. Farther to the left, Temple III defines the equinoctial sunset position as seen from Temple I, while the highest of the skyscraper pyramids — Temple IV, on the right — fixes the sunset position on August 13 as seen from Temple I.

Thus, as will become apparent from the discussion to follow, there is good reason to believe that the highest pyramid of the five — that labeled by the archaeologists as Temple IV — was actually the first to have its site established. It was constructed on the water-divide directly in line with the sunrise position over Victoria Peak on December 22. (It should be kept in mind that staking out the site of a pyramid and completing its construction are two very different things; the lintel of Temple IV was not put into place until after A.D. 741.)

However, because Victoria Peak is not easily visible on the southeastern horizon, the Maya erected a second pyramid to mark this alignment as seen from Temple IV (no doubt following the pattern of architecturally reinforcing key astronomical alignments which seems to have already been established at Uaxactún). This was Temple III, which was

Figure 49.
The eastern horizon at Tikal as seen from Temple IV. While neither Temple I nor II intersects the horizon as seen from this highest of the pyramids in the Maya capital, Temple III (on the right), by virtue of being surmounted by a triple-tiered roof comb, does just touch the southeastern horizon at the azimuth of the winter solstice sunrise (115°).

constructed on somewhat lower ground about 400 m (1300 ft) to the southeast. In order that it actually serve as a horizon marker, it was necessary to surmount the pyramid with a massive roof-comb, an architectural embellishment which the Maya frequently used to give their otherwise squat-looking structures more impressive height. And, in the case of Temple III, the roof-comb was a full three tiers high — not just for aesthetic reasons but quite obviously for the practical one of intersecting the horizon. Thus, as viewed from the top of Temple IV, the middle of the triple-tiered Temple III will be seen to just intersect the distant horizon at the azimuth (i.e., 115°) where the winter solstice sunrise occurs over Victoria Peak. (Radiocarbon dating reveals that the finishing touches were not put on Temple III until after A.D. 810.)

With the location of Temples IV and III now worked out, the position of Temple I was automatically fixed. It would be located directly east of Temple III so that priests standing atop the latter structure could calibrate the equinoctial sunrises (i.e., on March 21 and September 21) over

Temple I. (Of course, once both pyramids were in place, priests standing atop Temple I could use the backsight to Temple III to calibrate equinoctial sunsets as well.) Temple I's exact distance from Temple III, about 300 m (1000 ft), would be determined by the intersection of the equinoctial sunrise line with the point from which the August 13 sunset could be viewed against the midline of Temple IV's doorway. In other words, priests standing atop Temple I could calibrate their most important day — "the day the world began" — by sighting to the middle of the doorway of the highest pyramid the Maya ever constructed.

After the positions of the first three pyramids had been worked out, the siting of a fourth structure (Temple V) could now be established. For this a hill about 250 m (800 ft) to the southwest of Temple I was chosen. The exact position of Temple V, however, forms an alignment which makes a perfect right angle with that of Temples I and IV. Ironically, Thompson, for all his fascination with and love for the Maya, was not terribly impressed with their architecture, and candidly makes the claim that they were incapable of constructing a right angle (Thompson, 1974, 94). However, the alignments between Temples IV, I, and V at Tikal convincingly prove him wrong (Hartung, 1977, 114).

But what was the purpose of Temple V, oriented as it was to Temple I in the same way as the axis of the "Street of the Dead" was aligned at Teotihuacán? It is unlikely that a line of sight to the horizon was intended at an azimuth of 15°.5 from Temple V or at an azimuth of 195°.5 from Temple I, because such alignments could only have served to mark the positions of stars. Due to precession, the rising and setting positions of stars would have changed all too rapidly to give them anything other than a transitory value. However, because Temple V is clearly oriented toward the north, there definitely seems to have been an alignment in that direction which the Maya sought to mark, and if it was not with Temple I, one is tempted to suggest that it must have been with its lower, more squat counterpart across the central plaza, Temple II.

The latter is the lowest and most unpretentious of the five skyscraper pyramids. Indeed, when one stands atop Temple I and views the western horizon, the equinoctial sight-line to Temple III and the August 13 sight-line to Temple IV bracket Temple II on either side. Although it might seem that Temple II's function was merely to serve as an architectural

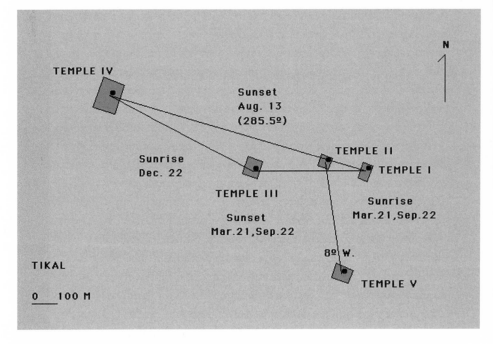

Figure 50.
The five major pyramids of Tikal were all constructed within a 40-year period beginning in the mid-eighth century A.D., apparently as part of an ingeniously designed astronomical matrix. The sight-line between Temple I and Temple IV (the highest of the pyramids) marks the sunset position on August 13, whereas the sunrise position at the winter solstice is perpetuated in the sight-line between Temple IV and Temple III. Because Temple I and Temple III are sited due east-west of each other, they mark sunrise and sunset alignments at the equinoxes. Although there was no star located directly above the earth's pole of rotation in Maya times, a sight-line from Temple V to Temple II appears to have marked the most westerly position of the Maya's equivalent to a polestar, Kochab.

counterweight to Temple I, its construction for such a purpose would have represented a sizable commitment of both manpower and resources solely for aesthetic reasons. Moreover, the site of Temple II — offset slightly to the south, allowing unobstructed sight-lines between Temples I, III, and IV — suggests that aesthetics alone did not dictate its placement. Furthermore, when the azimuth of Temple II as viewed from Temple V is found to be 352°, or 8° west of north, one cannot help but remember that the Olmecs had used that same orientation for the layout of La Venta nearly 1800 years earlier.

In the case of La Venta we had argued that the point in the heavens toward which its central axis was aligned was the closest thing to a pole star that existed for the Olmecs in 1000 B.C. Naturally, any point so close to the north celestial pole would be circumpolar and therefore have no rising or setting position which could be marked against the horizon. On the other hand, the star Kochab (magnitude 2.07), with a declination of 83°.5 in the year 1000 B.C., was only about 6°.5 away from the pole of rotation in that year and was thus the celestial body with the smallest radius of movement. However, in the intervening 1800 years, precession had caused Kochab to shift its declination to just under 79°, so by the year A.D. 800 it was 11° away from the pole. But, in the same time period, the star Polaris (magnitude 2.02) had precessed from being just over 17° away from the pole in 1000 B.C. to the point where its declination was 82°.7, or just under 8° away from the pole in the year A.D. 800. Thus, by the time the Maya were reaching their apogee, Polaris had replaced Kochab as being the closest bright star to the pole of rotation— but even then it was still a good 8° away from where it is today. In fact, the present generation of humanity is one of the few which can actually think and speak in terms of a "polestar," for at no other time in recorded history has a highly visible celestial body stood so close to the pole of rotation as Polaris does now.

THE MOON FINALLY BEHAVES

The discovery of the Dresden Codex in the Yucatán speaks to much of the Maya's lunar research having been carried out in that region, most likely at places like Edzná and Uxmal. However, it would appear that the ultimate breakthrough for the Maya came at their astronomical site of Copán, in the mountains of western Honduras, some eight years after the base dates recorded in the Codex, for in 763 an event of singular importance took place there. For well over half a century debate has centered on what this remarkable event must have been, for the date of its occurrence is engraved no fewer than eight times on seven different altars, stelae, and buildings (Carlson, 1977, 105). Initially, Herbert Spinden proposed that an astronomical congress must have taken place on that occasion, for the date is accompanied by portraits of what seem to be important personages seated on pillows (Spinden, 1924). Epigraphers have more recently suggested that the much-repeated date commemorates the accession to power of an important king. Although I cannot evaluate the merits of either of these arguments, I can point out that on the date in question a total lunar eclipse, visible from Copán, took place just after sunset. When the difference of longitude between Honduras and London is factored in, the Maya Long Count date (using Thompson's original correlation value) and Oppolzer's date agree perfectly. (The multiply recorded Maya Long Count date is 9.16.12.5.17 6 Caban 10 Mol, which equals Maya day-number 1,415,637. Adding the GMT correlation factor of 584,285 yields Julian Day number 1,999,922, which equates to June 29, A.D. 763. Since the midpoint of totality occurred at 7:10 P.M. Honduras time, it was then 1:10 A.M. in London, where a new Julian Day had begun at midnight. Thus, the lunar eclipse in question, listed as number 3050 in Oppolzer's catalog, is recorded as having taken place on Julian Day number 1,999,923, which is, of course, what the date then was in Europe.) It would appear, therefore, that coming so shortly after the "near misses" which had been calculated in the Dresden Codex (see Chapter 6), the eclipse at Copán may well have been the first such event which the Maya successfully predicted. Indeed, it may well be that they were so certain of their success, that for the occasion they had convened an astronomical congress to witness it.

In pointing out that a lunar eclipse visible at Copán did in fact occur on this oft-repeated date, I am left wondering why an event of such transcendental importance, coming so shortly after the debacle the Maya astronomers had experienced with the Dresden Codex, was not given more prominence than it was. David Stuart, one of the leaders of the new epigraphy movement, not only states that the "astronomical conference" hypothesis has long since been refuted (1992, 170), but goes on to describe the accession to power of Ruler 16 on that date (178). In the discussion which follows, we also learn that a mysterious "Personage A" was likewise "seated" on that date, as well as a chieftain known as Yax K'am Lay (180). Stuart admits that he is not certain to what these "seatings" refer, but cautions us that a "seating" event does not necessarily imply a ruler's inauguration, nor do they point to patterns of corulership. Thus, at least

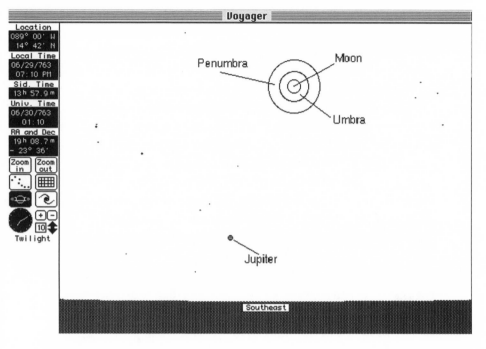

Figure 51.
This screen display produced by the VOYAGER computer program recreates the total lunar eclipse of June 29, A.D. 763, as seen from the major Mayan astronomical center of Copán in present-day Honduras. The sky has been 'whitened' for ease of reproduction and the author has superimposed upon it explanations of the various symbols. As explained in the text, the author's identification of this eclipse as the event which occasioned the multiple recordings of the Mayan date of 9.16.12.5.17 6 Caban 10 Mol at Copán strongly argues for the validity of the initial Thompson correlation rather than for his "revised" one. (The VOYAGER program is a product of Carina Software, San Leandro, CA 94577.)

we can be assured that Copán did not acquire three new chieftains on the day the eclipse took place.

Of course, in pointing out my uneasiness with even this one result obtained by the epigraphers who, in Coe's words, have "broken the Maya code," I realize that I have already defied one of the most outspoken professional warnings that I have ever seen in print, to wit this quote from Linda Schele: "The decipherment has occurred. There are two ways to react to it. One is to embrace it, and if you can't do it yourself, get someone on your side who bloody well can. The other is to ignore it, to try and destroy it, to basically dismiss it" (Coe, 1992, 273). On the other hand, if anyone has any doubts about the solsticial and other alignments which figure so prominently in the exposition presented here, he or she can either replicate my observations in the field or make the required measurements on large-scale maps for themselves.

The much-recorded lunar eclipse at Copán seems to have represented the triumphal solution to a problem which had first begun to intrigue Olmec priests nearly eight centuries earlier. It is therefore all the more ironic that this climactic breakthrough came as late as it did, for in little more than another half century, the Maya went into a decline from which they never totally recovered. One can only wonder whether they might have gone on to even greater intellectual achievements had their civilization not collapsed so abruptly in the ninth century. Surely, no other native people or culture within the Mesoamerican region would ever reach the same levels of sophistication or attainment again.

THE ROLE OF VENUS IN MAYAN ASTRONOMY

After the sun and the moon, the planet Venus is the brightest object in the heavens. Small wonder, then, that for the peoples of pre-Columbian Mesoamerica it figured prominently in both their mythology and religious rituals. Unlike the ancient Greeks who only belatedly realized that the "morning star" and the "evening star" were one and the same body, the Mesoamericans recognized it as a single celestial object which passed through a cycle having four distinct phases, even though they did so without ever truly understanding what occasioned these respective changes. Among the Maya, who formalized their observations of Venus in the Dresden Codex, it was described as a morning star for a period of 236 days, followed by a 90-day period of invisibility when it was assumed to be in the "underworld." This, in turn, was followed by a 250-day period when the planet was seen as an evening star, after which there was another 8-day period when it again "disappeared" into the underworld. Although the lengths of the individual phases were certainly not as precise as suggested by the above numbers, the complete Venusian cycle according to the Maya totaled 584 days, a value which is remarkably close to the planet's 583.92 day synodic period recognized by modern astronomers. (As David Kelley has pointed out, however, the Venusian interval varies from 579.6 days to 588.1 days within a given five-year period, so the 584 value is really a mean [Kelley, 1977, 58].)

The mysterious disappearances of Venus into the underworld were, of course, the result of its conjunctions with the sun. In other words, as the planet revolves around the sun on an orbit which is inclined at 3°.4 to the plane of the ecliptic, there are two positions in its path when it comes visually so close to the sun that it can no longer be seen. One of these is when Venus is directly in line *between* the Earth and the sun—a position which astronomers call inferior conjunction. In this position it can approach to within 24 million miles of the Earth, reaching its maximum brightness just before it visually disappears. At the reduced radius of its inferior conjunction, Venus moves very rapidly through its invisible phase—indeed, as we have seen above, in what the Maya measured as a period of eight days. On the other hand, when the orbit of Venus takes it *behind* the sun—a position which astronomers call superior conjunction—it may be as distant as 162 million miles from the Earth. Its daily horizontal motion is then so small that it took 90 days, according to the Maya, between the time it disappeared as a morning star and when it reappeared as an evening star.

These differences can perhaps best be understood by examining the following tables which present critical data relating to two of Venus's most recent conjunctions with the sun. In both tables, the rising and setting times of the sun and Venus are as they would have been experienced from the major ceremonial site of Cholula on the Mexican plateau. Cholula was chosen for this example because (1) it is known to have been a key center for the worship of Quetzalcóatl, the god-king who was believed by the Nahuatl-speaking peoples of the *meseta* to have been reincarnated as the planet Venus, and (2) it is considered by many anthropologists to have been the source of the Codex Borgia, the primary indigenous account of the planet's movements stemming from the Mexican plateau (Krickeberg, 1982, 193). In the first table, the superior conjunction of June 13, 1992, is presented statistically, whereas in the second, the inferior conjunction of April 1, 1993, is displayed in the same manner.

Table 4 – Superior Conjunction, Venus/Sun — June 13, 1992

Date	Time of Sun Rise	Sun Set	Time of Venus Rise	Venus Set	Angular Separation*
4/15	5:15 A.M.	5:50 P.M.	4:30 A.M.	4:43 P.M.	15°43′
4/30	5:05 A.M.	5:54 P.M.	4:30 A.M.	5:02 P.M.	11°52′ (D)
5/5	5:02 A.M.	5:56 P.M.	4:30 A.M.	5:09 P.M.	10°33′ (B)
5/15	4:58 A.M.	6:00 P.M.	4:33 A.M.	5:24 P.M.	7°54′
6/13	4:55 A.M.	6:10 P.M.	4:56 A.M.	6:10 P.M.	0°12′
7/1	4:58 A.M.	6:14 P.M.	5:21 A.M.	6:35 P.M.	4°59′
7/15	5:03 A.M.	6:13 P.M.	5:43 A.M.	6:49 P.M.	8°51′
7/22	5:06 A.M.	6:11 P.M.	5:54 A.M.	6:54 P.M.	10°47′ (B)
7/28	5:08 A.M.	6:09 P.M.	6:04 A.M.	6:57 P.M.	12°26′ (D)
8/1	5:09 A.M.	6:07 P.M.	6:10 A.M.	6:58 P.M.	13°31′

*B — Limit of invisibility according to the Codex Borgia.
D — Limit of invisibility according to the Dresden Codex.

Although no Mesoamerican observer could have known when the actual moment of conjunction took place, had he been privy to the calculations contained in the Dresden Codex he would have expected the planet's disappearance on April 30 and its reappearance on July 28. As can be seen from table 4, this meant that the Maya were essentially unable to distinguish the planet's position any closer than about 12° from the sun at the time of superior conjunction. Someone employing the calculations of the Codex Borgia would have anticipated the planet's disappearance on May 5 instead, when its angular separation from the sun had narrowed to about 10°.5, and its reappearance on July 22, when its angular distance had once more widened to about the same value. In other words, using the naked-eye astronomy available at the time, there was an angular discrepancy of at least 1°.5 — equivalent to about 6 days in time — in the two observational records, revealing how difficult it was to actually pinpoint the planet's location with any degree of accuracy. However, recent calculations by Anthony Aveni have demonstrated that the 8-day period of invisibility used in the Dresden Codex at inferior conjunction can actually vary from as few as 3 days to as many as 16, depending on the ecliptic's orientation to the horizon (Aveni, photocopy preprint, 8).

In contrast to the very slowly changing positions of the sun and Venus during superior conjunction, it will be seen from table 5 how rapidly they move first toward one another and then away from one another at the time of inferior conjunction. Again, the Mesoamerican observer would not have been able to precisely establish the time of their closest passage, but anyone employing the Codex Borgia would have anticipated the planet's disappearance on March 26 and its reappearance about 12 days later on April 7. In this instance, the angular separation of the two bodies would have diminished to just under 12°. Using the Dresden Codex, the disappearance of Venus would have been calculated as occurring on March 28 and its visual return would have been anticipated some 8 days later on April 5. Interestingly, in this instance the visual extinction of Venus would occur when the angular distance between the sun and Venus fell below 10°. Though the angular values are identical to what they were at the time of superior conjunction, they have here been reversed in the two indigenous sources, again reinforcing the difficulty which the early Mesoamericans had in pinpointing the planet's true position during its supposed absence in the underworld.

According to Lucrecia Maupomé (1986, 44), most scholars believe that the ancient Mesoamericans used the inferior conjunction of Venus to define the length of its cycle, although both Eduard Seler and Martínez Hernández are dissenters to this view. In any event, Aveni's findings concerning the variable length of Venus's disappearance at inferior conjunction scarcely makes that any more reliable an indicator of the planet's location in the sky than any of the other longer phases.

Despite their difficulties in defining the phases of Venus with any precision, the Mesoamerican skywatchers could not have failed to have

Table 5 – Inferior Conjunction, Venus/Sun — April 1, 1993

Date	Time of Sun Rise	Sun Set	Time of Venus Rise	Venus Set	Angular Separation*
3/20	5:36 A.M.	5:43 P.M.	6:13 A.M.	6:56 P.M.	20°00'
3/24	5:33 A.M.	5:44 P.M.	5:51 A.M.	6:32 P.M.	15°02'
3/26	5:31 A.M.	5:45 P.M.	5:40 A.M.	6:20 P.M.	12°36' (B)
3/28	5:29 A.M.	5:45 P.M.	5:28 A.M.	6:07 P.M.	10°23' (D)
4/1	5:26 A.M.	5:46 P.M.	5:06 A.M.	5:40 P.M.	7°52'
4/5	5:23 A.M.	5:47 P.M.	4:44 A.M.	5:14 P.M.	9°44' (D)
4/7	5:21 A.M.	5:48 P.M.	4:33 A.M.	5:02 P.M.	11°49' (B)
4/10	5:19 A.M.	5:48 P.M.	4:18 A.M.	4:44 P.M.	15°23'
4/14	5:16 A.M.	5:49 P.M.	4:00 A.M.	4:22 P.M.	20°16'

*B — Limit of invisibility according to the Codex Borgia.
 D — Limit of invisibility according to the Dresden Codex.

been intrigued by the striking reinforcement which the planet's cycle provided to their numerological and calendrical systems. They seem to have been relatively quick to realize that five revolutions of Venus around the sun (5 × 584 days = 2920) equaled eight similar revolutions by the Earth (8 × 365 days = 2920). Thus, on the eve of every eighth of their "Vague Years" — the name which astronomers have given to the 365-day interval used throughout Mesoamerica — Venus could be expected to appear in virtually the same place in the sky that it had eight years earlier. For a people seeking order in nature, this realization of such a completed cycle must have been reassuring indeed, especially with respect to a celestial body whose cosmic importance was so great and whose behavior otherwise seemed so erratic.

Before leaving this point, however, it should be emphasized how important it is to "get the horse before the cart" in our thinking on this matter. Some researchers, most recently Maupomé (1986), have argued that the Mesoamerican calendars are based on the phases of Venus. If true, this would mean that one of the most difficult of all celestial cycles was worked out first, and into this the interlocked 365-day "Vague Year" and 260-day sacred almanac were then fitted. (An explanation of how the latter interval came into being is not even attempted.) Such an explanation defies common sense, for only after a meaningful interval of time like a "Vague Year" has been defined will it even be possible to recognize that eight such intervals correspond to five of the longer and less precise cycles of Venus. In other words, you begin with a "yardstick" of known units to determine the length of something unknown, and not the other way around.

(To be sure, there were other numerological "twists" to the Venusian cycle which must have excited the priests equally or more so than the correspondence of five Venusian years with eight "Vague Years." If a Venusian year is divided by eight it yields an interval of 73 days, which is the same result which one obtains when dividing a "Vague Year" by five. Eight plus five yields the sacred number of 13, and this multiplied by the other key numeral, 20, corresponds to the length of their sacred almanac, or "Calendar Round" [260 days]. Seventy-three Calendar Rounds in turn equal 18,980 days, which equate with 52 "Vague Years"—the length of the Maya "century," and the interval between "the binding of the years" as practiced by the Nahuatl-speaking peoples of the Mexican plateau. And although 52 is not evenly divisible by 8, a double "century" of 104 years is, meaning that 146 Calendar Rounds equate not only to 104 "Vague Years" but to 65 Venusian cycles as well.)

However, the fact that the details of Venus's movements were not defined by the Maya until the early seventh century—to wit, the base date of the Dresden Codex, which is 9.9.9.16.0 1 Ahau 18 Kayab = February 6, A.D. 623—reveals how elusive the solution of this riddle must have been, even for a people with such a sophisticated mathematical system as the Long Count. Even so, as Michael Closs observes (1977, 97), they chose a nonastronomical base for their count, suggesting to him that the Maya sought to correlate the movements of Venus to its supposed "birthday" on 1 Ahau, in order to facilitate their computations using the Long Count. On the other hand, for those peoples living on the Mexican plateau who were not the cultural beneficiaries of the Long Count, the answer seems to have come even later still, judging from the fact that the Codex Borgia dates to Aztec times.

To be sure, in both instances the Venusian cycle could only have been worked out by long and patient counting. Having the Long Count against which to tally such a lengthy series of observations would surely have helped the Maya to expedite record keeping and insure its overall accuracy, but it would not have been essential to the process itself. Indeed, the major purpose of the "Venus table" in the Dresden Codex seems to have been to assist the Maya priests in making periodic corrections to their calculations, for in any 104-year period the planet got 5.2 days out of phase with the table (Kelley, 1977, 58). (For a detailed discussion of how the Maya shifted the base of their calculations to keep Venus "on track," see Closs, 1977, 89–99.)

Of critical importance, however, was finding a well-defined starting point from which the cycle could be calibrated. (The difficulty of using the planet's disappearances we have already discussed.) But what, after all, is fixed about a "star" that shows up in the eastern sky before dawn for *nearly* eight months, disappears for *about* two and a half to three months, then reappears in the western sky shortly before sunset for *something over* eight months, and disappears again for *between* 8 and 12 days? Indeed, as Aveni has shown, the Maya appear to have incorporated lunar observations into the Dresden Codex in an effort to pin down the movements of Venus, assuming somewhat naively that the motions of one celestial body probably controlled or influenced those of another (Aveni, photocopy preprint, n.d., 11). Kelley, on the other hand, makes the reverse argument, stating that there are indications that Venus's movements were "somehow used in predicting eclipses" (1977, 70). As Thompson has pointed out, "Both phenomena [solar eclipses and the heliacal risings of the planet Venus] were greatly feared by the Maya" (1972, 111).

In any event, if the *times* of Venus's appearance and disappearance were so difficult to pin down, might one have found it easier to fix its *places* of appearance and disappearance instead? Surely in a society accustomed to horizon-based astronomy like that of Mesoamerica, the movements of Venus might have been more convincingly calibrated against some static feature in the landscape than against some nebulous temporal formula. Certainly such a model was already in place for most Mesoamericans with respect to the movements of the sun — save for the Maya in the featureless expanses of the Yucatán — so why not, by extension, apply the same "principle" to Venus? Indeed, as we have seen, it was the Maya, alone of all the Mesoamerican cultures, who managed to pin down the eclipse cycle of the moon. What they lacked in horizon landmarks they more than made up for with the Long Count and the construction of their own survey markers in the landscape (as we have seen with their construction of "La Vieja" at Edzná). That is why Horst Hartung's discovery of the alignment between Uxmal and the pyramid of Nohpat out in the featureless plain of northern Yucatán is so important: It marks the extreme southerly rising point of the planet Venus (Hartung, 1971). (We shall return to the subject of the horizon observation of Venus later on.)

If the Maya's efforts to accurately predict eclipses were crowned by success so late in their history (i.e., A.D. 763), then their struggle to define the phases of Venus appears to have come even later still. Indeed, Floyd Lounsbury (1983) argues that the Maya "Venus table" was historically set in motion on the Long Count date of 10.5.6.4.0 1 Ahau 18 Kayab, which equates to November 20, A.D. 934. On that morning, a heliacal rising of Venus occurred which Lounsbury has called "a unique event in historical time," because it came exactly three Great Cycles (146 × 260 days) after the base date of the Dresden Codex. Lounsbury believes that the Maya astronomers did not recognize the need to shift bases (i.e., correct their calculations) until a full Great Cycle had elapsed. Ironically, attaining such precision at such a late date must have been small consolation indeed for a society whose very foundations were already crumbling beneath them.

Chapter 9

The Twilight of the Gods

THE FALL OF TEOTIHUACÁN

For almost 900 years following its founding in the wake of Cuicuilco's destruction and abandonment, Teotihuacán had flourished as the greatest commercial and cultural center of the entire New World, reaching at the peak of its wealth and power a population which probably numbered close to 200,000. Its trade relations extended down into the Gulf coastal lowlands of eastern Mexico and most likely as far as Soconusco as well, for its architectural innovations are seen at Kaminaljuyú, on the outskirts of modern Guatemala City. Its religious and artistic influences were felt even amongst the lowland Maya, and artisans and merchants from virtually all parts of Mesoamerica frequented its markets and bazaars. No other native culture in the Americas ever produced a larger, more dynamic or impressive a metropolis than Teotihuacán, and in its heyday it ranked as one of the three greatest cities in the world, along with Rome in Europe and Beijing in Asia.

For all its economic power and architectural grandeur it was, however, a "forward capital"—an exposed outpost on the northern edge of the Mesoamerican cultural realm, a geographic location which gave it only half a hinterland. In this regard, it was more similar to Beijing than to Rome, for the former also lay near the northern perimeter of the Chinese cultural realm. And, like Beijing, its hinterland was defined by the limits of agriculture, for beyond it to the north stretched the arid wastes of the Mexican plateau, just as its Asian counterpart confronted the endless steppes of Mongolia and the shifting sands of the Gobi. Rome, on the other hand, not only lay near the middle of the Mediterranean basin but also near the middle of the then-known *oekumene*, or habitable world, of Western civilization.

But unlike either Beijing or Rome, both of which saw themselves threatened by peoples beyond the agricultural pale and therefore sought to protect themselves from that quarter, Teotihuacán apparently never contemplated the likelihood of danger from the northern deserts. Whereas the Romans set their boundary across the narrows of northern England along Hadrian's Wall and on the mainland of Europe along the Rhine River, a line of palisaded forts through southwestern Germany known as the Limes, and the Danube River, and the Chinese constructed the Great Wall from the shores of the Yellow Sea for more than 3000 km (2000 mi) into the wastelands of western China, Teotihuacán took no such precautions against the nomads of the Mexican plateau. Surely the cultural boundary between "civilized" and "barbarian" was just as sharp in the New World as it was in the Old, but any threat that this might have implied seems to have been totally ignored or discounted in the case of Teotihuacán.

Ironically, all three of these world metropolises ultimately suffered the same fate: Each of them fell to barbarous nomads from the north. Perhaps the greatest irony was that of Rome, which had the greatest defense in depth between itself and its northern enemies and yet was the first to succumb to their depredations (in the fifth century A.D.). Beijing, thanks at least in part to its elaborate Wall, managed to hold off the Mongols until the thirteenth century, whereas Teotihuacán was overrun about the middle of the eighth century A.D.

That a city of nearly a quarter of a million people could fall before the onslaught of a mere handful of nomadic hunters and gatherers may seem a highly unlikely scenario; it was not, to be sure, a foretaste of the

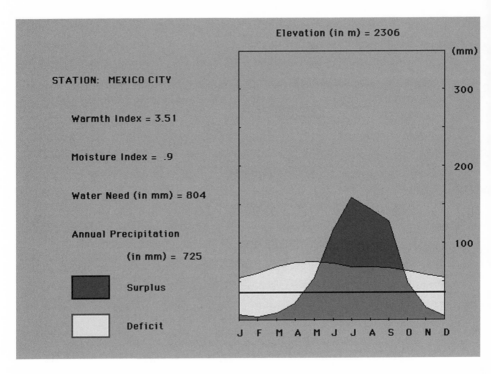

Figure 52.
The water budget for Mexico City (Aztec Tenochtitlán) demonstrates the characteristic monsoonal variation from low-sun drought to high-sun rains, with the annual precipitation total falling just slightly short of what is required for forest cover. Thus, the native vegetation of the Valley of Mexico is grassland, though only a few score meters (a couple hundred feet) upslope in the cooler, moister mountains good stands of pine and oak may be found. Because the elevation of Tenochtitlán averaged about 2350 m (7700 ft), the climate in which the Aztecs found themselves was neither tropical nor even quite subtropical, the boundary for the latter being a warmth index of 4.0. Of course, both warmth and moisture fall off to the northwest, resulting in a climate which is inimicable to growing corn and hence a region which remained the preserve of the hunting-and-gathering Chichimecs.

destruction to be wreaked on the Aztec capital of Tenochtitlán eight centuries later by a few hundred Spanish conquistadores, for that uneven struggle was between a Stone Age people and a small army that was equipped with horses, mastiff dogs, steel swords, and firearms and which had the psychological advantage of a confused mythology surrounding it. Teotihuacán appears to have lacked not only defensive preparations but also any kind of military organization to come to the city's aid in time of attack. With no ramparts to protect it and no militia it could muster, Teotihuacán must have seemed a plum just waiting to be picked by the first band of nomads who felt themselves bold enough to attempt such a move. Those invaders appear to have been the Otomís, a semisedentary buffer group who were caught in the path of an advance wave of Uto-Aztecan, or Nahuatl-speaking, peoples, spreading southward across the Mexican plateau during the first half of the seventh century A.D.

We can only guess at what triggered the southward movement of the Uto-Aztecans: Perhaps it was the growing desiccation of their original homelands in what is now the southwestern United States, in the same way that drought had so frequently served as a mechanism in setting off migrations of nomadic peoples in the heart of Asia. (In fact, so widespread and recurring were these periods of dryness in the heartland of that vast continent that Yale geographer Ellsworth Huntington spoke of the climate of the region as "the pulse of Asia.") At the same time that the Petén region of northern Guatemala — the core area of the Maya civilization — seemed to be experiencing a gradual increase in moisture (again, according to Huntington), the homeland of the northern nomads may well have been undergoing a progressive diminution in rainfall. (Indeed, the global climatic model developed by the CLIMAP project confirms that from ca. A.D. 850 until 1250 temperatures warmed and precipitation decreased over the Mexican plateau [Messenger, 1990, 27]. It is not impossible that these trends could have already set in a century or two earlier in the American Southwest, whence came the original Uto-Aztecan peoples. There is evidence that Mesoamerican cultural outliers in the north of Mexico began disappearing shortly after A.D. 600 [Adams, 1991, 284].) In a region already marginal in the extreme, such a nudge from the climate may have been all that it took for the hunters and gatherers of the northern desert to turn ever more covetous eyes on the rich and thriving city to their south.

Thus, the arrival of the Otomís in Teotihuacán was probably the result of both a "push" from a steadily deteriorating climate and a "pull" exerted by a large, prosperous, and totally defenseless city. In any event, confronted with the choice of standing their ground in the face of the advancing nomads on the north or of seeking refuge in the grandiose city to the south, the hapless Otomís opted for the latter. Their own intentions may not have been hostile, but certainly the Teotihuacanos could hardly have been expected to welcome them with open arms. The economic, social, and political dislocations which resulted from having a horde of refugees overrun the great city were probably more than it could endure. Even so, the Otomís were merely "the tip of the iceberg," for the real collision of cultures came somewhat later when the Uto-Aztecans themselves burst into the Valley of Mexico. With the arrival of the Toltecs, the city's fate was sealed, for the charred timbers of Teotihuacán's palaces reveal that it was put to the torch about A.D. 750.

What the Toltecs could have gained by destroying this great metropolis — other than perhaps some temporary alleviation of hunger amongst their clansmen — is difficult to imagine. By "beheading" the nerve center of the Mesoamerican world, the Toltecs all but demolished the vast commercial network of which it was the focus. And by slaughtering such of its priests and chieftains who had not fled at their coming, they all but extinguished the very religious and cultural basis of its society. Of course, on both of these scores, the Toltecs were scarcely any different from the Goths in Rome or the Mongols in Beijing; immediate and pressing motives took precedence over any thought of the wider implications their actions might ultimately have. At the moment, none of the invaders could have foreseen the devastating effects that each of their moves would have on the forward march of civilization in their respective parts of the world, and even if they had, they probably could have cared less. It is only we, in retrospect, who can appreciate the full sense of tragedy which these events portended.

It can hardly be imagined what the fall of Teotihuacán must have meant to the peoples and cultures of Mesoamerica. By way of a modern analogy, it could perhaps be likened to the repercussions that the total destruction of a New York or London would have on the world's economic and cultural life today. Yet, because it was the *only* metropolis of its size and significance in the New World, its loss must have been even more keenly felt.

Not only did the fabric of long-distance trade break down, but it was as though the very heart and brain of the region had suddenly stopped. Refugees from the city fled to the south and east taking with them only what they could carry in their arms and minds. Some sought sanctuary on a mountaintop near the present-day city of Cuernavaca where they built a defensively conscious ceremonial center which we know today as Xochicalco. Others poured across the mountains into the basin of Puebla, finding only temporary refuge at Cholula, for the Toltecs soon overran that place as well. Still others continued downslope into the eastern rain forests where they took up residence in the ceremonial center of El Tajín, almost hidden amidst the karstic hills of what is now northern Veracruz state. But these survivors of the holocaust — the elite, without question — could only have been a small number of the original population of Teotihuacán, the remainder of whom now found themselves struggling to keep alive without the infrastructure and security of an urban exchange system. For them, the great majority, it was as though the clock had been turned back to the days of a subsistence economy.

It was not just the physical destruction of the city itself nor the breakdown in food supply lines which caused such agony and suffering, severe though that must have been; it was also the psychological shock of witnessing a great metropolis collapse into anarchy — without any semblance of law and order, without any feeling of personal security, without any meaning to its social or political or religious structure, without any promise of a future. Surely, the fall of Teotihuacán sent shock waves of despair throughout Mesoamerica, for ultimately no people or culture within the region could escape its repercussions.

THE ARRIVAL OF THE PURÉPECHA

Ironically, it was just as Teotihuacán was undergoing the trauma of its conquest and destruction that the Maya were nearing the peak of their development. While the palaces of the Teotihuacanos were being put to the torch on the edges of the northern desert, the skyscraper pyramids of Tikal were rising, tier upon tier, out of the jungles of Petén. Probably the first reports the Maya had of their great rival's demise came with runners from the north bearing the evil tidings. In the months that followed, the slow but steady shrinkage and then abandonment of all trade with the northern metropolis took place. This, in turn, must have been succeeded by increasing dislocations of peoples on the northern periphery, as tribes and cultures in the path of the fleeing refugees and advancing warriors were forced to give way to the southward-pressing nomads.

It was not, however, just the advance of the Nahuatl-speaking migrants coming out of "la gran Chichimeca," as the Spanish came to call the desert north of Mexico, that occasioned this growing cascade of peoples from the borderlands of Mesoamerica. Sometime about the eighth or ninth century A.D. a seaborne people appear to have arrived on the west coast of Mexico in sufficient numbers to have had a disruptive effect on the settlement pattern which had previously existed. Calling themselves the Purépecha, which in their own language meant "latecomers" or "recent arrivals," they seem to have made their original landfall in the vicinity of the mouth of the Balsas River and then spread inland and upstream from there. Apart from the coastal fringe of the river mouth itself, the country in which they found themselves was the hottest and driest part of southern Mexico—the desert basin of the Balsas Depression—a region which may well have been a population void before their arrival. In any event, the Purépecha quickly realized that the Balsas had little to offer them other than metallic ores, such as copper, silver, and gold, and while they had the technology and skills to smelt and fashion metals, they certainly could not derive their sustenance from them. Thus, it was almost inevitable that they would seek the solace of the cooler, damper, forested uplands where they could cultivate their crops and build their homes. The region that beckoned them was the volcanic highland of Michoacán, an upland of productive soils and pine-clad mountains liberally sprinkled with sparkling lakes teeming with fish and aquatic birds. That such a land had gone previously unsettled seems hardly likely, but just which peoples the Purépecha displaced to take possession of it is somewhat unclear. Surely, the Mixtecs, or "cloud people," on their southeast were probably jostled by their arrival, for about this time the Mixtecs began a concerted southward advance against their longtime neighbors in the valley of Oaxaca, the Zapotecs. And the Otomís may have been pushed to the north and east, spilling into the basins of Mexico and San Luis Potosí at this time. Another people set adrift by these migrations seems to have been the Chiapanecs, whose original homeland is unknown but who ended up pushing southward during this same time frame into the northwestern corner of Chiapas

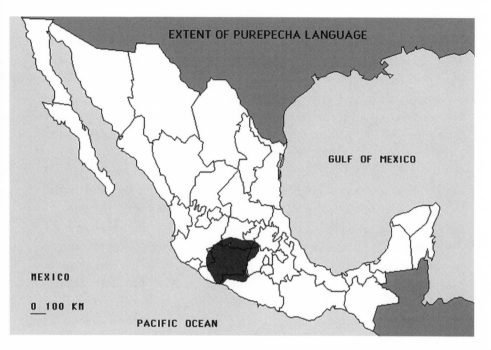

Figure 53.
The distinctive character of Purépecha, or Tarascan, place-names makes it relatively simple to outline the extent of the settlement area which the Purépecha occupied at the time of the Spanish conquest. It seems rather unlikely that the area which they occupied before the Conquest was larger, for none of their neighbors could match them either in terms of armaments or military organization.

state—to which they gave their name—and there being ultimately absorbed by the Zoques. The Purépecha dominions came to coincide almost perfectly with the drainage basin of the Balsas, which today coincides nearly exactly with the state boundaries of Michoacán; both of these natural and political regions can, in turn, be delimited by the areal extent of the Purépecha language and its place-names.

The Purépecha were in almost every way strikingly different from their neighbors. Not only was their language totally unrelated to any of the native tongues around them, but their culture was quite unlike that of the Mesoamericans. They dressed differently, they cut their hair differently, they knew the use of metal and their neighbors did not, and their gods and religion were different. Obviously, the Mesoamerican calendar with its intertwined pantheon of gods and rituals was totally unknown to them, and despite their precocity in fashioning metals, they seem to have been notably lacking in mathematical and astronomical knowledge. Quantification to the Purépecha was defined as "one, two, and many," whereas their interest in celestial matters seemed to focus on the Southern Cross — suggesting that their native home may well have been in western South America, from which they brought the knowledge of metallurgy (Adams, 1991, 284).

Although the Purépecha practiced agriculture, they were described by their later Aztec neighbors as being primarily hunters and fishermen; indeed, *Michoacán* in Nahuatl means "the land of the fishermen." Their principal deity was the god of fire, but whether this was a carryover from their original homeland or an innovation that arose as a result of finding themselves (*a*) in a region of active volcanism or (*b*) in a region of plentiful firewood is impossible to say. Certainly, in the moist uplands of Michoacán there was not the same preoccupation with the seasonal lack of precipitation which prompted most Mesoamerican societies to place the rain-god near the top of their pantheon. Thus, while the Purépecha remain in many ways an enigma in the already puzzling framework of prehistoric Mesoamerica, their belated arrival, coinciding closely with the southward push of the Nahuatl-speaking nomads from the north, may have helped to set off the chain reaction of population dislocations which overwhelmed much of the region within the century or two which followed.

THE COLLAPSE OF THE MAYA

In their semi-isolation amidst the rain forests of the Petén and the scrub forests of Yucatán on the southeastern borderlands of Mesoamerica, the Maya were literally the last of the pre-Columbian cultures to feel the impact of the population movements on the region's northern and western frontiers. Indeed, apart from the Nahuatl-speaking Pipiles and the Nicarao who inexplicably made a "long march" off the Mexican plateau, down through the Pacific coastal lowland of Soconusco, and into what are today the countries of El Salvador and northwestern Nicaragua, the southern margins of Mesoamerica seem not to have been actively involved in the movements of peoples per se, at least not initially. The impact which they experienced was perhaps more an economic and psychological one than a physical one, though the former may eventually have locally translated into the latter as well. It may well be compared to the course of revolution running through Latin America in the early nineteenth century, modeled on events which had previously taken place in the United States and France but which Latin Americans had only heard about rather than directly experienced. In any case, the cause of the collapse of the Maya, just as they seemed to be reaching the zenith of their civilization, has been a source of much speculation and long debate among scholars.

Evidence for the decline of the Maya may be read from both their calendrical inscriptions and their architectural activity — or more accurately stated, from their gradual cessation. Beginning in the first half of the ninth century, at one ceremonial center after another the practice of erecting stelae to commemorate the completion of a *hotun,* or *katun,* was abandoned. (The *hotun* was an interval of five "Vague Years.") This, of course, suggests that an interest in or a concern with calendrical matters had for some reason disappeared, and in a society which heretofore had been obsessed with timekeeping, it was as if the very essence of their religious structure or belief system had been altered. Similarly, no great public works of construction or renewal of pyramids or palaces was undertaken, meaning that the very physical infrastructure of their society was beginning to fall apart. Thus, even the meager clues we have at hand suggest that both the spiritual and material existence of the Maya began to deteriorate markedly from about the 840's onward.

Among the many hypotheses advanced to explain the demise of the Maya civilization have been those which sought to invoke both physical, or environmental, factors and cultural, religious, sociological, and/or political factors. Some theorists have looked for internal causes within the Maya homeland in Petén, while others have suggested external forces from outside their core area as the impetus for their decline. Let us examine each of these major arguments in an effort to evaluate how they may have, individually and collectively, contributed to the society's downfall.

On the physical or environmental side of the argument, two rather different scenarios have been proposed, one predicated on a change in climate and the other on an essentially static climate within the region. In the first scenario, championed initially by Huntington in the period about the time of the First World War, a gradual increase in rainfall took place in the Petén region beginning about the eighth century. Not only did the vegetation grow back more rapidly, making it difficult for the Maya to keep their cornfields from being overgrown, but the shorter dry season made periodic burning difficult as well. Moreover, the soils were increasingly leached of their nutrients, resulting in declining crop yields at the same time that population growth was reaching a peak. Increasingly unable to feed themselves any longer, much less the growing numbers of the urban elite dependent upon them, the Maya farmers were pushed to the limits of their endurance. Certainly, there would be no "spare time" left over for such "frivolous" pursuits as building or reconstructing pyramids at the whim of the priest or chieftain. The net result was the breakdown of the food supply system coupled with a gradual dissolution of political control and religious authority: in short, a physical collapse which resulted in a cultural implosion.

But what evidence did Huntington employ on which to build such a hypothesis? As it turns out, his primary source material was derived from the growth rings of the sequoia trees of California, a region which he argued had a climate which was inversely related to that of the Petén. In other words, when it was relatively wet in California, it was dry in the Petén, whereas if California underwent a drought, Petén would receive more than its normal share of precipitation. Thus, at the peak of the so-called Old Empire of the Maya, from about A.D. 300 to 900, the tree-ring evidence from California suggests normal rainfall in that area with consequent drought in the Petén, but beginning about the end of that era, a prolonged period of drought set in, in the American Southwest, which was paralleled by heavier than normal rainfall over Central America.

The Mayanist Sylvanus Morley, for one, did not "buy" Huntington's argument, for he questioned how the climate in one part of the world could possibly be instrumental in occasioning a change in another 3000 km (2000 mi) away. Of course, at the time that both Huntington and Morley wrote, nothing was known of the jet stream, the El Niño phenomenon, or of what climatologists have subsequently come to call "teleconnections": the interrelationships between climatic factors over long distances. But as the latter concepts have increasingly come into the tool kit of the discipline, such teleconnections are no longer so "unthinkable." Indeed, an anecdote from my own firsthand field experience may speak directly to such a circumstance, for during the late 1970's while California was undergoing a severe drought, abnormally heavy rains throughout the Gulf coastal region of Mexico and the Petén region of northern Guatemala caused large-scale flooding in those areas. A blocking "high" in the Pacific off of California produced a northward "kink" in the jet stream which sent Pacific airmasses ashore in the Northwest, which, once they had crossed the Rockies, were shunted deeply southward over the Gulf of Mexico where they collided with maritime tropical air and resulted in a sustained period of heavy precipitation. Thus, even though Huntington may not have totally understood the mechanics of such an interrelationship, his hypothesis may have been closer to the truth than his detractors, both then and later, have been willing to acknowledge. (Indeed, it is interesting that the computerized global climatic model created by the CLIMAP project strongly supports Huntington's basic premises: During the Classic Period, the southern Maya region was cooler and drier than normal, whereas beginning about A.D. 850 the Maya lowlands became considerably wetter. On the other hand, this contradicts entirely the drought hypothesis reported in Adams [1991, 266]. As suggested above, in most rain forest environments it is not drought that presents a threat, it is additional rain!)

In the second physical hypothesis, no climatic change is postulated. Now the burden of collapse falls squarely on soil depletion; after many generations of farmers repeatedly growing corn on the same plots of land, the soils simply wore out, especially as the increasing pressures of population growth precluded their fallowing for any restorative period. With the breakdown of the food supply system, the further scenario of administrative and social collapse was inevitable.

Hypotheses that look to a cultural explanation of the Maya's downfall tend to stress war, civil unrest, or disease as a causative factor of societal decay. It has long been recognized that the idealistic view of the Maya as a peace-loving, intellectually oriented people was the figment of the imagination of certain early scholars who were prone to simplistically compare the Maya to the Greeks and the Aztecs to the Romans. The evidence of war among the Maya may be seen in ceremonial centers such as Becán, in the southern Yucatán, founded early on in the "Old Empire," for it was fortified by both a wall and a dry moat. Walls have also been found running through the jungle to the north and south of Tikal, though they did not prevent the city from being subjugated by its neighbors to the east. Indeed, Edzná itself, perhaps the oldest major Maya urban agglomeration (dating to the second century B.C.), also boasts a moated fort of sizable proportions. Therefore, warfare seems to have been endemic among the Maya city-states right from the outset, so whether it could have taken such a drastic upturn in the mid–ninth century that the very existence of the ceremonial centers themselves was undercut remains to be conclusively demonstrated.

As regards the civil unrest hypothesis, any number of possible "triggers" suggest themselves: A farmers' rebellion against repeated levees of public-works projects by the priestly caste has already been mentioned. Internal bickering between heirs apparent to the power structure could have factionalized the public as well. (Maybe there were too many rivals being "seated" in new offices at the same time, as the epigraphers suggest happened in Copán!) Or perhaps new or different interpretations of religious dogma became the divisive "straw that broke the camel's back." One could, of course, go on suggesting all manner of such potential causes for dissension, but alas, without the satisfaction of knowing which, if any, of them is correct. In the same way, any evidence that there might have been of widespread mortality caused by disease is totally lacking, for in the humid climate of the Petén, especially, skeletal remains are quickly decomposed.

Having framed the discussion in terms of internal versus external causes, we are again at a loss for historical evidence, particularly of the latter. We do know that at least one band of Toltecs, supposedly driven out of their society by an internecine struggle for the kingship, migrated from the Valley of Mexico, through Cholula to the Gulf coast, and then sailed to the Yucatán in the late tenth century. This exploit not only gave rise to a Toltec cultural overlay in such places as Chichén Itzá but also provided the fabric of a legend which ultimately had far-reaching effects on the history of Mesoamerica, namely the promised return of Quetzal-cóatl to rightly claim his throne. However, by the time this episode took place, the "Old Empire" of the Maya in the jungles of the Petén was all but over, and such vitality as it still possessed was then found in the city-states of the drier scrub country of the northern Yucatán. By then warfare had reached a new level of ferocity with leagues of city-states grouping themselves around the leadership of such places as Chichén Itzá, Uxmal, and Mayapán. The latter fortified itself with a great enclosing wall, as did the smaller but strategic seaport center of Tulúm, but to little ultimate advantage. The so-called New Empire of the Maya (from A.D. 900 to 1200) represented something of a desperate last gasp of a people who had already seen most of their grandeur and knowledge slip away from them. Their calendar had degenerated into a Short Count in which there was no longer any span of time recognized other than the 52-year intervals between the meshing of the sacred and secular counts. Their architecture had become almost a caricature of what they had built earlier, as witnessed in the shoddy temple structures of a place such as Tulúm. And their elaborate religious pantheon seems to have given way, as least in part, to a form of phallic worship, as evidenced by the crude stelae found at some of the "New Empire" sites. In short, the glory that had been the Maya's was already long gone at the time of the arrival of the Spanish; it only remained for the latter to extirpate virtually all of the remaining material evidence of their civilization by burning whatever indigenous records and books they could find.

Concerning our earlier discussion on the role of climate in the demise of the Maya, there is intriguing geomorphic evidence which lends further support to Huntington's thesis of an increasingly wet climate in southeastern Mexico during the Late Classic Period (A.D. 600–900). The westernmost site ever constructed by the Maya was Comalcalco, which lies in the heart of the swampy lowland called Chontalpa, some 40 km (25 mi) to the northwest of the modern city of Villahermosa, the capital of Tabasco state, and some 16 km (10 mi) from the coast of the Gulf of Mexico. It is located on the right bank of the Río Seco ("Dry River") at an elevation scarcely 10 m (33 ft) above sea level. Situated in the midst of an extensive alluvial lowland, Comalcalco had no easy access to building stone of any kind; hence, in this one place and nowhere else the Maya constructed their buildings of fired brick, giving the site a totally unique character among Mesoamerican ceremonial centers.

But Comalcalco is unique in another way as well. At the time of its construction, it apparently served as a seaport—most probably for Palenque and the hinterland of the Grijalva Valley, which lay to the southwest. In its heyday, Comalcalco may, in fact, have lain on or immediately back of the coast, for the continuous sedimentary deposition of the great rivers in this region has since pushed the shoreline farther and farther out into the shallow waters of the adjacent Gulf. At the same time, the block of the earth's crust beneath this giant, compound delta has been sinking under the weight of the accumulating sediments, for today the footings of most of Comalcalco's buildings are standing in water—not too unlike the conditions found in Venice.

However, it is not the Po plain of Italy which affords the closest parallel with the Chontalpa region of Tabasco but rather the plain of the Yellow River in North China. There, the mighty Hwang Ho, also known as "China's Sorrow," has changed its course at least nine times in the last 25 centuries. Probably the most disastrous of these course changes occurred in 1854 when, just downstream of the city of Kaifeng, the river abandoned its old channel which led southeastward out into the Yellow Sea and turned sharply northeastward to find an outlet in the Bo Hai instead. Not only were immense areas flooded in the process, but it is also estimated that the inundation took the lives of over a million persons trapped in its path. The present mouth of the Yellow River lies on the north side of the Shandong Peninsula, fully 250 miles from its former outlet to the south of that peninsula.

I would argue that much the same kind of a catastrophe befell the Chontalpa region sometime in the Late Classic Period. In this instance, the Grijalva River, presently credited with ranking seventh in volume among the rivers of the world, made a similar drastic shift in its channel just upstream of the present-day city of Cárdenas. Turning sharply eastward, it abandoned its older, more direct route to the Gulf and spilled into the vast swampy basin where the Río de Teapao, Río Tacotalpa, Río Macuspana, Río Tulijá, and the immense Río Usumacinta and its myriad tributaries all come together. Comalcalco, the former seaport and gateway to the great Grijalva Valley, was now left "high and dry" along the empty watercourse of the Río Seco — without a hinterland to serve and quite cut off from any overland contacts it may have earlier had with the Maya core area to the east. Certainly, if there had been any Maya settlements and ceremonial centers in the immensely fertile river valleys between the Grijalva and the Usumacinta — and it seems almost unthinkable that the Maya had not seen fit to utilize this region — all traces of them were swept away in the resultant flood. Although the effects of this cataclysm may have been limited to the immediate Chontalpa region, it is very possible that they were, in fact, just the most dramatic manifestation of a changing climate which was soon to engulf the entire Maya society. What we do know is that the wave of collapse moved across the Maya lowlands from west to east, with the first Maya center to go under being Palenque about A.D. 810. Yaxchilán and Piedras Negras on the mighty Usumacinta followed soon after (by 825), and Altar de Sacrificios farther up the valley was essentially abandoned by 910. Within the next few decades the rain forests of the Petén had swallowed up most of the remaining cities, and what had once been a thriving urban population of perhaps 12 million had fallen to an impoverished rural population of less than 2 million (Adams, 1991, 264).

Chapter 10

Dawn in the Desert: The Rise of the Toltecs

THE CHICHIMEC WORLD

Mexico's geographic location within the trade wind belt means that most of the country's moisture is derived from the Gulf of Mexico to the east. Were it not for the fact that the folded ridges of the Sierra Madre Oriental rise to heights of over 3000 m (10,000 ft) within little more than 100 km (60 mi) of the coast, the greater part of the country might be expected to have been lush and green. However, because of that "accident" of topography, most of Mexico lies in a "rain-shadow" behind the mountains, with the result that water is in critically short supply through much of the year.

Nowhere is that deficiency more in evidence than in the northern interior of the country, because as the latitude of 30° is neared, the winds become more southerly, paralleling the Mexican coast and bringing their moisture ashore in Texas and the Gulf coastal areas of the United States instead. Along Mexico's east coast, the last great river flowing out of the interior is the Río Pánuco, which reaches the sea where the bustling oil and industrial port of Tampico now stands. For all intents and purposes, the Pánuco marked the northernmost boundary of the Mesoamerican cultural realm because beyond it, maize — the indigenous staff of life — could no longer be grown with dependable regularity.

Once the verdant crests of the Sierra Madre Oriental with their stands of oak and pine forest are passed, the landscape quickly changes into one of creosote bush, yucca, and cacti. With all but the highest mountain uplifts now cut off from the trade winds, the vast interior of northern Mexico is a region almost totally dependent for its water supply on the scattered and sporadic monsoonal downpours of summer. As temperatures over the high plateaus of northern Mexico and the southwestern United States build up with the northerly advance of the sun, an upper-level flow of moist air starts moving in off the Pacific, triggering thundershowers that are as spotty in their distribution as they are short and violent in nature. These monsoonal rains begin earlier and last longer in the south of the Mexican plateau than they do in the north, and how far they penetrate or how much precipitation they produce can vary markedly from one year to another. As in Monsoon Asia, a very careful timing of the agricultural cycle might produce a successful crop, but in just as many if not more instances a total disaster could result as well. Small wonder then, that the local inhabitants found little opportunity and even less incentive to attempt to gain their livelihood in other than the most rudimentary manner, that is, through collecting (gathering and hunting).

To be sure, during the Pleistocene ice age things were rather different. That was the time of the "pluvials," or heavy rains, which were occasioned by the equatorward displacement of the midlatitude storm tracks. At that time large parts of the Mexican plateau supported a dense grass cover which enabled a rich fauna of prehistoric grazing animals to inhabit the region. But as the climate warmed and the continental ice sheets retreated, so did the storm belts shift northward, nudging the Mexican plateau toward the semiarid and arid climate which it experiences today. While some of the great herds of deer, elk, and bison survived by moving northward, many species — such as the native camels and horses, as well as the great lumbering mammoths and mastodons — became extinct as the temperatures rose, the rains ceased, and the grasslands degenerated into desert and scrub. What had been a Paleolithic

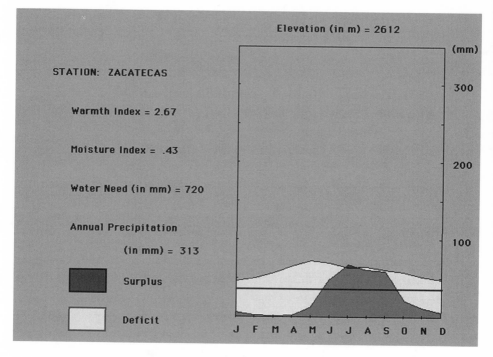

Figure 54.
The climatic station of Zacatecas is representative of a large part of the northern Mexican plateau and as such typifies the environment in which the nomadic Chichimecs were found. Although the warmest month is May, the water need (and hence the temperature) is moderate throughout the year, due both to the place's northerly latitude and to its high elevation. Frosts can occur in the low-sun (winter) months, but the greatest drawback to agriculture is the deficiency of moisture. A monsoonal distribution of precipitation is still apparent, but barely meets the moisture requirements of plants for more than a couple of months. As a result, the prevailing vegetation of the region surrounding Zacatecas is of a short-grass steppe or semidesert variety.

hunter's paradise had turned into a harsh and niggardly expanse inhabited chiefly by small rodents and reptiles, and the occasional larger predator. Indeed, one of the most productive local environments continued to be the waters of the temporary playa lakes which occupied the floors of many of the mountain basins, for there both fish and waterfowl could be found, at least seasonally.

The higher crests of the Sierra Madre Occidental on the western edges of the Mexican plateau formed something of a green oasis in the drab brownness of the northern desert. Here a slightly greater annual rainfall coupled with cooler temperatures made the moisture effective enough to support extensive forests of pine, but once the descent of the western slopes was made, so too was there a return to semiarid conditions, only now in company with tropical temperatures. The aridity of the Pacific versant of the Sierra Madre Occidental is relieved only here and there by the waters of some larger river snaking its way to the coast. Northward beyond the great delta of the Río Grande de Santiago in what today is Nayarit state, the patches of green become smaller and more scattered the farther up the coast one goes. It was in these little alluvial plains along such rivers as the Sinaloa and the Fuerte that the last outposts of the Mesoamerican culture realm were to be found, clinging to their existence as tiny islands of corn cultivation in a vast surrounding sea of nomadism.

Although the boundaries between the settled agriculturalist and the nomadic hunter-gatherer were fairly rigidly drawn by nature itself, this did not prevent the two culture-worlds from interacting with one another. Perhaps much of this interaction was the peaceful interchange of goods and ideas, because we do know that trade items from Mesoamerica reached well up into the American Southwest and that some especially prized commodities, such as native copper, found their way from as far away as the shores of Lake Superior to Central Mexico. In the same way, certain cultural traits like the ritual ball game and sacrifices to the morning star spread well beyond the limits of Mesoamerica into adjacent regions of North America. But inevitably some of this cross-cultural interaction was also of a more violent nature, and raids by hungry nomads into frontier areas of agricultural production must have been both frequent and repeated. Thus, depending on a given nomadic tribe's geography, they might have been drawn into the expanding web of civilization either early or late, either to a great degree or perhaps not at all. In any case, for at least a half dozen centuries following the founding of Teotihuacán, the line of contact between city dweller and barbarian must have fluctuated uneasily through the barren desertlands of the Mexican plateau just a few score kilometers beyond the horizon from the Pyramid of the Sun.

THE LEGACY OF CONQUEST

Following their successful onslaught on Teotihuacán, the Toltecs must have experienced a certain numbing realization of what they had done. In place of the large, thriving metropolis that had tempted their incursion in the first instance now lay the glowing embers of a dead and vacant city — the humble homes of its people in ruins, its vast, sprawling marketplaces silent, its artisan quarters abandoned, its religious and ruling elite gone. Once its stores of foodstuffs had been ransacked and its objects of art had been pilfered, there was nothing left but the hulking masses of its great pyramids standing as mute witnesses to the death of a great civilization. How long it took for Teotihuacán's terrified and impoverished populace to shrink back into the countryside is difficult to imagine; certainly, the exodus must have been a rapid one because with the supplies of food and water cut off, the city's inhabitants would have had to flee quickly to other, more congenial areas of subsistence or perish in the attempt. The pandemonium, panic, and sheer human suffering which engulfed the survivors must have been catastrophic. The loss in life was no doubt staggering; the loss in cultural and intellectual terms was almost irreparable.

Ironically, it was probably the latter which troubled the Toltecs the most. The total fabric of the city's life was gone. Its social structure was in tatters. Its religious being was in question. Existence had suddenly become meaningless. It was as though the gods had forsaken them, for without the priestly elite, there was no interpretation of their will, no ordered timetable by which to commemorate them. Time itself had lost its meaning, for without the calendar one day was the same as any other.

Surely, the mysterious malaise which settled over the survivors of Teotihuacán could not have long gone unnoticed by the Toltec conquerors. What was this "calendar" of which everyone seemed to speak? How had it ordered the lives of the people, and why was there such an empty void without it? Was there something unseen — invisible in the city itself but nevertheless real and powerful — through which the priests had communicated with the gods? No nomads, lurking on the desert fringes of the great metropolis, would have suspected that in addition to the pyramids and palaces and marketplaces and workshops — which they *could* see — was a mystical force that drove the entire engine of civilization, but which they *could not* see. It was something of which they would only belatedly become aware once the engine had stopped.

In their quest to find out what this "calendar" was all about, the Toltecs probably had to rely primarily on untutored, secondary sources, for the priests who were the custodians of such privileged information had long since fled. Indeed, the native sources tell us that at the first sign of threat and turmoil, the priests of Teotihuacán had assembled their books and religious paraphernalia and abandoned the city for a land in the east. Nevertheless, the Toltecs must have come into possession of enough of the priestly records to recreate the calendrical system almost exactly, though at the same time they clearly availed themselves of the opportunity to make some distinctive modifications and embellishments of their own.

A CALENDAR REBORN: THE NAHUA MODEL

The basic structure of the Toltec calendrical system was unmistakably patterned on that of its Teotihuacano predecessor, for 13 numerals alternated with 20 day-names to form the basis of a "sacred almanac" whose primary function was to divine the fortunes of individuals and schedule major religious festivities. Another count containing 18 groups of 20 days followed by 5 additional days which were considered "unlucky" measured the length of a "year" — the latter being a concept with which the Toltecs must have had only a most rudimentary acquaintance. The two counts ran simultaneously and only after 52 years had passed would the numbers and names of the days once again be the same as when the count began. This point, in particular, must have impressed the Toltecs, because it was as though it proved that history repeated itself. To the primitive mind, it may also have suggested the necessity for humans to do something special — to make the appropriate offerings to the gods — so as to ensure that the world would continue for another 52 years, for such a provision was built into the Toltec version of the calendars from the very start.

To identify specific years within any given 52-year "bundle," the Toltecs also imitated the practice of their Teotihuacano forebears by naming each year for the day of the sacred almanac on which it *ended*. Because the least common divisor of both calendars was 5, this meant that the secular year could only end on one of the same four day-names (20 ÷ 5), though the numeral would vary from 1 through 13 within each 52-year "bundle" of years. Thus, in effect the days which became the "year bearers" of the Nahua peoples were those named "Rabbit," "Reed," "Flint-Knife," and "House," or *Tochtli, Acatl, Tecpatl,* and *Calli* in their own language.

Another characteristic of the Toltec calendar which was derived from earlier Mesoamerican practice was the calibration of the beginning of the secular year with the southward zenithal passage of the sun. At the latitude of Tula (20° N), the Toltec capital city, this event occurred on July 24. Yet, to these newly acculturated nomads, this event must have seemed far less auspicious than the zenithal passage of the Pleiades (the distinctive asterism of seven visibly clustered stars which has intrigued peoples throughout the world), for they made this latter passage the occasion to mark the end of each of their 52-year cycles with a special celebration called the "binding of the years."

Perhaps geography explains much of the Toltecs' fascination with the Pleiades, for no other native people of Mesoamerica who came under the influence of the calendar lived so directly beneath this star group. Indeed, at the latitude of Tula, the Pleiades transited the zenith each year at midnight on the evening of October 9. Although the position of all stars in the heavens changes with time due to precession (the very slow wobble of Earth on its axis), throughout the entire duration of the Toltec Empire this star cluster remained within 2° of the zenith. Even by the end of Aztec times it was within 2°.5 of the zenith, and at the present time the Pleiades are little more than 4° from the zenith as measured from Central Mexico.

Although the Toltec 52-year cycle began with "1 Rabbit," thanks to Nahua mythology the "binding of the years" ceremony took place in the second year of the cycle, "2 Reed." This stemmed from the Toltecs' understanding that there had been four previous creations of the world, or "suns," —each of them associated with one of the cardinal points, each lasting for 676 years (13 multiples of 52), and each having been terminated by such disasters as being devoured by jaguars, consumed by fire, destroyed by wind, or submerged by flood.

After this last cataclysm it supposedly took a year to "raise the heavens again," and in the second year a feast was prepared for the gods (Krickeberg, 1980, 24). Since by tradition fire was first acquired on this occasion, the ceremony itself involved putting out all the fires of the past era and rekindling new ones. Thus, in the Nahua mind the fateful moment in which the Pleiades passed through the zenith — in relative proximity to Orion's Belt, which they visualized as a "fire drill" — provided an appropriate opportunity for demonstrating humankind's gratitude to the gods for giving them fire. To the Toltecs — and later the Aztecs — this meant cutting out the heart of a sacrificial victim and kindling the first new fire in his chest cavity. Indeed, some form of human sacrifice was to become an integral part of the celebration of the end of each 20-day "month," as well as on the occasion of an ominous day called "4 Movement." The Nahua peoples believed that the present "world," or the "fifth sun," had been created on a day with that name and that it would end on another day named "4 Movement" when devastating temblors would destroy the earth.

Any researcher who would attempt to reconstruct the calendrical system of the Toltecs must necessarily take into account the facts and fictions by which they lived. Certainly the most exhaustive study that has been made of the Nahua calendar was that carried out by the Mexican scholar Alfonso Caso (1967), who based his correlation on the correspondence of certain key dates of the Spanish conquest and native Indian sources. The events which he chose to demonstrate this correspondence included Cortés's arrival in Tenochtitlán (November 9, 1519), his forced retreat from the city known as *La Noche Triste* (June 30, 1520), and his ultimate destruction of the Aztec capital and capture of the emperor Cuauhtémoc (August 13, 1521). On the basis of these correspondences, Caso concluded that the Nahua calendar had to have begun with the "month" of Atlcahualo, although of 42 sources which he surveyed ranging from the sixteenth through the twentieth century, he found a wide difference in opinion. (Remember that what we term a "month" in the Mesoamerican calendar is in fact an interval of 20 days, and had nothing to do with the length of the period of the moon's revolution.) Like Caso, 14 of the sources opted for the "month" of Atlcahualo, another 14 preferred Tlacaxipehualiztli, 7 cited Izcalli, 3 chose Tititl, 2 Atemoztli, and 1 each Panquetzaliztli and Toxcatl. Thus, no fewer than 7 of the 18 "months" have been suggested as the starting point of the Aztec year. Even the two earliest chroniclers, the Spanish clerics Sahagún and Durán, disagreed: The first cited a beginning Julian calendar date of February 2; the second, March 1.

By devising a computer program which permitted me the flexibility of testing *all* of the "months" of the Aztec year as potential starting dates, I was able to establish that *any* of the first 8 "months" would have produced the same three correspondences as Caso's correlation. However, if the calendar had begun with the 9th month, *La Noche Triste* would have fallen during the *nemontemi*, or 5-day unlucky period, whereas from the 10th through the 18th "months" it would have occurred on the day 3 Huey Tecuilhuitl rather than on 18 Tecuilhuitontli as Caso argued. From "month" 13 on, the most critical of the three dates—the fall of Tenochtitlán—would have occurred on 7 Xocotl Huetzi rather than 2 Xocotl Huetzi, thereby rendering the last 6 of the Aztec "months" as impossible candidates for the beginning of their year. Thus, while any of the first 8 Aztec "months" produced totally as accurate results as Caso claimed for Atlcahualo, when they were tested against a fourth well-known date from the Conquest—namely, that of the great Cholula massacre carried out by Alvarado on May 23, 1520—both the 7th and 8th "months" had to be dismissed as well.

Having now narrowed the field to the first 6 "months" of the Aztec year, I proceeded to test each of them to determine on which day of the secular calendar the final day of the sacred almanac fell. This was important because Caso argued that the name of the year took its name from that day; and since Caso had selected Atlcahualo as the first "month" of the year, he concluded that the critical day would have been 20 Tititl.

Choosing the final celebration of the "binding of the years" in 1507 as my test case, I found that all 6 of the "months" produced exactly the same results: the day "1 Rabbit" of the sacred almanac fell on 20 Tititl of the secular calendar (corresponding to January 22, 1507). One round earlier in the sacred almanac, however—i.e., on May 7, 1506—the secular calendar which began with "month" 1, Izcalli, would again have reached the date 20 Tititl, whereas those versions of the secular calendar which began in "months" 2 through 5 (including Caso's choice, Atlcahualo) would all have recorded 20 Huey Tozoztli. On the other hand, the version of the secular calendar which began with "month" 6 would have reached the date 5 Nemontemi, the last of the so-called 5 unlucky days. Thus, through this test I had further narrowed the field of possible candidates for the secular year's starting "month" to the only two with truly distinctive characteristics—"month" 1, Izcalli, and "month" 6, Toxcatl.

Caso claimed that the Toltecs would never have chosen the name of one of the 5 unlucky days as the name of the year, and therefore had ruled out the possibility of Toxcatl having served as the beginning of the secular year. Nonetheless, several earlier writers including Bernardino Sahagún had commented on how similar the celebrations of its festival—the greatest of the entire year—were to those of the "binding of the years," so I was not about to discount it quite yet. A further correlation was required to narrow the choices between Izcalli and Toxcatl.

All researchers examining the Mesoamerican calendars have been struck by how closely the Nahua version mirrors that of the Maya. Indeed, a comparison of the day-*numbers* of the sacred almanac in each of the Nahua and Maya versions reveals that they are only two days apart! For example, what would have been the day 12 Ik in the Maya almanac corresponded to the day "1 Rabbit" in the Aztec count. (Remember that after the numeral 13 is passed in the sacred almanac the day-numbers begin with 1 again.) One of the days in this discrepancy could easily have resulted from a lapse in the count occasioned by the chaos attending Teotihuacán's fall, while the other might well derive from a difference in counting techniques—the Olmecs and the Maya starting from sunset and the Toltecs and the Aztecs from sunrise.

However, when the day-*names* of these two dates are combined with their respective numbers, we find that the relative positions of these dates in the sacred almanac are actually 106 days apart. This is because 12 Ik is day 142 of the Maya count whereas "1 Rabbit" is day 248 of the Aztec count. Thus, from 142 to 248 represents a shift of 106 days. In other words, when we correlate individual days of the Maya sacred almanac with their counterparts in the Nahua count, we find that the advance of the latter over the former amounts to five 20-day "months," an additional 5 days for the unlucky *nemontemi* period, and an extra day because the Toltecs and their heirs did not use zeros with which to count. (To illustrate this point, a day which would have been numbered 0 Pop by the Maya would have been 1 Pop to the Aztecs. It seems likely that the pragmatic Nahua saw no value in a number which meant "in progress" or "not yet complete." By the same token, their failure to grasp the notion of zero probably likewise accounts for their having abandoned sunset as the time from which to tabulate their count of the days and substituted sunrise instead.) Of course, this 106-day interval can also be thought of as a restatement of the remainder between one round of the 260-day sacred almanac and one round of the 365-day "Vague Year" expressed according to the Nahua counting mode.

Naturally, with a displacement of 106 days between corresponding dates in the two calendars, we can no longer argue for some casual lapse having taken place between them but must recognize instead that a carefully calculated and conscious shift had been made of the starting point of the secular calendar. This recognition therefore led me to test the date of zenithal sun passage over Tula as it might have been recorded in the *unaltered* Maya secular calendar and then compare that to the date as it would have been recorded in a version of the Aztec calendar based on Caso's correlations. (For this test, I used the example I cited above in which the day of the Maya almanac equated to 12 Ik and that of the Aztec to "1 Rabbit.") According to the unaltered Maya secular calendar the day was 0 Yax, while in the Aztec version it was 1 Izcalli. This meant that I had now established a correlation between the "months" of the Maya and Aztec secular calendars, for if Yax corresponded to Izcalli, then Zac would correspond with Atlcahualo, and so on.

However, to get the *position* of 12 Ik in the Maya almanac to match that of the *position* of "1 Rabbit" in the Aztec almanac I would have to advance the count of the latter by five "months" and six days, as I described above. When I did this, I found that the date on which "1 Rabbit" was reached was on 1 Toxcatl, but only if the *nemontemi* had also been inserted somewhere ahead of 1 Toxcatl. (Of course, it doesn't matter where the *nemontemi* is inserted between Izcalli and Toxcatl to obtain such a result, but all early accounts of the structure of the calendar suggest that the 5-day unlucky period immediately preceded the beginning of the new cycle—i.e., it was positioned just ahead of the "month" of

Toxcatl. Only with such a configuration will the Aztec secular calendar mesh exactly with the Maya secular calendar.

Once a convincing correlation had been established between these two versions of the Mesoamerican calendrical system, I reasoned that the chronology of the Nahua time-count should now be as secure and reliable as that of the Long Count. It should, therefore, be possible to devise a computer program to run the Nahua secular calendar "backward" in the same manner that I had done with the Maya calendar in order to establish when it had actually come into being. I was well aware that, because the "Vague Year" of the Nahua "slipped" forward one day in every four years just as the Maya secular calendar did, the "month" of Toxcatl would have "migrated" widely through the year. Thus, in 1521, when Cortés conquered the Aztecs, the first day of Toxcatl fell on May 4; in 1403, on June 3; in 1091, on August 20; and so on. Therefore, it was necessary to insert a "flag" in my program which would search out the closest correspondence between the beginning of Toxcatl and the "binding of the years" ceremony, which in our calendar would have occurred in the month of October. Concurrently, I would be looking for a "suitable" beginning date for the southward zenithal passage of the sun — in other words, one which would have made "good sense" to a group of pragmatic nomads — in short, a straightforward beginning of the secular year with a day numbered "1" in both the sacred and secular counts. (While the Toltecs would have been no more likely to tamper with the religiously sanctified sacred almanac than any other Mesoamerican people ever were, they had good reason to shift around the secular calendar to suit their needs, just as the Maya had done back in A.D. 48.)

As I ran the computer program "backward," I discovered that the closest correspondence between the beginning of Toxcatl and the "binding of the years" occurred in the year 883 ("2 Reed") when they were just two days apart. However, if the secular calendar had begun in the previous year ("1 Rabbit"), as tradition indicated it had, then the July 24 zenithal passage of the sun would have occurred on the date 7 Atlcahualo — certainly not a rational day of "beginnings." Going back a further 52-year cycle, I found that the beginning of Toxcatl fell on October 24 in the year 831 (some 15 days after the zenithal passage of the Pleiades), whereas the southward passage of the zenithal sun took place on July 24, 830. In the secular calendar, this happened on 14 Izcalli — again hardly an auspicious day on which to begin a calendar. If, however, we go back yet one more interval of 52 years, we find that Toxcatl would have commenced on the day November 6 (a full 27 days following the zenithal passage of the Pleiades), but that the southward passage of the zenithal sun on July 24, 778, would have coincided with the day 1 Cuetz-pallin ("Lizard") of the sacred almanac and 1 Izcalli of the secular count. Although there is every reason to believe that a considerable period of planning and anticipation had to have preceded this date, the internal structure of the calendar itself argues for its having been inaugurated on July 24, 778. Indeed, this conclusion finds strong reinforcement in the research of Krickeberg (1980, 209), who states that the Nahua believed that the present "sun," or "world," came into being in the equivalent of our year 726. When we realize that this notion places the creation of the "Toltec world" exactly 52 years before the starting date of their calendar, we can appreciate how quickly these recent nomads from the desert had come to embrace one of the most fundamental concepts of Mesoameri-can civilization — to wit, the cyclical repetition of history.

By selecting 1 Cuetzpallin 1 Izcalli as the beginning date of their sec-ular calendar, the Toltecs also assured that their first celebration of the "binding of the years" — on October 9, 779 — fell on the auspicious day of "1 Death" in the sacred almanac. By the same token, if they had re-tained an awareness of the 52d sunset after the summer solstice — i.e., August 13 — they could not have failed to appreciate that it fell on 8 Cuetzpallin 1 Atlcahualo, exactly one "month" after the southward pas-sage of the zenithal sun. And similarly, they would have found that the autumnal equinox (September 22) occurred on 9 Cuetzpallin 1 Tozoz-tontli, so they must have felt quite satisfied in having established such an impressive measure of consonance with the rhythms of the heavens. It is also interesting that by inaugurating their secular count on July 24, 778, the Toltecs had, in fact, made Izcalli the first "month" of their year. However, unlike the Maya and the other Mesoamericans whose 5-day unlucky period fell just ahead of the beginning of the secular year, the Toltecs had chosen to shift it so that it more closely approximated what they considered to be a celestial event of yet greater significance — the midnight zenithal passage of the Pleiades—hence its insertion just ahead of the "month" of Toxcatl.

In addition to the astronomically fixed celebrations of the zenithal passages of the sun and the Pleiades, there were the equinoxes and solstices that occupied defined positions in the ritual year as well. Of these, it would appear that it was the winter solstice that became the occasion for the most important celebration, because the sun was then at its farthest remove south and there was need to ensure its return to more northerly latitudes. One of the lasting legacies of the Nahua calendar is the annual celebration which now serves to mark the feast day of the patron saint of Mexico, Our Lady of Guadalupe. In 1531 a newly converted Indian peasant by the name of Juan Diego, trudging across the hillside at Tepeyac just north of Tenochtitlán, claims to have seen the Virgin. Although the Spanish bishop was at first dubious, a shrine was erected there which has since become the most important pilgrimage site in Catholic Mexico. Sahagún, in writing about the place in the 1580's, was already "suspicious" about both its name and its function, for by then it had become known as "Our Lady of Guadalupe-Tonantzin," the latter appelation being that of the Aztec sun-goddess. He also observed that the temple of the sun goddess had stood on the same hill in pre-Conquest times, and he was at pains to explain why, of all the churches dedicated to the Virgin, this was the only one at which the Indians worshiped (Sahagún, 1981, 329). Had he looked more deeply into the matter, he would likewise have been intrigued by the fact that the annual feast day falls on December 12, which in the Julian calendar marked the winter solstice!

In the same vein, one cannot help wondering how, in the wake of the Spanish conquest, the various individual Indian villages of Mexico and Guatemala came to choose their local patron saints from among the array which the Catholic church offered them, and whether the choice of any given "saint's day" might not have been simply a thinly veiled artifice for continuing a time-honored religious celebration from the pre-Columbian past.

In addition to the fixed religious festivals of the Nahua year were those which "migrated" through the seasons with the slippage of the secular calendar. The final day of each 20-day "month" provided the occasion for a celebration which almost invariably involved some form of human sacrifice, as did the occurrence of the feared day "4 Movement." By Aztec times, these ritualized killings had reached such a peak that the birth of each new day was greeted by the offering of a human heart.

TOLTEC HISTORY AND THE CALENDAR

Because Itzcóatl, the fourth emperor of the Aztecs, had all the history books of earler civilizations burned, the fragmentary and contradictory records that we have of the Toltecs derive chiefly from two sources: Ixtlilxóchitl's *Historia Tolteca-Chichemeca* and the *Anales de Cuauhtitlán*, both of which are post-Conquest documents that purport to list the Toltec kings and the lengths of their respective reigns. Although each of them lists 10 rulers, only three names are common to both lists and only one of their reigns overlaps the same period of time. Indeed, the *Historia's* list is particularly suspect, because six of the rulers are therein said to have reigned for exactly 52 years and the last — Quetzalcóatl — supposedly reigned for 74.

Moreover, because the Toltecs lacked the Long Count, considerable debate has arisen among scholars as to the particular 52-year cycle in which any given event may have taken place. Contributing to the confusion has been the contention of some researchers that the Toltecs used a modified version of the Mixtec calendar, which caused their dates to be 12 years at variance with (i.e., earlier than) the time-count inherited from the Olmecs (Davies, 1977, 441–466). As Caso has pointed out, however, such an argument is totally at odds with what we know about the precision of Mesoamerican timekeeping; indeed, it does nothing to explain the striking correspondences between the later Aztec calendar and the earlier Maya version of the same time-count which we discussed earlier. Therefore, the chronology given below is that based on the version of the Aztec calendar in use at the time of the arrival of the Spaniards.

If we disregard for the moment the more legendary accounts of the earliest nomad chieftains (for example, the earliest chieftain, Mixcóatl, or "Cloud Serpent," supposedly laid the groundwork for the first Toltec capital at Ixtapalapa, to the southeast of modern Mexico City), then perhaps one of the first events recorded in Toltec history to which we can assign a reasonably reliable date was the birth in the year Ce Acatl ("1 Reed") of the chieftain-king who took the name "Quetzalcóatl" and who later was deified by his subjects. (One should keep in mind, however, that the original deity named Quetzalcóatl was a culture hero who supposedly first acquainted the peoples of Mesoamerica with agriculture and the calendar and whose representation as a feathered serpent is repeatedly juxtaposed with a second deity—Tlaloc, the rain-god—on the façade of one of the principal pyramids at Teotihuacán. It is likewise interesting that in this representation, Quetzalcóatl is clearly associated with seashells, implying a link with the distant sea.) The son of another chieftain named Mixcóatl and his wife Chimalman, the boy was named "Ce Acatl Topiltzin," the latter appelation meaning "our prince." The year which most convincingly coincides with this event was A.D. 947. In the year "2 Rabbit" (974) his father established the Toltec capital at Tulancingo, but when Quetzalcóatl ascended to the throne three years later (in the year "5 House"), he moved his capital to Tula, some 100 km (60 mi) to the west. (Sanders believes that the Toltecs had occupied the region surrounding Tula as early as A.D. 700 [Adams, 1991, 220], while Krickeberg dates the actual founding of the city to the year 856 [1980, 424]. Although the terrain surrounding Tula would have made a gridded master plan difficult to carry out, at least a part of the city is laid out with an orientation based on the August 13 alignments found at Teotihuacán [Adams, 1991, 231].) This move appears to have been a response to pressure exerted by the so-called historic Olmec, or "Olmec Uixtotin," who at that time controlled both the valleys of Mexico and Puebla. Despite having enjoyed a relatively long reign of peace and prosperity in his new capital, Quetzalcóatl was forced by a power struggle within the Toltec hierarchy to flee with his retinue to the Gulf coast in the next year named "1 Reed" (999). Although the deposed king died on reaching the coast, legend has it that he was subsequently reincarnated as the morning star (the planet Venus), having vowed to return one day rightfully to reclaim his throne. His retinue continued to the east, arriving on the coast of the Yucatán, and then moved inland to subjugate the by then almost moribund Maya city-state of Chichén Itzá.

Meanwhile, back in the Toltec capital of Tula, new chieftain-kings came and went. Matlacxóchitl is reported as having died in the year "10 Rabbit" (1034), whereas Nauhyotzin, his successor, passed away in the year "12 House" (1049). Matlaccoatzin then assumed the throne and ruled until his death in the year "1 House" (1077). He was followed on the throne by Tlicohuatzin, who reigned until the year "9 Rabbit" (1098). The subsequent events of Toltec history all took place within the reign of a king called Huémac.

Little else comes down to us in the way of Toltec history apart from certain "innovations" which they developed in carrying out their calendrical rituals. In the year "7 Rabbit" (1122), for instance, we are told that the Toltecs initiated the practice of sacrificing children to the rain-god, and in the year "8 Rabbit" (1162), as a consequence of certain "auguries," they note that they began sacrificing prisoners by shooting them with arrows, a practice they claim to have learned from the Huastecs. When war broke out five years later (in the year "13 Reed," or 1167), the Toltecs report that they began the sacrifice of prisoners by flaying them. Ironically, though most "civilized" societies would have found such practices totally repugnant, for the Toltecs they represented evidence of their advance from nomadic hunting and gathering to a life as settled cultivators, for these innovations in human sacrifice must be seen as attempts to propitiate newly acquired agricultural deities, such as Tlaloc and Xipe. None of these "refinements" seem to have stayed the hand of destiny, however, for in the following year, "1 Flint-Knife," Chichimecs swarmed in from the northern desert and laid waste Tula, causing Huémac to flee southward with his court. It was at this time that Huémac relocated the Toltec capital to Chapultepec, on the western outskirts of present-day Mexico City. His kingdom lost and his subjects scattered over the countryside, a despondent King Huémac committed suicide in the year "7 Rabbit" (1174). Although bountiful harvests were recorded in the year "2 Reed" (1195) — when the Toltecs celebrated what was to be their final "binding of the years" ceremony to ensure the world's survival for another 52 years — this belated stroke of good fortune was not enough to rekindle their vitality as a people, and in the year "1 Flint-Knife" (1220) they disappeared as an organized force from the pages of pre-Columbian history.

THE ROLE OF VENUS IN THE CEREMONIAL LIFE
OF THE NAHUA PEOPLES

Although what passes for Toltec history is a mixture of legend and fact, it does provide us with a temporal framework against which we can assess certain of the key events whose commemoration by the Aztecs speaks to the continuance of a lengthy tradition. For the purposes of studying how the Toltecs actually used the calendrical information to which they fell heir, we should keep in mind that their domination of the Mexican plateau lasted roughly 500 years — i.e., from the late eighth to the early thirteenth century.

Within that time span, there were nine celebrations of the "binding of the years," namely, in 779, 831, 883, 935, 987, 1039, 1091, 1143, and 1195. Within the same period, there were four times when the Venusian double-cycle coincided with such an event. These occasions were in 831, 935, 1039, and 1143. Therefore, if any correspondence is to be found between the calendars as handed down to the Aztecs and the Venusian events, it must focus on these four years, in all of which a superior conjunction took place.

We have already remarked how the Nahua peoples of the Mexican plateau defined the four phases of Venus in the Codex Borgia, assigning a 243-day period to its existence as a morning star, followed by a 77-day period of invisibility, then a 252-day period as an evening star, and finally another 12-day disappearance into the underworld before it returned once more as a morning star.

We have also commented on the difficulty which the Mesoamericans had in accurately defining the planet's movements, due to their failure to understand the nature of its "disappearances." While modern astronomers can mathematically pinpoint the moment of Venus's conjunctions with the sun, the Mesoamericans had to rely on their first visual sightings of the planet, either as an evening star just after sunset or as a morning star just before sunrise.

In one of the more valuable papers to emanate from the 1984 Symposium on Archaeoastronomy held at the National Autonomous University of Mexico, J. Daniel Flores Gutiérrez presented a detailed computer analysis of the trajectories of Venus as they occurred over more than 300 years of Mesoamerican history. In addition to making the point that the "binding of the years" festivals of the Toltecs and Aztecs were of two alternating types—Venus as an evening star in the years 1195, 1299, 1403, and 1507, and as a morning star in the years 1247, 1351, and 1455—his study revealed that, regardless of the type of festival, no Venusian event (e.g., the planet's disappearance, reappearance, or elongation—the latter being its angular distance from the sun) correlated with any key date of the solar year whatsoever. The author was thus left expressing the hope that someone might yet find one or more of the planet's periods—i.e., of 584 days, of 8 years, of 104 years, or of 260 years—in the structure of the codices (Flores Gutiérrez, 1991, 353).

However, because we are unable to make any sense out of the motions of Venus against the background of our own calendar, before we abandon all hope of finding a meaningful temporal pattern to its movements, we should examine them in reference to the indigenous Mesoamerican calendar. In table 6, all of the conjunctions of Venus, superior as well as inferior, that occurred in the years "2 Reed"—i.e., at the time of the "binding of the years"—are listed according to the dates of their occurrence in both Julian and Nahua calendars.

It is readily apparent from table 6 that with each successive celebration of the Venusian 104-year "double-cycle," the conjunction of the planet with the sun moved forward in the year about a month, according to the Julian calendar. However, because during this same period the Mesoamerican calendar had "slipped" forward some 26 days (i.e., 13 days during each 52-year "bundle" of years), according to the indigenous time-count the date of any given pair of conjunctions never varied by more than 2 days—the greatest discrepancy having taken place in the twelfth century. On the other hand, between any two successive pairs of conjunctions a 4-, 5-, or 6-day hiatus did, in fact, occur. However, whereas a forward shift of more than seven months took place according to the Julian calendar, there was no more than a 33-day forward movement in the date of the Mesoamerican sacred almanac—i.e., from 12 Ollin to 5 Cuetzpallin. Moreover, as can be seen, with the exception of the first four occurrences and two of the last three occurrences, all the conjunctions of Venus took place within the Nahua "month" of Tozoztontli.

Table 6 – Dates of Conjunctions of Venus, A.D. 727–1507

Year	Date	Type*	Day of Toltec/Aztec Calendar
727	November 2	S	12 Ollin 9 Huey Tozoztontli
779	October 20	I	12 Ollin 9 Huey Tozoztontli
831	October 1	S	6 Ozomatli 3 Huey Tozoztontli
883	September 18	I	6 Ozomatli 3 Huey Tozoztontli
935	August 31	S	1 Miquiztli 18 Tozoztontli
987	August 17	I	13 Coatl 17 Tozoztontli
1039	July 31	S	9 Cipactli 13 Tozoztontli
1091	July 17	I	8 Xochitl 12 Tozoztontli
1143	July 2	S	6 Tecpatl 10 Tozoztontli
1195	June 17	I	4 Cozcacuauhtli 8 Tozoztontli
1247	June 4	S	4 Cozcacuauhtli 8 Tozoztontli
1299	May 18	I	13 Malinalli 4 Tozoztontli
1351	May 6	S	1 Acatl 5 Tozoztontli
1403	April 18	I	9 Tochtli 20 Tlacaxipehualiztli
1455	April 6	S	10 Atl 1 Tozoztontli
1507	March 19	I	5 Cuetzpallin 16 Tlacaxipehualiztli

*S—Superior; I—Inferior.

As mentioned earlier, it was not, however, the conjunctions of Venus and the sun which the Mesoamericans were defining but rather the planet's mysterious disappearances into the "underworld." Because they never understood the celestial mechanics behind its disappearances, they could never really pinpoint the planet's nearest actual approach to the sun. Instead, all they could do is record its last visual sighting in the east (in the case of a superior conjunction) and its first sighting in the west. Therefore, all they were really aware of was that Venus — on its longest visit to the underworld — usually disappeared during the "month" of Atlcahualo and usually reappeared during the "month" of Toxcatl. A greater precision than this was impossible to obtain, but how this correlated to the reconvergence of the sacred almanac and the secular calendar is not readily apparent, for in each of these years the initial date of the year, "1 Rabbit," fell anywhere from 2 to 3 Julian months ahead of conjunction and always about a Julian month ahead of the planet's disappearance.

It is, therefore, quite apparent that, when calibrated against the Mesoamerican calendar, the movements of Venus showed a remarkable cyclicity, suggesting that, on average, the planet's disappearances and reappearances could often be "predicted" within a day or two. Indeed, never would Venus fail to reach its expected place in the heavens for more than six days. Perhaps by modern scientific standards a prediction this approximate would not constitute "precision," but it must nevertheless have sufficed to reinforce the confidence of the masses in the priestly hierarchy, which was probably a consideration of some importance in itself.

However, to me, the lack of a precise correspondence between one of these Venusian events and the solar year strongly suggests that scholars have been looking in the wrong place to calibrate the planet's movements. Instead of trying to match either the last day that Venus is visible before a conjunction or the first day it is visible after one with the beginning of one 104-year period or the end of another, perhaps we should be attempting to calibrate the planet's cycle against the solar year at a time when we are certain that it will be visible against some fixed horizon marker. This might be Venus's extreme northerly or southerly rising or setting position — as delineated by such an alignment as that discovered by Horst Hartung from Uxmal to the pyramid of Nohpat in the flat expanse of the Yucatán—or by its rise over some commanding topographic feature in a region of more rugged terrain.

Inasmuch as it was Venus's heliacal rise as the morning star that most concerned the Mesoamericans, it seems very probable that the "binding of the years" festival with which it is supposed to have coincided had to have been one of the "morning star" variety—i.e., one that occurred in the 104-year cycle associated with the years 1247, 1351, and 1455. (Note that each of these dates falls within the Aztec era rather than in Toltec times. Furthermore, it is well established that a Venusian period *did not* coincide with the Aztecs' final celebration of the ceremony in 1507.) It is also known that, although the ceremony itself was held in a year named "2 Reed," such as 1455, the new 52-year cycle actually began in the previous year which was "1 Rabbit."

Among the Nahuatl-speaking peoples of the Mexican plateau, one of the principal centers for the worship of Venus was Cholula on the western edge of the Puebla basin. (Others were Teotitlán del Camino and Tehuacán in the valley between Cholula and Oaxaca.) Indeed, Cholula was known to have been both an important market center and also the primary pilgrimage site of highland Mexico. After the fall from grace of the Toltec king Quetzalcóatl and his banishment from Tula, he stopped first at Cholula on his way into exile in the east.

For anyone surveying the eastern horizon from Cholula, there is no question but that the most impressive feature within view is the great snow-capped cone of Orizaba, Mexico's highest mountain (5701 m, 18,700 ft). It is interesting and no doubt significant that in Nahuatl the peak is known as Citlaltépetl, or "the mountain of the star." One has good reason to believe that the "star" in question might well have been Venus, because throughout Toltec and Aztec times, the brightest star to rise in the vicinity of Orizaba was Spica (magnitude 0.97), but even it rose 6° away to the south. It is true, however, than in Teotihuacáno times Spica rose near Orizaba for about a century, but it seems very unlikely that the Nahuatl name for the peak would have commemorated an event which had not been observed for nearly a millennium. (Even stranger is the explanation given for the mountain's name by the Spanish writer Clavijero, who claims that it received its appelation in colonial times after the peak had experienced a 20-year series of eruptions beginning in 1545 [Macazaga Ordoño, 1979, 45].)

From the clues at hand — namely, that Cholula was a major pilgrimage center dedicated to the worship of Quetzalcóatl (i.e., the planet Venus), that the most striking physical feature within view of Cholula is the cone of Orizaba, that the native place-name for the feature was "mountain of the star," and that no bright star (other than possibly Venus) rose anywhere near the peak — the hypothesis which remains to be tested is this: If Venus does indeed rise over the mountain, when does it do so, and does this in any way coincide with the beginning or ending of the solar year as known to the Nahuas?

Using a computer, a detailed study of the trajectory of Venus as seen from Cholula was made for the entire period of Nahua ascendancy over the Mexican plateau — i.e., from the eighth through the fifteenth century. This allowed seven full 104-year Venusian cycles to be examined, beginning in 830 and ending in 1454. One of the results of this exercise was the discovery that Venus was found to rise six times over Orizaba in any given eight-year period. This cyclical pattern is sketched out in table 7.

Thus, every eight years these Venusian events are repeated at the same place in the sky within a day or two of the time they were last witnessed. In the second and seventh years of the cycle Venus puts in no appearance over the mountain at all, whereas in the third, fifth, and eighth years it rises over Orizaba in the spring (March and April). However, in the first, fourth, and sixth years of the cycle the heliacal rise of Venus over Orizaba will be seen to occur in the autumn months of October and November. It is on these occasions, of course, that its fateful appearance most closely coincides with the midnight zenithal passage of the Pleiades. Even so, from the early twelfth century to the mid–fifteenth century, the date of Venus's rise over Orizaba advanced about 10 days (from November 11 to November 1), so a truly convincing case for a horizon-based calibration of the planet's movements with the "binding of the years" ritual still remains somewhat in doubt.

Table 7 – Dates of Venus's Rise over Orizaba

Year of Cycle	Approximate Dates
1	Late October–Early November
2	——
3	Late April (19–21)
4	Mid-November (10–12)
5	Late March (25–28)
6	Mid-October (15–18)
7	——
8	Early April (8–10)

THE GEOGRAPHIC SCOPE OF TOLTEC INFLUENCE

At the peak of the Toltecs' power their capital city of Tula probably numbered between 30,000 and 40,000 inhabitants, and its trading network extended from as far south as the Nicoya Peninsula of Costa Rica (from which it imported polychrome ceramics), eastward into the Yucatán Peninsula, and as far northward as the present-day southwestern United States (where the architectural influences of both Tlaloc, the rain-god, and Quetzalcóatl, the feathered serpent, may be identified). Interestingly, although Plumbate pottery from Soconusco shows up in Tula, no metal has ever been found there, despite the fact that the Toltec period is known to have coincided with the first appearance of metallurgy in Mesoamerica. (Antagonism with the Purépecha, the first practitioners of the new craft, may well be the explanation.) Nonetheless, mining colonies had been established in the northern desert—probably as early as Teotihuacáno times—to supply semiprecious stones to the civilizations of Central Mexico, but about the year A.D. 600 a southward retreat had begun which had all but abandoned the Chichimec "outback" to the nomads by 850. A Toltec reexpansion into this region appears to have taken place about 900, and Casas Grandes in northwestern Chihuahua seems to have been a thriving Toltec trading outpost by about 1050. Although Central Mexican influences had begun to show up in western Mexico at such sites as Ixtépete near modern Guadalajara and at Ixtlán del Río in the borderlands of Nayarit from about A.D. 300 onward, these contacts were considerably strengthened during Toltec times. Contact with the Maya area of the Yucatán was not limited to commerce as we have seen, for about the year 1000, Toltec warriors moved in to establish a new militaristic regime in the old ceremonial center of Chichén Itzá, not only giving that place a new lease on life but materially altering its architecture, art, and religion as well. Not the least of these cultural influences was the introduction of the cult of Quetzalcóatl, who became known to the Maya by the name of Kukulkan.

Geographically closer at hand were such ceremonial centers as Cholula and Xochicalco which, despite their proximity to the Toltec heartland, managed to retain a fairly strong Teotihuacáno character. It would seem that the neighbors nearest to the Toltecs who received the most cultural impact were the Mixtecs. Although they had originally received the calendar by way of the Zapotecs, together with the hieroglyphic system of dots and bars to record numerals, under Toltec influence they abandoned the use of bars. As a result, we find that all of the beautifully colored Mixtec codices which have been preserved define calendar dates only with dots.

XOCHICALCO AND THE ZENITH TUBE

Situated on a mountaintop about 20 km (12 mi) south-southwest of Cuernavaca (latitude 18°.8 N) is the fortified Late Classic ceremonial center of Xochicalco. Its architecture shows the strong influence of Teotihuacán, and it has been argued by some scholars that the hilltop city represented one of the refuges of the fleeing elite of that great metropolis as it came under attack from the desert nomads. Quetzalcóatl finds vivid representation there along the sides of the main pyramid, and the site also boasts one of the largest ball courts of all Mesoamerica. Astronomically, the city's chief claim to fame is its zenith tube and observation chamber hollowed out of the living rock. Having an aperture of 40 cm (16 in.), the vertical tube opens into a subterranean cavern some 8.5 m (27.9 ft) beneath it and was obviously used to calibrate the zenithal passage of the sun (Broda, 1986, 92). At Xochicalco's latitude, this is an event which takes place on May 15 and July 29 each year. It would appear that the inspiration for this device was the similar feature found in Mound P at Monte Albán, which heralded the heliacal rise of the star Capella (magnitude 0.08) on the morning of the first zenithal sun passage over that site. Interestingly, in the seventh century A.D., when the city was probably founded, the heliacal rise of the Pleiades took place on May 15 over Popocatépetl, as seen from Xochicalco. Since no evidence has ever been presented to argue for a separate and independent calendar beginning on May 15, it must be presumed that the zenith tube served the function of calibrating a locally observable phenomenon within the existing Mesoamerican calendar.

The German geographer Franz Tichy has argued that Pyramids C and D at Xochicalco served to mark key astronomical alignments as viewed from the altar of glyphs, which is located directly between them. Looking eastward, he finds that the northern corner of Pyramid C marks the sunrise azimuth on the summer solstice, while the southern corner of the same structure defines the sunrise azimuth at the winter solstice. Turning toward the west, he finds that the northern corner of Pyramid D is aligned to the sunset azimuth on the days of the zenithal sun passage—i.e., May 15 and July 29. A line drawn through the middle of both pyramids and over the stela on the intermediate altar divides the solar year exactly in half, he states (Broda, 1986, 85). It seems clear, therefore, that although Teotihuacán had itself fallen victim to the barbarians, in places like Xochicalco, the torch of astronomical knowledge had still not been extinguished in Late Classic times.

EL TAJÍN AND THE PYRAMID OF THE NICHES

Nestled in the karstic hills of northern Veracruz is the architecturally elaborate and intriguing site of El Tajín. Although evidence of settlement in the area goes back as far as 1500 B.C. (Adams, 1991, 232), life at the village level appears to have emerged by Late Preclassic times but seemingly without noticeable Olmec influence. The region surrounding El Tajín appears to have been solidly within the Totonac cultural sphere then just as it is today. During its earlier stage of city growth (A.D. 100–500), El Tajín was strongly influenced by Teotihuacán and may well have served as a commercial outlier for the plateau metropolis in the supply of lowland tropical products. However, its greatest development architecturally and influentially occurred as Teotihuacán's power waned and finally disappeared (A.D. 500–1100), and therefore the construction of most of its spectacular urban core occurred about the same time as the emergence of the Toltecs.

Although no fewer than 11 ball courts have been found at the site, testifying to the great ritual importance of the game, the crowning architectural achievement of El Tajín is the so-called Pyramid of the Niches. It received this name because each of its four sides is decorated by box-like niches whose number is invariably described in the literature as totaling 365. This in turn has prompted the suggestion that the structure commemorated the length of the solar year and that small stucco figurines representing the prevailing deity of each day may have occupied the niches.

However, it is readily apparent to anyone taking the time to actually count the niches that their number does not total 365. The reason for this is that the front, or east, side of the pyramid is surmounted by a staircase which disrupts the basic symmetry of the structure, requiring some of the niches to have been telescoped to about half of their standard size. Even so, one can count only 26 such features on each side of the staircase, yielding a total for the east face of 52. Inset into the median of the staircase itself are five panels, the four lowest of which are each composed of three smaller niches. It is uncertain whether the topmost fifth panel, which is noticeably damaged, likewise contained three niches or whether this contained only one central niche, yielding a total of 13 rather than 15 such embellishments in the staircase as a whole. It is additionally uncertain whether these 13 or 15 smaller niches are to be reckoned into the total for the structure as a whole. If not, the front face contains 52 niches; when they are included, it contains either 65 or 67 niches.

Figure 55.
The front, or east, face of the Pyramid of the Niches at El Tajín in northern Veracruz state. A major ceremonial center of the Totonac people (one of whom is seen in traditional dress in the foreground) at least since A.D. 600, El Tajín shows the influence of both Teotihuacán and the Toltecs. As explained in the text, there is some question as to how the structure shown above could have functioned calendrically, because it contains considerably fewer than the 365 niches so often stated in the literature.

Despite the destruction of most of the pyramid's top tier, it appears that each of its four sides could have contained 5 niches, yielding a total of 20. However, if the top tier of the pyramid actually served as an open temple, its front, or east, side may have had a doorway in place of 3 of the niches and still preserved its structural symmetry. Thus, we must add either 17 or 20 additional niches at the top of the pyramid, bringing the total for the east side and topmost tier to a minimum of 69 (if we disregard the small staircase niches and allow for an open temple at the top) or a maximum of 87 (if we count all the staircase niches but allow for no open temple at the summit).

The remaining three sides — i.e., the south, west, and north — are symmetrical in that each of them has a total of 87 niches. Thus, together these three faces yield a total of 261 niches, which when added to those on the east side and top tier of the pyramid come to either 330 or 348, depending on how you wish to count the latter. (However, so pervasive has the contention been that El Tajín's architectural jewel contains 365 niches that the scale model of the pyramid which was constructed for display in the Museum of Anthropology in Mexico City was *distorted* so that it would total this number!) When I attempted to point out in a scholarly article the discrepancy between the actual number of niches which can be counted and the theoretical figure of 365, my observation was dismissed with the comment that "the remaining [17 to 35] niches were buried beneath the staircase." If true, such an argument pointedly begs the question of how the pyramid could then have functioned as a counter for the length of the solar year.

If, on the other hand, we recognize the futility of attempting to argue that the niches served to record a 365-day count, especially when anywhere from 17 to 35 of the niches were hidden beneath the staircase, quite another reading of the pyramid's purpose is possible. Suppose we take the 52 niches on the east face as one count, the 13 (or 15?) smaller niches in the staircase as a second count, and the 20 niches (or were there only 17?) in the top tier as a third count, we find three of the key multiples of the Mesoamerican calendar neatly defined in three separate architectural components of the structure. If the remaining three sides of the structure are conceived as forming a fourth count (totaling 261 niches), we have as close an accommodation to the length of the sacred almanac as architectural symmetry permits. It is thus possible that the Pyramid of the Niches *may* have functioned as a calendrical counter, but if so, it was more likely to have done so for the 260 days of the divinatory almanac than for the 365 days of the solar year.

The dating of El Tajín's florescence and the overwhelming emphasis of its sculptural detail on human sacrifice (Kampen, 1972) strongly suggest that the site received considerable Toltec influence. Hieroglyphics repeatedly refer to a figure identified as "13 Rabbit," who may have been one of the city's leading rulers. Depictions of "Eagle Knights" also strengthen the impression that warriors and militarism played key roles in the city's development. But, aside from the possible calendrical associations of the Pyramid of the Niches, El Tajín demonstrates no real involvement in matters astronomical. Ensconced amongst a myriad of low limestone hills, it has a situation which all but precludes any kind of long-distance orientation, be it solsticial or otherwise. Located on the lower slopes of the Sierra Madre Oriental, it experiences a climate which is dominated by overcast skies and light drizzle through much of the year. Indeed, its very name commemorates the storm-god, and El Tajín has itself fallen victim to the destructive force of hurricane-driven rains. Commemorating astronomical cycles in stone appears to have been El Tajín's sole, but very distinctive, contribution to the evolution of the Mesoamerican calendar.

THE THREE STONE RINGS OF ZEMPOALA

Unlike the sequestered ceremonial center of El Tajín, Zempoala, the Totonac capital, was situated in a far more open setting near the coast of the Gulf of Mexico, about 40 km (25 mi) north of present-day Veracruz. No doubt because of its accessibility, it had very early been reached by Olmec influences from the south, for as we have already noted, it was one of the first ceremonial centers in the central Veracruz region to demonstrate a solsticial orientation — in this instance, to Orizaba, or Citlaltépetl, on the winter solstice sunset. Its proximity to Cortés's toehold in Veracruz also made it the first Mesoamerican city of any size to be visited by the Spanish conquistadores.

In the central plaza of Zempoala, just beneath the massive pyramids that frame its northeastern corner, are three intriguing rings of stone, each fashioned of rounded beach cobbles cemented together to form a series of small, stepped pillars. The largest of the rings contains 40 of the stepped pillars, the middle-sized ring has 28 such features, and the smallest ring numbers 13 stepped pillars around its circumference. It would appear that the three rings were used to calibrate different astronomical cycles, possibly by moving a marker or an idol from one stepped pillar to the next with each passing day (in somewhat the same way that has been suggested for recording the passage of time at the Pyramid of the Niches).

Deciphering the smallest, 13-pillar ring is probably the easiest and most straightforward task, for one cycle of this ring very likely constituted a so-called *trecena*, or 13-day interval, of the sacred calendar. Used in conjunction with the middle-sized, 28-pillar ring, it could very well

Figure 56.
The three stone rings of Zempoala as viewed from the top of the main pyramid. Inasmuch as the three rings are surmounted by 13, 28, and 40 steplike pillars, respectively, it appears that they were used by the Totonac priests as counting devices to keep track of eclipse cycles.

have defined a 364-day "year," much like that found by our "New World Hipparchus" at the outset of his calendrical experimentation. Or it might have defined the number of lunations in a year.

But what was the base from which the 28-pillar ring was derived? Was it simply the number of *trecenas* within a given year? If so, it certainly would have been possible to distinguish between the first 20 and the last 8, so as to define the length of the sacred almanac, if that was desired. Or was the 28 derived from an approximation of the number of days between full moons? Or from the number of "lunar mansions" in which the moon "rested" on its never-ending celestial journey? (The latter concept is familiar in early Middle Eastern and Asian astronomy.) Whether it was used alone or in conjunction with the 13-pillar ring, a lunar association seems very likely.

The largest ring is the most enigmatic, for no cycle based on 40 is known from Mesoamerica, although it obviously could have served to define two cycles of 20. Naturally, if it had been used as one component in defining a "year," then we might have expected to find some means of recording nine full circuits of the ring—i.e., $9 \times 40 = 360$—but no such "device" is present. If it had been used in conjunction with the middle-sized ring, it would, of course, define an interval of 1120 days (40×28), which bears no relationship to either the sacred or secular calendar. However, had it been used together with the smallest ring of 13 pillars, it could have calibrated two full cycles of the sacred almanac, or $40 \times 13 = 520$ days. The latter, known as a double *tzolkin* in Mayan terminology, equates to three eclipse half years, and thereby provides a useful interval in predicting eclipses. (An eclipse year is the length of time it takes for the sun to move from one of its intersections with the path of the moon, or node, until it returns to the same intersection, or node. It measures 346.62 days in length. Hence, an eclipse half year totals 173.31 days, and three eclipse half years add up to 519.93 days. In Mesoamerican terms, this value would be rounded to 520 days, or the equivalent of two rounds of the 260-day sacred almanac.) It is, therefore, quite possible that by using the three rings together, the Totonac priests were able to calibrate the movements of the moon closely enough so as to know when it might next be "devoured." In any event, there is every reason to believe that the three stone rings of Zempoala afford yet another bit of evidence testifying to the intellectual curiosity and architectural ingenuity of the early Mesoamericans.

Chapter 11

People of the Pleiades: The Aztec Interlude

FROM TULA TO TENOCHTITLÁN

Perhaps the most eloquent testimony to the geographic diffusion of the calendar by the Toltecs is the fact that we have indisputable evidence of its presence in the far reaches of western Mexico by at least the early decades of the twelfth century. As the Codex Botturini makes abundantly clear, when the Aztecs began the migration which took them from their homeland in the marshes of Aztlán to the small rocky islets in Lake Texcoco, which ultimately became the spectacular capital city of the vastest indigenous empire Mesoamerica was ever to know, each move along the way was documented both in space and in time. Whereas the identification of many of the place-names they used can only be guessed at (e.g., "place of the sand spider," or "place where spear-throwers are made"), the temporal sequence of the events which transpired can be precisely pinned down year by year.

The Aztecs record that their departure from their island home (subsequently identified as Mexcaltitán on the coast of Nayarit) occurred in the year "1 Flint-Knife." Because they already knew the significance of the "binding of the years" ceremony, they celebrated four such events in the years "2 Reed" while en route. Four years after the last celebration — in the year "6 Reed" — the narrative ends abruptly, due to the Codex Botturini having been damaged. Yet, from the evidence at hand, it is obvious that their migration took some 187 years to complete. This is because there are 27 years between "1 Flint-Knife" and the first occurrence of "2 Reed," and 52 years between each recurrence of a year of that name, followed by four additional years — i.e., 27 + 52 × 3 = 27 + 156 = 183 + 4 = 187. Inasmuch as their arrival in the Valley of Mexico is known to have taken place about the beginning of the fourteenth century, this would mean that their departure date was most probably in the year 1116.

Ironically, most of the ancient native accounts herald the beginning of the Chichimec period with the next time the year "1 Flint-Knife" occurred — i.e., 52 years later in 1168. This is because earlier in the decade, Tula, the capital of the Toltecs, had been overrun by barbarian Chichimecs and put to the torch. In the Codex Botturini the Aztecs record that they had left the "place of the reeds," or Tula, in the year 1163, so there is strong circumstantial evidence that it was the Aztecs themselves who had been the culprits. Just as the Toltecs had been the undoing of Teotihuacán, so the Aztecs appear to have been responsible for bringing down the remnants of the first Nahua civilization on the Mexican plateau.

Ultimately, the irony was to become even greater, for once they became fully aware of what they had done, the Aztecs revived the memory of the Toltecs as the greatest people who had ever lived. They were heralded as the first people who had learned to count, the first to understand the movements of the sun and to measure the passage of time, and the most consummate artisans who had ever molded clay or worked in feathers or textiles. Indeed, the highest compliment an Aztec could pay to anyone was to liken him to a Toltec!

As might have been expected, the Aztec migration essentially followed the line of least resistance. This was the corridor afforded by the Río Grande de Santiago, Mexico's second-largest Pacific-flowing river, and by its major tributary, the Lerma, whose headwaters rise in the highland basin of Toluca, some 100 km (60 mi) to the west of the Valley of

Mexico. The basin of Toluca, however, was not an especially attractive goal in its own right, for it was the loftiest of all the intermontane basins of the Mexican plateau. With an elevation of 2640 m (8660 ft), it was both cold and arid compared to the Valley of Mexico just over the next mountain ridge to the east. Moreover, in the middle course of the Río Lerma, the Aztecs most probably ran afoul of the Purépecha, or Tarascans, and therefore may have been obliged to detour north and eastward along the valley of the Río Turbio instead, thus ending up in the open plains to the north of Tula. On the other hand, it is just as likely that the urban metropolis of the Toltecs was their goal from the outset, and that they had moved upstream toward it as directly as they could. In any event, as the Codex Botturini informs us, the Aztecs had reached Tula by the year 1145 and did not depart until 1163.

Whereas the place-name evidence indicates that the first phase of the Aztec migration had brought them into what is now the state of Hidalgo, most of the places mentioned in the second phase of their account have been identified with localities in the present state of México. At the close of this second phase, they had reached Chapultepec, on the western outskirts of modern Mexico City, and celebrated their fourth "binding of the years" ceremony in 1299. Of the third and final phase of their migration, all of which focused on the Valley of Mexico, only the fragmentary record of four years remains, though it is generally agreed that the actual founding of Tenochtitlán can be assigned to the year 1325.

The Valley of Mexico not only lay some 400 m (1300 ft) lower than that of Toluca, and thus enjoyed a somewhat more temperate climate, but it also embraced the largest body of water on the entire Mexican plateau—a feature sometimes known as the Lake of the Moon. Although it consisted of basically one extensive articulated basin, it had three major components, partially separated from one another by higher ridges of land which formed irregular peninsulas. The southernmost arm of the body of water was known as Lake Chalco, whereas the largest and most central portion was known as Lake Texcoco, and the northern arm was called Lake Xaltocán. The marshes along the edges of the lake had very early come to be appreciated for their abundance of waterfowl and for such aquatic animals as the axolotl, a large salamander which was esteemed for its flesh.

Technically, the Lake of the Moon was what the geomorphologist calls a playa lake. As such, it was chiefly fed by run-off from the adjacent mountains, and therefore it was seldom very deep. Depending upon the amount of summer rainfall received, the lake was often very irregular in volume and in shape as well. Naturally, the longer the dry season continued, the more the water evaporated and the more the lake's shorelines contracted. At the same time, the brackishness of the water increased as the proportion of dissolved salts in the remaining water rose toward the saturation point and then began to crystallize out in the form of salt pans along the edges of the lake.

Had the Lake of the Moon been a classic playa lake, it would, of course, never have been the magnet for human settlement that it actually was. This is because, in addition to the summer run-off, its water supply was augmented by seepages of groundwater out of the volcanic formations on the south and especially the southwest sides of the lake. Because this water had percolated through lava rather than through limestone it contained little or no dissolved salts and was therefore fresh rather than brackish. Indeed, having been filtered through the volcanic formations, it was also cold, clear, and pure, so a more fortuitous combination of circumstances can scarcely be imagined — a plentiful supply of water on the very edge of a semidesert basin. (The Aztec glyph for Chapultepec very pointedly depicts the flow of water from beneath the mountain.)

Unlike typical playa lakes in other of the highland basins of the Mexican plateau, the Lake of the Moon had drawn settlers to its shores through all of human history. We know, for example, that prehistoric man was hunting mastodons on the shores of the lake at Tepexpán as early as 9000 B.C., and we have already spoken of the first agricultural villages of El Arbolillo and Zacatenco dating to about 1500 B.C. The earliest Olmec-inspired settlements at Tlatilco, Tlapacoya, and Cuicuilco were sited near the western and southern edges of the lake as well, perhaps at least in part because the freshest waters of the lake were to be found in these quadrants. Certainly by the time the Aztecs arrived in the Valley of Mexico in the late thirteenth century, all of the best land surrounding the lake had long since been occupied. Indeed, at the time of their arrival, the western, southern, and eastern shores of the lake had been consolidated into the three distinct kingdoms of Atzcapotzalco,

Culhuacán, and Coatlinchán, respectively, so it was into this political constellation that these newly arrived barbarians from the west intruded at the beginnings of the fourteenth century.

Needless to say, the Aztecs were not particularly welcome in the already relatively densely settled Valley of Mexico, for it was all the local inhabitants could do to feed themselves in this marginal semiarid upland environment. According to the Aztecs' own tribal legend, the god of war, Huitzilopochtli, had promised that their migration would be over when they found an eagle with a rattlesnake in its beak sitting on a cactus on a small rocky island—surely a combination of signs that they would not be likely to miss. Perhaps it was this augury which led them to look in the middle of the Lake of the Moon for their "promised land." On the other hand, another version of their arrival in the basin of Mexico states that when they asked for land on which to settle, they were offered a couple of small rocky islets in the middle of the lake roughly equidistant from each of the existing cities—essentially a no-man's land inhabited only by rattlesnakes and scorpions. Indeed, it has been suggested that this was done in the hope that the latter would make short work of the Aztecs, but apparently the willingness of a starving Chichimec to eat almost anything had probably been overlooked. In any case, to acquire sufficient land on which to settle, the Aztecs set about driving stakes into the shallow lake bottom and then scooping up mud and stones to build out the perimeters of their islands, much as they witnessed had been done in the heavily cultivated *chinampas* (sometimes erroneously referred to as "floating gardens") around Xochimilco at the south end of the lake. Thus, with an immense input of arduous and disciplined labor, the Aztecs gradually transformed the little rocky islands of Tenochtitlán and Tlatelolco into the nuclei of two intensely cultivated garden cities, the former serving as their religious and political nerve center while the latter increasingly took on the functions of a busy marketplace.

It should be noted in passing that whatever scenario one prefers for the founding of the Aztec capital, its siting had nothing to do with such concerns as solsticial orientation. There was no real choice as to where the city should be located, for its foundations were fixed by the geographic "accident" of the two little islands in the middle of a lake in which none of the original inhabitants of the Valley of Mexico had any interest or saw any value. It was an extremely difficult site on which to build any kind of a permanent settlement, but once the city had begun to take shape the advantages of its location gradually became increasingly apparent. From a commercial standpoint it was easily accessible to water craft carrying foodstuffs and other bulky supplies from the adjacent shores of the lake, and from a military standpoint it was sufficiently buffered by the surrounding expanses of water to enjoy a very defensible location. Therefore, although Tenochtitlán possessed none of the astronomical significance of many earlier Mesoamerican ceremonial centers, what was initially a very difficult site was ultimately transformed into a central place with a situation of paramount importance.

Several decades were to pass, however, before this vigorous, upstart people were to have so securely established themselves as to ensure their survival in the hostile physical and cultural environment in which they had settled. All the while, they remained the political tributaries of the king of Atzcapotzalco, but by the 1360's they felt that they were ready to found a kingdom in their own right. However, because they were sorely aware that they lacked the proper "pedigree" of nobility, they requested that a prince from Culhuacán become their king. Of course, such a choice linked them dynastically to a southern rival of Atzcapotzalco and in that sense it was a brilliant tactical move as well. Thus, in 1364 Acamapichtli ascended the throne in Tenochtitlán, becoming in the process the first of the monarchs of the Aztecs.

Acamapichtli's 40-year reign was largely a peaceful one, for it definitely was in the interests of the Aztecs to maintain as friendly relations as possible with the more powerful city-states that surrounded them. His successor, Huitzilíhuitl, also made an advantageous move by marrying one of the daughters of the king of Atzcapotzalco and then inducing her to implore her father to reduce the onerous tributes he had been exacting from the Aztecs, which he agreed to do.

On the death of Huitzilíhuitl in 1417, Chimalpopoca, a nephew of the king of Atzcapotzalco, became the third regent of the Aztecs. In the following year, he led his armies in the defeat of Coatlinchán, seizing the southeastern mainland of the lake for the growing Aztec city-state. However, within the decade an environmental crisis brought the Aztecs and their recently acquired relatives-by-marriage likewise to the point of blows. The expanding island city-state of Tenochtitlán was rapidly out-growing its supply of fresh water, both for domestic consumption and for irrigating the chinampas on which its food was grown. Whether the request for help which they addressed to the rulers of Atzcapotzalco was rudely phrased or not, the latter used this as an excuse to move against what they now perceived was an alarmingly expanding rival. Secret emissaries were sent into the Aztec capital, and in 1426 both the king Chimalpopoca and his son were assassinated. This treacherous act was followed by an economic blockade of the island towns which, together with the increasingly desperate water supply problem, obliged the Aztecs to react with violence.

What ensued depends on whose account one wishes to believe, that of the Aztecs or that of their confederates, the nearby city-states of Tacuba and Texcoco. According to the Aztec version, they alone resisted the attacks of Atzcapotzalco and finally rose up to conquer their oppressive neighbor in 1428. Tacuba and Texcoco, on the other hand, argued that it was their alliance with the Aztecs which ultimately turned the tables on Atzcapotzalco. In any event, what is certain is that, following the election of Itzcóatl, the son of Acamapichtli, as king and the establishment of a supreme council of advisors, the Aztec state was launched upon an entirely new course of action from that time forward. Although the council included the first Montezuma (Motecuhzoma Ilhuicamina), a son of Huitzilíhuitl; Nezahualcóyotl, the poet-king of Texcoco; and Tlacaélel, another son of Huitzilíhuitl, it was the latter more than any other single individual who came to shape the destiny of the Aztec people.

THE TORCH IS PASSED

For the better part of the next fifty years, three different kings occupied the Aztec throne, but throughout this entire time the real power resided with the royal counselor, Tlacaélel. At his direction, Itzcóatl began a series of reforms granting titles to the nobles and redistributing landholdings to enhance their status. Perhaps Tlacaélel's chief contribution was to forge a "historic conscience" among the Aztecs by burning the books of conquered peoples and the old accounts of his own people. He rewrote history to exalt the origins of the Aztecs and to establish a genealogical link with the Toltecs. He elevated Coatlicue, the hideous mother of Huitzilopochtli, the god of war, to a special position of honor in the Aztec pantheon, and gave a new interpretation to the Aztecs' religious philosophy. The present world of "the fifth sun" had begun, he argued, with the sacrifice of the gods, especially of Quetzalcóatl, at Teotihuacán. Thus, if the gods had sacrificed themselves so the sun would move and man could live, then man should sacrifice himself so that the sun could live. This, he maintained, was the only way to postpone the final cataclysm. For Tlacaélel, war was not alone a tool of conquest, subjugation, and exploitive tribute acquistion, but also a means of ensuring a continuous supply of human victims for the sacrificial altars of the Aztec temples. He not only planned and carried out the first military campaigns of the Aztecs, securing control over the Valley of Mexico, but he also launched the so-called "flower wars" whose divine mission it was, in alliance with Huitzilopochtli, to subjugate all other peoples and nations in order to preserve the world. As the champions of such a noble cause, he assured the Aztecs that they would be invincible in battle.

When Itzcóatl died in 1440, he was succeeded on the throne by Motecuhzoma Ilhuicamina. Although the kingship was first offered to Motecuhzoma's half-brother Tlacaélel, the latter refused, no doubt because the reigns of government were already firmly in his hands. Under his guidance, the "first Montezuma" proceeded to build a great new temple in honor of their father. However, the precariousness of Tenochtitlán's food and water supply manifested itself again in 1454 when a famine struck the Valley of Mexico and took a heavy toll of life during the following two years. Perhaps in part to ensure that such privation would not endanger the growing city-state again, the construction of an aqueduct from Chapultepec was begun and a military campaign was launched into the Gulf coastal region which concluded with the annexation of the area around Veracruz in 1463. This lush tropical coastland provided the Aztecs with a treasure house of resources, including corn, beans, fruit, cotton, wood, and medicinal plants as well as gold dust, jewelry, precious stones, rock crystal, feathers, live birds, jaguars, seashells, and turtles. After 13 years of labor, the Chapultepec aqueduct was finally completed in 1466.

It was also during the reign of the "first Montezuma" that the Aztecs carried out an expedition which probably ranks as the closest thing to a scientific endeavor that they ever mounted. At Tlacaélel's urging, a party was sent out to look for Aztlán, the original Aztec homeland, and to learn if Coatlicue, the mother of the war god, was still living there. Given such a sponsor and such a questionable goal, it is small wonder that, when the expedition returned after an appropriate length of time, it could happily report that Coatlicue was indeed alive and well and that she sent her greetings!

Motecuhzoma's passing in the year 1468 once more provided Tlacaélel with an opportunity to reign as king, but again he declined, and Axayácatl, the grandson of Itzcóatl, next assumed the mantle of royal leadership. In 1473, the market center of Tlatelolco was finally and formally annexed by Tenochtitlán, having remained a separate political entity ever since its founding at the same time as the Aztec capital. It was in the same year that the great calendar stone which has since become the virtual hallmark of the Aztec civilization was also dedicated.

However, five years further along, when the Aztec armies turned their attention westward toward Michoacán, they suffered a disastrous defeat at the hands of the Tarascans, or Purépecha. Some reports state that as many as 30,000 Aztec warriors died in this one battle on the approaches to the Tarascan capital. Undoubtedly, the Tarascans' mastery of advanced metallurgy and possession of superior weapons were of decisive importance in the campaign's outcome, but some scholars have likewise attributed the Tarascan victory to their superb military organization. Wherever the truth may lie, we do know that the defeat was extremely demoralizing to the Aztecs. It was as though the war-god had abandoned them, their sacred mission to save the world had been aborted, and the myth of Aztec invincibility had been shattered. It was clear that, as a result of this single bloody disaster, the violent and short-lived Aztec Empire had already passed its psychological peak, and within a matter of months Tlacaélel is reported to have died. Axayácatl himself is said never to have recovered from this stunning blow, and after a lingering malaise of three years, he too passed away.

In 1481 Tizoc, the brother of Axayácatl, was elected king, but his reign was both brief and depressing. No doubt in a vainglorious attempt

Figure 57.
This reproduction of the Aztec calendar stone found in the National Museum of Anthropology and History in Mexico City shows how brilliantly the original was painted. In the third ring from the outside are depicted the 20 symbols of the days of the sacred almanac. They are meant to be read in a counterclockwise direction, beginning at the top left.

to rekindle Aztec pride and fervor, he began the construction of the largest temple to the war-god ever undertaken, but he died in 1486 before he saw it completed. At this juncture, a third brother, Ahuízotl, was elected king, and the following year the new temple was dedicated in the presence of invited dignitaries from tributary states both far and near. (Even the king of the hated Tarascans was reputedly in attendance.) The Aztecs "pulled out all the stops" to make this event the most memorable that had ever been witnessed up until that time, for over the course of the four days that the celebration went on, it is variously reported that between 20,000 and 80,000 human victims had their hearts torn out on the sacrificial stone at the temple's top. The continuing "flower wars" with nearby Tlaxcala helped to supply many of the victims, but new military campaigns against the Huastecs to the northeast and the Zapotecs to the south also made their contributions.

If Tenochtitlán's thirst for blood was in any measure satisfied by this horrendous ceremony, that satisfaction was only temporary at best. Just as pressing, if not more so, however, was the growing city's thirst for water, and in 1499 a new aqueduct was opened into the city from the southwesterly precinct of Coyoacán. Although the entire project was carried out against the advice of some of the earlier residents of the district, the Aztecs soon found that the volume of water they had directed into the city was far too great to be satisfactorily contained. As a result, lake levels were seriously upset and the Aztec capital was flooded, apparently with a considerable loss of life. Indeed, Ahuízotl himself was injured during the inundation, and after a lingering illness passed away in 1502.

Against this sobering backdrop, his son, Motecuhzoma Xocoyotzin (the "second Montezuma"), assumed the throne, intent on restoring whatever grandeur he could to the Aztecs. His first move was to deify himself, but in order to do this, he had to arrange for the assassination of most of the court officials who had earlier served his father, for they obviously knew too much to go along with his grandiose ambitions. When his supposed ally, Nezahualpilli, the king of Texcoco (actually a secret enemy), came forward with ominous predictions as to the imminent demise of the Aztec Empire, Montezuma was visibly shaken, and the subsequent occurrence of other mysterious omens only served to heighten his anxiety. Visions of men on horses, a smoking comet in the sky, and the destruction of the temple of Huitzilopochtli by fire unnerved him further. Worst of all was Nezahualpilli's prophecy that Quetzalcóatl would soon return to rightfully claim his kingdom, for such a warning the exiled king of Tula had himself delivered, as all the heirs of the Toltecs well knew.

When Montezuma led his people in the celebration of the "binding of the years" in 1507, he may well have doubted whether the world as he knew it would endure another 52 years. Perhaps already then the first reports were beginning to reach him of "great white houses" out upon the sea amidst the islands of the rising sun. Certainly, within a few years, these Spanish exploring vessels were being sighted off the coast of Mexico itself, and with an almost inexorable rhythm, the approach of impending doom cast its lengthening shadow over the melancholy emperor and his terror-ridden state. In what has to be one of the most remarkable coincidences of all human history, Hernán Cortés and his small band of conquistadores landed on the beach at Veracruz in the fateful Aztec year of "1 Reed" — a year of the same name as that of Quetzalcóatl's birth and therefore one in which all Mesoamericans would have expected him to return. Paralyzed with a fear instilled by the prognostications of his own sacred calendar, the hapless Montezuma was at a loss as to how he should receive the strange white "gods" who had arrived on his shores.

It is beyond the scope of this work to discuss the Spanish conquest, but if there is any further irony to be appended to this account of the rise and fall of Mesoamerican civilization, it can only be this: The flame of Mesoamerican intellect which had first been kindled with the passage of the zenithal sun over Izapa at noon on August 13, 1359 B.C., was extinguished on the causeways of the Lake of the Moon as the sun was setting on August 13, 1521. With all the poignancy of a Greek tragedy, the cycle had now come full circle. Tenochtitlán lay in ruins, and Cuauhtémoc, the last emperor of the Aztecs, was in chains. The Mesoamerican age was over.

Chapter 12

The Long Journey: A Retrospective

The civilization that died on the 13th of August, 1521, was the last in a long parade of Mesoamerican indigenous cultures. Indeed, apart from that of the Incas in the highlands of the Andes, the Aztec Empire represented the final flowering of native genius in the Americas. Within a decade or two following the European arrival, the toll taken by conquest, enslavement, and disease had all but erased the hard-won achievements of the Mesoamerican peoples during the past three millennia. Because so many of their written records had the calendars as their focus, and these were so intimately interlaced with their religion, the Spanish were especially assiduous in consigning as many such books to the flames as they could find.

Ironically, it was precisely this interconnection between religion on the one hand and astronomy, mathematics, hieroglyphics, and architecture on the other that had stalled the forward progress of intellectual development within Mesoamerica. Despite their use of such sophisticated tools as the Long Count and the concept of zero, their presumed discovery of magnetism and of the celestial pole, their knowledge of the length of the Venusian cycle, their ability to predict eclipses, and their success in having located both the Tropic of Cancer and the parallel of latitude on which the sacred almanac was born, the priestly elite of Mesoamerica never apparently probed beyond the supernatural to find a rational explanation for, or a logical cause-and-effect relationship between, the phenomena they observed. For example, although the Mesoamericans recognized the planet Venus as being both the "morning star" and the "evening star"—whereas the Greeks considered them two separate bodies, Hesperos and Vesperos—the native American cultures found no other explanation for Venus and its strange "behavior" than that it represented the god Quetzalcóatl periodically visiting the underworld. Indeed, the Maya seem to have attempted to "massage" the measures of its various phases into such a structured pattern that, according to the calendar, it would always make its heliacal appearance on its "birthday"—the day 1 Ahau. While this is but one illustration of their "bending the rules" or "fudging the results," there seems to have been enough of this kind of evidence of the Maya's employing the calendar to serve their religious needs to prompt Thompson to conclude that they were more astrologers than they were astronomers. In other words, their study of the heavens was not motivated by the desire to acquire knowledge for knowledge's sake, but rather to further an ideological agenda.

In the preceding chapters, I have attempted to demonstrate how geography influenced the development of some of the key aspects of the intellectual life of pre-Columbian Mesoamerica. Our focus has been on the unique, interlocking pair of sacred and secular calendars which were devised in this region and which ultimately became the very hallmark of indigenous civilization on the North American continent. Insofar as it has been possible, I have traced the diffusion of these ingenious innovations from their birthplace on the southern margins of Mesoamerica through both time and space to embrace the whole of the region. Naturally, in a journey as encompassing in time and space as this has been, it was only inevitable that there would be changes and omissions, advances and retreats, triumphs and failures. Perhaps the most remarkable fact of all is that the Mesoamerican calendars could have touched the lives of so many people in so many places for so long a time, given that most of them were preliterate and that their only means of overland movement was by foot.

We have seen how a convergence of clues—astronomical, historical, and geographical—led to the identification of the calendars' cradle in Izapa and how the association of time with space was first recognized there in terms of a solsticial alignment. We likewise traced the calendars' diffusion both southward along the coastal plain of Guatemala as far as the western reaches of what today is the country of El Salvador and also northwestward along the Pacific shore of Chiapas into the Tehuantepec Gap. From the earliest Olmec ceremonial center at San Lorenzo, we watched the tide of civilization sweep through the Gulf coastal plain of Mexico, radiating toward the north and west onto the Mexican plateau, toward the south and west into the highlands of Oaxaca, and eastward into the Petén and Yucatán.

The initial wave of calendar adoption and city building found its furthest limits in the moisture requirements of maize, and there, on the very edge of the Chichimec world, gave rise to the greatest urban agglomeration that the pre-Columbian Americas ever produced. Indeed, it was under the aegis of Teotihuacán that the two most "scientifically motivated" expeditions of the era were undertaken—one into the northern desert to find the Tropic of Cancer and one into the southern jungles to locate the place "where time began."

From its "high water mark," or golden age, in the sixth century A.D., Mesoamerican civilization began an inexorable decline—precipitous on occasion, slow and faltering at other times. More than anything, it was the Chichimecs of the north—the Nahuatl-speaking nomads—who were responsible for its collapse, for with their advance we see the retreat of intellectualism back toward the south and east. At the same time that the Toltecs were substituting warriors for priests at the top of their social and political hierarchy and institutionalizing increasingly innovative forms of human sacrifice as part of the calendrical rituals they had "inherited" by virtue of their conquest of Teotihuacán, the Maya were putting the finishing touches on their centuries-long effort to predict eclipses and define the cycle of Venus. Yet, within little more than a century they, too, had been swept away—no doubt by a combination of circumstances, but among which military pressures from the uncivilized north must certainly have played a substantial part. It may have been fitting that the Toltecs were themselves overrun and put to flight by yet

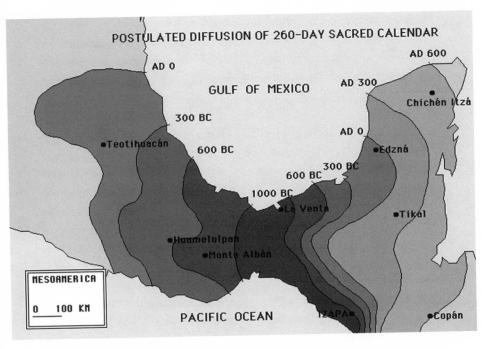

Figure 58.
This map summarizes the diffusion of the Mesoamerican calendrical system from its hearth in Soconusco by using isochrones of 300–400 years. Once through the Tehuantepec Gap, the calendars spread both westward onto the Mexican plateau and eastward into the Maya region. Though both dots and bars were initially used to record numerals everywhere, on the Mexican plateau and southward into the Mixtec and Zapotec country, Nahua (i.e., Toltec and later Aztec) influence resulted in the abandonment of the practice of using a bar for "5" and in the substitution of dots for all numerical notations.

another sweep of Nahuatl-speaking nomads out of the north, the Aztecs, but in the process Mesoamerican civilization was set back even further. Now, as militarism and war were elevated to instruments of statecraft and human sacrifice reached the scale of mass murder, the calendar was largely reduced to a timetable for execution and the numerical hiero-glyphs became mere tools for tribute extraction. With the notable excep-tion of persons like Nezahualcóyotl, whose contributions to poetry and engineering made him probably the closest thing to the Renaissance man in Aztec times, the intellectual apogee of Mesoamerican civilization had already long since been reached and passed before the Spanish arrived.

Tragic as their fanatical siege of book burning was, it simply marked the final chapter in a story which the Aztecs themselves had undertaken for reasons of "historical legitimacy" and which the Toltecs had, perhaps unwittingly, launched when they put the priests of Teotihuacán to flight nearly a millennium earlier.

SOCONUSCO: HEARTH OR BRIDGEHEAD?

Among the many questions which remain unanswered despite our lengthy inquiry is at least one which goes back to the very origins of the calendar and civilization itself. If, as we have hypothesized, the region of Soconusco was indeed the cradle of these developments within Mesoamerica, was it because these innovations arose out of the response of local people to local environmental needs or stimuli or did they simply represent the transmission onto the North American continent of ideas born elsewhere? In other words, we are confronting the classic dichotomy of "independent invention" versus "diffusion": Was Soconusco a true hearth of innovative genius in its own right, or was it merely a bridgehead where the calendars first "came ashore" on the Middle American mainland from some other birthplace overseas?

In our exposition up to now, we have tacitly assumed that Soconusco was a "hearth" and not a "bridgehead," but is this assumption justified? After all, no less a scientist than Alexander von Humboldt — one of the fathers of modern geography — commented as early as the beginning of the nineteenth century on the amazing similarity between the "Tibetan" and "Tartar" calendars of the Old World and the Aztec calendar of the New. He pointed out not only that both calendars were based on cycles that combined numbers and animal names, but also that there was a striking correspondence in the very names of the animals that appeared in each of the calendars. He was also impressed by the commonalities between the 28 "lunar mansions," or *nakshatras*, used by the Hindus and what he called the "Mexican zodiac" (Humboldt, 1810). Subsequent writers have drawn numerous parallels between the Chinese and Mesoamerican time-counts; several have gone so far as to strongly suggest, if not openly state, that the former was undoubtedly the forerunner of the latter.

Implicit in such claims and conjectures, of course, is some form of transpacific contact. Indeed, if the dates we have assigned to the origins of the Mesoamerican calendars are correct, then such voyages would have to have been undertaken at least as early as the fourteenth century B.C. — a possibility to which almost no reputable archaeologist or anthropologist is willing to subscribe. On the other hand, as we have seen, there is bountiful evidence of early and repeated seaborne contacts with South America through a long span of pre-Columbian history, at least some of which are known to have been with Soconusco as far back as the middle of the second millennium before Christ. Is it conceivable that the calendar might have been one of the innovations which accompanied the introduction of Ocós pottery, for instance?

Mention of ceramics in the same breath as conjectures regarding transpacific voyaging raises the spectre of a yet more ominous debate for most archaeologists, however. Some of the earliest known pottery to have been found in South America comes from the tiny fishing port of Valdivia on the desert coast of Ecuador (ca. 3800–3300 B.C.), and because it is consummately made and ornately decorated, it is obvious that it does not represent the bungling first attempts of some indigenous potter. It definitely has the appearance of an "import" with a long tradition of craftsmanship behind it. Moreover, and perhaps most unsettling of all, its design motifs bear a strong resemblance to those of Jomon pottery from southern Japan, whose antecedents go back to the sixth millennium B.C. But for any archaeologist to pose a geographic diffusion of the magnitude of a sea voyage from Japan to Ecuador — i.e., 8000 nautical miles — and especially in a time frame around 3500 B.C., would almost guarantee his or her being drummed out of the fraternity at the very least and perhaps committed to a mental institution at the very worst. Indeed, any "foreign intervention" in the cultural evolution of the Americas prior to the arrival of Columbus is considered by most anthropologists to have been highly unlikely, if not totally impossible.

Ironically, at the very time when modern geography is increasingly developing mathematical models and simulations to replicate the processes of diffusion, current anthropological thinking has virtually turned its back on it as an operating principle. Almost no effort is spared to substitute some other explanation — the gist of which inevitably revolves around some form of "independent invention"—to take its place. (For example, some of the most imaginative alternatives have been concocted to account for the spread of agriculture, that is, the introduction of various types of crops and livestock, across Europe—without the movement of human beings!) The idea of diffusion has become anathema, and anyone who attempts to apply it risks being labeled "out-dated" or "obsolete" in his or her research. In short, diffusion has become a "dirty word."

For the moment, we will put the "amazing coincidences" which von Humboldt noted between Old and New World calendars aside and concentrate instead on a possible South American origin. Although there is a noticeable reluctance on the part of many archaeologists to acknowledge even such linkages within the New World, the evidence is so overwhelming in favor of an early and sustained contact between the Andean countries of South America and western Mexico that there seems little reason to question the point any further. What remains to be established is whether or not any real antecedents of the Mesoamerican calendars can be traced to Colombia, Ecuador, or Peru prior to 1400 B.C.

Here the facts of geography are fully of as much importance in helping us to reach a sound conclusion as are any fragments of archaeological evidence. Like the Aztecs in Mesoamerica, the Incas in South America represented the final manifestation of indigenous civilization on their respective continents. This does not mean that either of them marked the culmination of native American achievement, because there is some reason to believe that the Tiahuanaco culture in the Lake Titicaca basin may have surpassed the Incas in intellectual creativity in the same way that the Olmecs had so far outshown the Aztecs; thus, in both regions, civilization may have reached its highest point long before its final chapter was written.

The Andean region of South America is characterized by three markedly different climatic aspects: First, on the east, in the *montaña*, we find a region of *selva*, or rain forest. Along the eastern slopes of Colombia, Ecuador, and Peru, the updrafts of warm moist air are almost unceasing, but are obviously much more vigorous during the warmer part of the day. The cloud forests of the *montaña* are constantly dripping with moisture and in many areas the total annual precipitation exceeds 5 m

(200 in.). Second, in the high mountains of the center, the sierra, we find a cool, semiarid climate whose most striking vegetation association is the puna, or alpine tundra. Precipitation is decidedly modest, seldom totaling more than about 750 mm (30 in.), and it likewise varies from a maximum in the high-sun season (December, January, and February) to a minimum in the Andean winter. Finally, bordering the Pacific coast over a distance of nearly 3000 km (1800 mi) is the Atacama Desert — the driest desert in the world. Cut off from the trade winds blowing across the Amazon basin and up the eastern front of the Andes by lofty ranges higher than 6000 m (22,000 ft) in elevation, the Pacific slope of South America is likewise paralleled by the intensely cold Humboldt, or Peru, Current. This combination of circumstances — a rain-shadow location exacerbated by offshore water so cold that almost no moisture is evaporated into the air above it — makes it virtually impossible for precipitation to occur. As a result, a place like Lima, the capital of Peru, a scant 20 km (12 mi) from the coast, receives an average of 25 mm (1 in.) of rain a year. To be sure, an occasional surge of Pacific air may drift the low-hanging fog onto the coastal sand dunes long enough to give rise to a brief and spectacular flowering of small plants whose seeds have lain dormant for perhaps a decade or more, but such *garuas* are not frequent. Perhaps somewhat more frequent but certainly more devastating are the periodic invasions of warm surface waters pushed into the coasts of Ecuador and Peru by the El Niño ("Christ Child") current, so named because it usually puts in its appearance around Christmas. When these "backwashes" occur, which is about every 7–8 years, the plankton in the cold fresh water of the Peru Current die back as the El Niño spreads a blanket of warm, saline waters over the sea surface. Cut off from their food supply, the fish move to deeper levels of the ocean or retreat southward with the colder water. And as the fish disappear, the hordes of seabirds that depend on them for food and that colonize the coastal cliffs die back, and in turn, the deposits of their excrement (guano) — a much prized fertilizer — also grow thin. Finally, culminating this ecological disaster are the rainstorms which are spawned by the high evaporation of the now-warm coastal waters. During an El Niño episode, as much rain can fall in the Atacama during a single storm as over an average 20-year

period. Indeed, in the one month of October 1967 as much rain fell at a station in northern Chile as the place would normally have received in the entire time since the Spanish conquest!

Thus, each of the Andean regions has its distinctive climatic hallmark. In the Amazon basin, it is almost always raining. In the Atacama, it almost never rains. And in the mountains between them it seldom rains much, but it tends to rain a little more in "summer" than in "winter."

The point to be made here is that only the latter region, the sierra, has an environment which would have seriously motivated anyone to develop a calendar. Indeed, elsewhere there would really have been no necessity for one. In the *montaña* there is sufficient warmth and moisture at all times of the year to grow virtually any crop imaginable. There is, in fact, good evidence that the people in southern Colombia, for example, around San Agustín, were already growing coca—possibly for export to Mesoamerica—as early as 500 B.C. Similarly, Chavín, the site of the classic Andean counterpart to the Olmec civilization, also on the east side of the Andes, was probably involved in the coca trade even 500 years earlier. In neither place was a means of timekeeping a prerequisite to agricultural success.

In the Atacama Desert, on the other hand, agriculture was impossible everywhere but in the 40-odd little exotic river valleys that cut their way down from the Andes to the shore of the Pacific. Here, amidst an otherwise waterless desert of sand and rock, the presence of these short, violent streams flowing out of the mountains presented the only opportunity for secure and continuing human settlement along the entire coast of Peru. To be sure, the coastal waters themselves could be counted on for some measure of subsistence, thanks both to the rich schools of fish and the aquatic birds that preyed on them—at least so long as El Niño did not put in an appearance. Indeed, these maritime resources were most likely the magnet that drew the early Ecuadorians and Peruvians out to sea and that gradually encouraged the coastal inhabitants to school themselves in the arts of raft building and navigation, and ultimately of exploration. But it was the narrow ribbons of green, irrigated cropland along the exotic rivers that made agriculture and ultimately town building possible. Although the cold offshore current keeps temperatures along coastal Peru relatively cool for being so near to the equator, there is more than adequate warmth for growing a variety of both tropical and subtropical crops. In the lowland oases these include maize, sweet potatoes, tomatoes, peanuts, and cotton, whereas in the mountains a greater dependence was placed on potatoes and quinoa, a hardy grain. Domesticated animals included the guinea pig in the coastal areas and the llama, alpaca, and vicuña at higher elevations.

From about 2300 B.C. onward—beginning with the Chavín culture at places like Cerro Sechín and continuing with such cultures as the Mochica, Nazca, and ultimately the Inca—an advanced civilization with imposing pyramids, planned cities, and elaborate irrigation works flourished in the coastal oases of Peru and in the highlands surrounding Lake Titicaca. As early as eight or nine centuries before Christ, Andean artisans had developed metalworking and not long afterward they were producing exquisite double-weave textiles. There is no question but that the South American "cultural hearth" had a very impressive lead over Mesoamerica in material goods, technology, and social organization for possibly as long as a millennium.

Such evidence as there is of contact between the South American "hearth" and Mesoamerica seems to have been traced more to Ecuador, and to a lesser degree, Colombia, than to Peru. How might this be explained? Once again, geography may hold the key. The total absence of suitable building materials for waterborne craft along the desert coast of Peru largely rules out the development of balsa rafts or reed boats in that area. Only along the estuary of the Guayas River in Ecuador and from northern Ecuador into Colombia do tropical forests come down to the Pacific shore. The totora reed, on the other hand, grows almost exclusively in freshwater lakes such as Titicaca.

However, Peru's lack of raw materials for raft or boat building was not its only impediment to contact with Mesoamerica; it also had the Humboldt Current to contend with. As Thor Heyerdahl's Kon-Tiki expedition vividly illustrated, any vessel swept along in this current's broad and forceful flow would be drifted far out into the Pacific, for it turns westward into the ocean just to the south of the equator. Its cold waters continue to depress temperatures and discourage the formation of rain clouds out past the Galápagos Islands and well beyond the Marquesas.

Any early navigator caught in this giant vortex of water would find that, once out of sight of the South American coast, his plight would worsen, because soon he would find himself pushed along by the trade winds as well. With both current and easterly winds against him, there would be little chance of his seeing the American mainland again.

To the north of Ecuador's westernmost promontory, both the ocean currents and the weather conditions are very different. The warm waters of the main branch of the Equatorial Countercurrent sweep northward along the coast of Colombia into the Gulf of Panama, and for part of the year the flow is strong enough to reach even as far as Soconusco and the south coast of Mexico. Thus, it wouldn't have taken much knowledge of navigation to drift northward along the coast of Central America in the summer months and to return again when the California Current intensifies its southward flow during the winter months. That Pacific Mesoamerica, then, should have had its earliest and most frequent contacts with Ecuador and Colombia, rather than Peru, is very largely a matter of the geography of timber resources and ocean currents. That both Ecuador and Colombia were themselves somewhat peripheral to the principal Andean cultural hearth in no way detracts from their importance as potential springboards of diffusion because even though they may have developed somewhat later than the Peruvian core area, they were still in close enough geographic proximity to the "center" to have been much more advanced than Mesoamerica.

We have already mentioned how the South American cultural hearth was responsible for the introduction of such items and ideas as ceramics, shaft tombs, and metallurgy into Mesoamerica and of human migrants like the Purépecha as well. On the other hand, we have also demonstrated that the climatic environments of the Andean region were such that the early civilizations which developed there had only the most rudimentary interest in or need for a calendar or timekeeping system. The Incas, for example, had a self-correcting calendar which began on the summer solstice (in the southern hemisphere, December 22). For this purpose, they had constructed four towers on the horizon above Cuzco to mark both the rising and setting positions of the sun on that date and on the winter solstice (June 22). They divided the intervals between the solstices into two periods of six 30-day months, allocating the remaining

5 days of the solar year to solsticial celebrations at each end of the annual cycle. Although they probably used certain key asterisms like the Pleiades and the Southern Cross as seasonal "mileposts" of the solar year, the Andean peoples do not appear to have been intellectually concerned with matters such as the eclipse cycle or the phases of Venus in the same way that the Mesoamerican cultures were. Impressive though their achievements in engineering, social organization, and statecraft may have been, the fact that they were preliterate societies and had not progressed beyond keeping numerical tallies on other than knotted, colored strings (called quipus) severely limited the development of the kind of mathematical sophistication which the Long Count had engendered. For all the Andean region's many cultural contributions to Mesoamerica, the calendar certainly was not among them.

THE CALENDARS OF ASIA AND THE MIDDLE EAST

With South America safely dismissed as a possible source of inspiration for the Mesoamerican calendars, we can now turn our attention westward across the Pacific to Asia to see whether their antecedents might be found there instead. For the moment we will lay aside all questions regarding transpacific diffusion and concentrate on (1) what kind of calendars existed on the peripheries of Asia and (2) when they had come into being. Only if they shared enough common traits to have been conceivable prototypes of the Mesoamerican models and had been developed before the middle of the fourteenth century B.C. would it even be germane to broach the subject of how they got from "there" to "here."

Lying on the western edge of the Pacific rim, China is known to have had "an embryonic form of a lunisolar calendar" as far back as the fourteenth century B.C. (Xi Zezong, 1987, 34). It differed from that of Babylon and Greece by (*a*) fixing the beginning of a month at the moment when the sun and the moon are at the same longitude (*shuo*), (*b*) fixing the beginning of the year at the winter solstice, and (*c*) dividing the year into 24 periods — 12 *jie* and 12 *qi*. Twenty of the latter had names connected with the seasons, showing that the calendar was primarily designed for agricultural purposes (35). In addition to *shuo* and *jie*, and *qi* the next basic element of the Chinese calendar was the "run" — an intercalary month used to calibrate the lunar and solar counts. Because the moon cannot be seen at the moment when the sun and the moon are at the same longitude (unless there is a solar eclipse), the "observation and calculation of eclipses became an inseparable part of Chinese calendar-making" (35). Beyond serving as an agricultural almanac, the Chinese calendar played an important role in statecraft, because astronomers were used by the emperor "to observe the heavens so as to investigate the change in human affairs on the earth" (34). Through the observation of celestial phenomena they were expected to divine such events as victory or defeat in a war, the rise and fall of a nation, the success or failure of the year's crop, and the actions of key members of the emperor's court.

For all of the many similarities that von Humboldt (and subsequently, others) claim to have discovered in the names of the Aztec days, months, and lunar mansions and those of their "Tibetan" or "Tartar" counterparts, the intrinsic character of the Chinese calendar was so different from that in Mesoamerica that it seems very unlikely that the one could have served as the model for the other. As we have seen, even though the Olmecs may have been recording eclipses by the time of the birth of Christ, their successors, the Maya, seem not to have discovered a surefire way of predicting them until as late as the eighth century, whereas calculating eclipses had been an integral mechanism of fixing the Chinese calendar from the very outset. Moreover, the Chinese system of using a duodecimal system for dividing their years had no counterpart in Mesoamerica, nor did the use of an intercalary month between their lunar and solar counts. And finally, whereas Xi Zezong mentions the establishment of an astronomical observatory in China as early as 2000 B.C. (38), he lays claim to only an "embryonic form of calendar" at the very time that the two Mesoamerican counts were coming into existence. Thus, a Chinese origin is all but ruled out for temporal reasons alone.

Turning yet farther westward, let us look to the Indian subcontinent next to see what that region's earliest astronomers had produced in the way of a calendar. Already during the so-called Vedic period (beginning with the arrival of the Indo-Aryan peoples from Central Asia, ca. 2000 B.C.), the sun had been identified as the "sole lightgiver of the universe," the moon was known to have shown by reflected sunlight, the five larger planets had been observed and named, and the celestial path of the sun and moon (the zodiac) had been divided into 27 or 28 asterisms called *nakshatras*, or "mansions of heaven" (Shukla, 1987, 9). The day was reckoned from sunrise to sunrise and the variability of its length was known. Six days formed a "week," five "weeks" constituted a month, and 12 months made up a year (10). The latter was composed of 366 days and was measured from one winter solstice to another. It was likewise divided into six seasons, each composed of two months, or 61 days. Twelve lunar months constituted a lunar year, and in order to keep the lunar and solar years in harmony, intercalary months were inserted at regular intervals (11).

Despite the antiquity of the Vedic calendars of the Indian subcontinent, it should be clear from the brief outline of their structure given above that they differed substantially from the Mesoamerican time-counts. Indeed, it is probably safe to say that the only similarities which the two calendrical systems had with one another were those which von Humboldt himself pointed out — i.e., some of the names of the animals used to identify the "mansions of heaven." That two early peoples, both inhabiting tropical environments, but in widely separated parts of the world, should "see" the same kinds of "animals" mirrored in the patterns of the stars is not too surprising. However, in view of all the critical differences between the two calendrical systems, this similarity is far too fragile a piece of "evidence" on which to base a claim for Hindu patrimony. Moreover, the "earliest work which exclusively deals with Vedic astronomy is the *Vedanga-jyautisa*," and although its date is controversial, the situation it describes can best be correlated either with 1150 B.C. or with 1370 B.C. (Shukla, 1987, 13). Thus, like that of China, the calendar of the Indian subcontinent was only coming into existence at the same time as our "New World Hipparchus" was at work in Soconusco, or perhaps even a couple of centuries later. Again, the very timing of its development rules it out as a model for the Mesoamerican calendar.

The only potential calendrical "donors" still remaining are Mesopotamia and Egypt, both of which well predate the beginnings of Mesoamerican calendrical experimentation. Although no objection can be raised on temporal grounds, the spatial relationship now becomes increasingly dubious. Diffusion from the Middle East to Soconusco would have involved vaulting not only the entire Pacific Ocean, but the Indian Ocean as well — and with no evidence of any intermediate stops underway, apart from those in India and China already discussed. Moreover, the very character of the Middle Eastern time-counts, based as they were on a sexagesimal system, is completely at odds with the Mesoamerican calendar. That they were the antecedents of the Indian and Chinese calendars, and likewise of the Greek and Roman, seems very likely, but surely not of those of the New World.

We can, therefore, with all good conscience hail our "New World Hipparchus" as a creative genius in his own right, not beholden to the ideas or ideology of any other people or region in the world. Indeed, in the time frame in which he lived and worked, he was as much a pioneer as the Chinese and Vedic astronomers who were at the same juncture of history, half a world away, developing their own distinctive calendrical systems — and at least a dozen centuries ahead of the great Greek astronomer to whom we are likening him. Soconusco may well have served as a bridgehead into Mesoamerica for a variety of South American cultural traits, but there seems little doubt that it constituted the very "hearth," or cradle, of the intellectual life of indigenous North America. The unique 260-day sacred almanac is the product of a convergence of time and space that may be traced directly to Izapa. All that we know of its creator was that he spoke the Zoque language, lived in the middle of the fourteenth century before Christ, and was intent on explaining the rhythms of the heavens. Never could he have imagined that the quest for understanding which he launched would set the stage for a calendar, a religion, and a civilization that would eventually become the very hallmarks of the cultural region which we know today as Mesoamerica, nor that they would touch the lives of so many people through such an immense span of time. It is perhaps only fitting that in the mountain fastnesses behind Izapa the 260-day count which he initiated continues to be tallied on wooden boards with sticks of charcoal to this very day.

References

Adams, Richard E. W. 1991. *Prehistoric Mesoamerica*. Rev. ed. Norman: University of Oklahoma Press.

"Amaizing Stories." 1993. *Economist*, May 8, vol. 327, no. 7810, pp. 89–90.

Andrews, George F. 1975. *Maya Cities: Placemaking and Urbanization*. Norman: University of Oklahoma Press.

———. 1989. *Comalcalco, Tabasco, Mexico: Maya Art and Architecture*. 2d ed. Culver City, Calif.: Labyrinthos.

Apenes, Ola. 1936. "Possible Derivation of the 260 Day Period of the Maya Calendar." *Ethnos* (Stockholm), vol. 1, pp. 5–8.

———. 1947. *Mapas antiguos del Valle de Mexico*. Mexico City: Universidad Nacional, Instituto de Historia, Publicación no. 4.

"Archaeological Map of Middle America: Land of the Feathered Serpent." 1968. Supplement to *National Geographic Magazine*, vol. 134, no. 4.

Aveni, Anthony F. 1975. *Archaeoastronomy in Pre-Columbian America*. Austin: University of Texas Press.

———, ed. 1977. *Native American Astronomy*. Austin: University of Texas Press.

Aveni, Anthony F., and Gary Urton. 1982. *Ethnoastronomy and Archaeoastronomy in the American Tropics*. Annals of the New York Academy of Sciences, vol. 385. New York: New York Academy of Sciences.

Aveni, Anthony F. 1980. *Skywatchers of Ancient Mexico*. Austin: University of Texas Press.

———, ed. 1982. *Archaeoastronomy in the New World: American Primitive Astronomy*. Cambridge: Cambridge University Press.

Aveni, Anthony F., Horst Hartung, and J. Charles Kelley. 1982. "Alta Vista (Chalchihuites): Astronomical Implications of a Mesoamerican Ceremonial Outpost at the Tropic of Cancer." *American Antiquity*, vol. 47, pp. 316–335.

Aveni, Anthony F., and Gordon Brotherston, eds. 1983. *Calendars in Mesoamerica and Peru: Native American Computation of Time*. Proceedings of the 44th International Congress of Americanists, Manchester, 1982. Oxford: B.A.R.

Aveni, Anthony F., ed. 1988. *New Directions in American Archaeoastronomy*. Oxford: B.A.R.

———. 1989. *Empires of Time: Calendars, Clocks, and Cultures*. New York: Basic Books.

———, ed. 1989. *World Archaeoastronomy*. Selected Papers from the 2d Oxford International Conference on Archaeoastronomy, held at Mérida, Yucatán, Mexico, January 13–17, 1986. Cambridge: Cambridge University Press.

Aveni, Anthony F., and Horst Hartung. 1986. *Maya City Planning and the Calendar*. Transactions of the American Philosophical Society, 0065-9746, vol. 76, pt. 7. Philadelphia: American Philosophical Society.

Aveni, Anthony F., ed. 1992. *Conversing with the Planets: How Science and Myth Invented the Cosmos*. New York: Times Books.

Barinaga, Marcia. 1992. "Giving Personal Magnetism a Whole New Meaning." *Science*, vol. 256, no. 5151, p. 967.

Benson, Elizabeth P., ed. 1968. *Dumbarton Oaks Conference on the Olmec*. Washington, D.C.: Dumbarton Oaks Research Library and Collection.

———. 1981. *The Olmec and Their Neighbors: Essays in Memory of Matthew W. Stirling*. Washington, D.C.: Dumbarton Oaks Research Library and Collections.

Bernal, Ignacio. 1969. *The Olmec World*. Berkeley: University of California Press.

Berrin, Kathleen, and Esther Pasztory, eds. 1993. *Teotihuacán: Art from the City of the Gods*. New York: Thames and Hudson.

Blom, Frans. 1924. "Report on the Preliminary Work at Uaxactun." *Carnegie Institution of Washington Yearbook*, vol. 23, pp. 217–219.

Brand, Donald D. 1943. "An Historical Sketch of Geography and Anthropology in the Tarascan Region." *New Mexico Anthropologist*, vols. 6–7, pp. 37–108.

———. 1960. *Coalcomán and Motines del Oro: An Ex-Distrito of Michoacán*. The Hague: Martinus Nijhoff.

Broda, Johanna. 1986. "Arqueoastronomía y desarrollo de las ciencias en el México prehispánico." In *Historia de la Astronomía en México*, ed. Marco Arturo Moreno Corral. Mexico City: Lito Ediciones Olimpia S.A.

Campbell, Lyle, and Terrence Kaufman. 1976. "A Linguistic Look at the Olmecs." *American Antiquity*, vol. 41, pp. 80–89.

Carlson, John B. 1975. "Lodestone Compass: Chinese or Olmec Primacy?" *Science*, vol. 189, no. 4205, pp. 753–760.

———. 1977. "Copán Altar Q: The Maya Astronomical Congress of A.D. 763?" In *Native American Astronomy*, ed. Anthony F. Aveni, pp. 100–109. Austin: University of Texas Press.

Carr, Archie. 1967. *So Excellent a Fishe*. Garden City, N.Y.: Natural History Press.

Caso, Alfonso. 1943. "The Calendar of the Tarascans." *American Antiquity*, vol. 9, pp. 11–28.

———. 1967. *Los Calendarios Prehispánicos*. Serie de cultura nahuatl. Monografías 6. Mexico City: Universidad Nacional, Instituto de Investigaciones Históricas.

Ceja Tenorio, Jorge Fausto. 1985. "Paso de la Amada: An Early Preclassic Site in the Soconusco, Chiapas, Mexico." *Papers of the New World Archaeological*

Foundation, no. 49. Provo, Utah: New World Archaeological Foundation, Brigham Young University.

Chadwick, R. 1971. "Archaeological Synthesis of Michoacán and Adjacent Regions." In *Handbook of Middle American Indians*, vol. 11, ed. Gordon F. Ekholm and Ignacio Bernal, pp. 657–693. Austin: University of Texas Press.

Chiu, Bella C., and Philip Morrison. 1980. "Astronomical Origin of the Offset Street Grid at Teotihuacán." Archaeoastronomy no. 2. *Journal for the History of Astronomy*, vol. 11, pp. S55–S64.

Cippola, Carlo M. 1964. *The Economic History of World Population*. London: Penguin Books.

Clark, John E., and Thomas A. Lee, Jr. 1984. "Formative Obsidian Exchange and the Emergence of Public Economies in Chiapas, Mexico." In *Trade and Exchange in Early Mesoamerica*, ed. Kenneth Hirth. Albuquerque: University of New Mexico Press.

Clark, John E., Michael Blake, Pedro Guzzy, Marta Cuevas, and Tamara Salcedo. 1987. *Informe al Instituto Nacional de Antropología e Historia. Proyecto: El Preclásico Temprano en la Costa del Pacífico*. Provo, Utah: New World Archaeological Foundation, Brigham Young University, and San Cristóbal de Las Casas, Chiapas, Mexico: Marzo.

Clark, John E. 1991. "The Beginnings of Mesoamerica: Apologia for the Soconusco Early Formative." In *The Formation of Complex Society in Southeastern Mesoamerica*, ed. William R. Fowler, Jr. Boca Raton, Fl.: CRC Press, Inc.

Clark, John E., and Dennis Gosser. 1994. "Reinventing Mesoamerica's First Pottery." In *The Emergence of Pottery*, ed. W. K. Barnett and J. W. Hoopes. Washington, D. C.: Smithsonian Press.

Closs, Michael P. 1977. "The Date-Reaching Mechanism in the Venus Table of the Dresden Codex." In *Native American Astronomy*, ed. Anthony F. Aveni, pp. 89–99. Austin: University of Texas Press.

Codice Botturini (Tira de la Peregrinación). 1975. Colleción de documentos conmemorativos del DCL aniversario de la fundación de Tenochtitlán. Mexico City: Secretaría de Educación Pública.

Coe, Michael D. 1960. "Archaeological Linkages with North and South America at La Victoria, Guatemala." *American Anthropologist*, vol. 62, pp. 363–393.

Coe, Michael D. 1968. *America's First Civilization*. New York: American Heritage.

Coe, Michael D., and Richard A. Diehl. 1980. *In the Land of the Olmec*. Austin: University of Texas Press.

Coe, Michael D. 1980. *The Maya*. 3d ed. New York: Thames and Hudson.

Coe, Michael D., and David Grove, organizers; Elizabeth B. Benson, ed. 1981.

The Olmec and Their Neighbors: Essays in Memory of Matthew W. Stirling. Washington, D.C.: Dumbarton Oaks Research Library and Collections, Trustees for Harvard University.

Coe, Michael D., E. P. Benson, and D. R. Snow, eds. 1986. *Atlas of Ancient America.* New York: Facts on File.

Coe, Michael D. 1992. *Breaking the Maya Code.* New York: Thames and Hudson.

Cowan, C. Wesley, and Patty Jo Watson, eds. 1992. *The Origins of Agriculture: An International Perspective.* Washington: Smithsonian Institution Press.

Craine, Eugene R., and Reginald C. Reindorp, eds. 1970. *The Chronicles of Michoacán.* Norman: University of Oklahoma Press.

Davies, Nigel. 1977. *The Toltecs until the Fall of Tula.* Norman: University of Oklahoma Press.

———. 1980. *The Toltec Heritage: From the Fall of Tula to the Rise of Tenochtitlán.* Norman: University of Oklahoma Press.

———. 1987. *The Aztec Empire: The Toltec Resurgence.* Norman: University of Oklahoma Press.

Demarest, Arthur A., Roy Switsur, and Rainer Berger. 1982. "The Dating and Cultural Associations of the "Pot-bellied" Sculptural Style: New Evidence from Western El Salvador." *American Antiquity,* vol. 47, pp. 557–571.

Demarest, Arthur A. 1992. "Ideology in Ancient Maya Cultural Evolution." In *Ideology and Pre-Columbian Civilization,* ed. Arthur A. Demarest and Geoffrey W. Conrad, pp. 15–36. Santa Fe: School of American Research Press.

Diehl, Richard A. 1983. *Tula: The Toltec Capital of Ancient Mexico.* London: Thames and Hudson.

Diehl, Richard A., and Janet C. Berto., eds. 1989. *Mesoamerica after the Decline of Teotihuacán, A.D. 700–900.* Washington, D.C.: Dumbarton Oaks Library and Collections.

Drucker, Philip, Robert F. Heizer, and Robert J. Squier. 1959. "Excavations at La Venta, Tabasco, 1955." Bureau of American Ethnology, Bulletin 179.

Durán, Fray Diego. 1971. *Book of the Gods and Rites of the Ancient Calendar.* Norman: University of Oklahoma Press.

Ekholm, Susanna M. 1969. "Mound 30a and the Early Preclassic Ceramic Sequence of Izapa, Chiapas, Mexico." *Papers of the New World Archaeological Foundation,* no. 25. Provo, Utah: Brigham Young University.

Flannery, Kent V. 1968. "The Olmec and the Valley of Oaxaca: A Model for Interregional Interaction in Formative Times." In *Dumbarton Oaks Conference on the Olmecs,* ed. Elizabeth P. Benson, pp. 79–110.

Flores Gutiérrez, J. Daniel. 1991. "Venus y Su Relación Con Fechas Antiguas." In *Arqueoastronomía y Etnoastronomía en Mesoamérica,* ed. Johanna Broda,

Stanislaw Iwaniszewski, and Lucrecia Maupomé, pp. 343–388. Mexico City: Universidad Nacional Autónoma de México.

Fuson, Robert H. 1969. "The Orientation of Mayan Ceremonial Centers." *Annals of the Association of American Geographers*, vol. 59, pp. 494–511.

Gadow, Hans Friedrich. 1908. *Through Southern Mexico; Being an Account of the Travels of a Naturalist.* New York: C. Scribner's Sons.

Girard, Rafael. 1948. *El Calendario Maya-Mexica: Origen, Función, Desarrollo y Lugar de Procedencia.* Mexico City: Editorial Stylo.

Goodman, Joseph T. 1905. "Maya Dates." *American Anthropologist*, vol. 7, pp. 642–647.

Gorenstein, Shirley, and Helen Perlstein Pollard. 1983. *The Tarascan Civilization: A Late Prehispanic Cultural System.* Nashville: Vanderbilt University Publications in Anthropology no. 28.

Graham, John A. 1989. "Olmec Diffusion: A Sculptural View from Pacific Guatemala." In *Regional Perspectives on the Olmec*, ed. Robert J. Sharer and David C. Grove, pp. 227–246. Cambridge: Cambridge University Press.

Greenberg, Joseph H. 1987. *Language in the Americas.* Stanford: Stanford University Press.

Grove, David C., and Susan D. Gillespie. 1992. "Ideology and Evolution at the Pre-State Level." In *Ideology and Pre-Columbian Civilization*, ed. Arthur A. Demarest and Geoffrey W. Conrad, pp. 15–36. Santa Fe: School of American Research Press.

Haberland, Wolfgang. 1974. *Culturas de la América Indígena: Mesoamérica y América Central.* Mexico City: Fondo de Cultura Económica.

Harter, James T., and Vincent H. Malmström. 1979. "Stenålderskalendar i Skåne?" *Forskning och Framsteg*, vol. 5, pp. 1–5.

Hartung, Horst. 1971. *Die Zeremonialzentren der Maya.* Graz: Akademische Druck- u. Verlagsanstalt.

Hatch, Marian Popenoe. 1971. "An Hypothesis on Olmec Astronomy, with Special Reference to the La Venta Site." *Contributions of the University of California Archaeological Research Facility (Berkeley)*, no. 13, pp. 1–64.

Hawkins, Gerald S. 1965. *Stonehenge Decoded.* Garden City, N.Y.: Doubleday.

Heyden, Doris. 1975. "An Interpretation of the Cave Underneath the Pyramid of the Sun at Teotihuacán, Mexico." *American Antiquity*, vol. 40, pp. 131–147.

Heyerdahl, Thor. 1961. "An Introduction to Easter Island." *Reports of the Norwegian Archaeological Expedition to Easter Island and the East Pacific, 1955–1956*, Monograph 24, pt. 1. Santa Fe: School of American Research.

Hosler, Dorothy. 1988. "Ancient West Mexican Metallurgy: South and Central America Origins and West Mexican Transformations." *American Anthropologist*, vol. 90, pp. 832–855.

Humboldt, Alexander von. 1810. *Vues des Cordillères et Monuments des Peuples Indigènes de l'Amerique.* Paris.

Kampen, M. E. 1972. *The Sculptures of El Tajín, Veracruz, Mexico.* Gainesville: University of Florida Press.

Kelley, David H. 1977. "Maya Astronomical Tables and Inscriptions." In *Native American Astronomy,* ed. Anthony F. Aveni, pp. 57–74. Austin: University of Texas Press.

Krickeberg, Walter. 1980. *Mitos y leyendas de los Aztecas, Incas, Mayas, y Muiscas.* Mexico City: Fondo de Cultura Económica.

———. 1982. *Las Antiguas Culturas Mexicanas.* Mexico City: Fondo de Cultura Económica.

Landa, Diego de. 1983. *Relación de las Cosas de Yucatán.* Mérida: Ediciones Dante, S.A.

Leon-Portilla, Miguel. 1962. *The Broken Spears: The Aztec Account of the Conquest of Mexico.* Boston: Beacon Press.

———. 1988. *Time and Reality in the Thought of the Maya.* 2d ed. Norman: University of Oklahoma Press.

———. 1992. *The Aztec Image of Self and Society: An Introduction to Nahua Culture.* Salt Lake City: University of Utah Press.

Lienzo de Jucutácato. Morelia, Michoacán: Museo Arqueológico del Estado de Michoacán.

Long, A., B. Benz, D. Donahue, A. Jull, and L. Toolin. 1989. "First Direct AMS Dates on Early Maize from Tehuacán, Mexico." *Radiocarbon,* vol. 31, no. 3, pp. 1035–1040.

Lounsbury, Floyd G. 1978. "Maya Numeration, Computation, and Calendrical Astronomy." *Dictionary of Scientific Biography,* vol. 15, pp. 759–818.

———. 1983. "The Base of the Venus Tables of the Dresden Codex and Its Significance for the Calendar Correlation Problem." In *Calendars in Mesoamerica and Peru: Native American Computations of Time,* ed. Anthony F. Aveni and Gordon Brotherston. Oxford: BAR International Series 174, British Archaelogical Series, pp. 1–26.

Lowe, Gareth W. 1967. Discussion. In "Altamira and Padre Piedra, Early Preclassic Sites in Chiapas, Mexico," *Papers of the New World Archaeological Foundation,* no. 20. Provo, Utah: Brigham Young University Press.

———. 1975. "The Early Preclassic Barra Phase of Altamira, Chiapas: A Review with New Data." *Papers of the New World Archaeological Foundation,* no. 38. Provo, Utah: New World Archaeological Foundation, Brigham Young University.

Lowe, Gareth W., Thomas A. Lee, Jr., and Eduardo Martínez Espinosa. 1982. "Izapa: An Introduction to the Ruins and Monuments." *Papers of the New World Archaeological Foundation,* no. 31. Provo, Utah: New World Archaeological Foundation, Brigham Young University.

Macazaga Ordoño, Cesar. 1979. *Nombres Geográficos de México.* Mexico City: Editorial Innovación, S.A.

MacNeish, Richard S. 1964. "Ancient Mesoamerican Civilization." *Science,* vol. 143, pp. 531–537.

Makemson, Maud W. 1943. *Astronomical Tables of the Maya.* Washington: Carnegie Institution of Washington, publication 586.

Malmström, Vincent H. 1973. "Origin of the Mesoamerican 260-Day Calendar." *Science,* vol. 181, no. 4103, pp. 939–941.

———. 1976a. "Knowledge of Magnetism in Pre-Columbian Mesoamerica." *Nature,* vol. 259 (Feb. 5), no. 5542, pp. 390–391.

———. 1976b. "Izapa: Cultural Hearth of the Olmecs?" *Proceedings of the Association of American Geographers,* pp. 32–35.

———. 1978. "A Reconstruction of the Chronology of Mesoamerican Calendrical Systems." *Journal for the History of Astronomy,* vol. 9, pp. 105–116.

Malmström, Vincent H., and Paul A. Dunn. 1979. "Pre-Columbian Magnetic Sculptures in Western Guatemala." Mimeo. (An abstracted version of this paper titled "The Fat Boys: A Pre-Columbian Mystery" was published on the Science page of *Time,* Sept. 3, 1979, vol. 114, no. 10.)

Malmström, Vincent H. 1981. "Architecture, Astronomy, and Calendrics in Pre-Columbian Mesoamerica." In *Archaeoastronomy in the Americas,* ed. Ray A. Williamson, pp. 249–261. Los Altos, Calif.: Ballena Press.

———. 1985. "The Origins of Civilization in Mesoamerica: A Geographic Perspective." *Yearbook of the Conference of Latin American Geographers,* vol. 11, pp. 23–29.

———. 1989. "The Spatial Dimension in Preliterate Time-Reckoning." *Geographical Review,* vol. 79 (Oct.), no. 4, pp. 422–434.

———. 1990. "Los Orígenes de la Civilización en Mesoamérica: Una Perspectiva Geográfica." *Anuario CEI III* (1989–1990). Tuxtla Gutiérrez: Centro de Estudios Indígenas, Universidad Autónoma de Chiapas.

———. 1991. "Edzná: Earliest Astronomical Center of the Mayas." In *Arqueoastronomía y Etnoastronomía en Mesoamérica,* ed. Johanna Broda, Stanislaw Iwaniszewski, and Lucrecia Maupomé, pp. 37–47. Mexico City: Universidad Nacional Autónoma de México.

———. 1992a. "Geographical Diffusion and Calendrics in Pre-Columbian Mesoamerica." *Geographical Review,* vol. 82 (April), no. 2, pp. 113–127.

———. 1992b. "Pre-Columbian Alignments in the Yucatán: Edzná." In *Geographical Snapshots of North America* (Commemorating the 27th Congress of the International Geographical Union and Assembly), ed. Donald G. Janelle. New York: The Guilford Press.

———. 1995. "Geographical Origins of the Tarascans." *Geographical Review,* vol. 85 (January), no. 1, pp. 31–40.

Mangelsdorf, Paul C. 1974. *Corn: Its Origin, Evolution and Improvement.* Cambridge: Harvard University Press.

―――. 1983. "The Mystery of Corn: New Perspectives." *Proceedings of the American Philosophical Society*, vol. 127, pp. 215–247.

―――. 1986. "The Origin of Corn." *Scientific American*, vol. 22, no. 2, pp. 72–79.

Matheny, Ray T. 1976. "Maya Lowland Hydraulic Systems." *Science*, vol. 193, no. 4254, pp. 639–646.

Matheny, Ray T., Deanne L. Gurr, Donald W. Forsyth, and F. Richard Hauck. 1983. "Investigations at Edzná, vol. 1, pt. 1: The Hydraulic System." *Papers of the New World Archaeological Foundation*, no. 46. Provo, Utah: New World Archaelogical Foundation, Brigham Young University.

Matheny, Ray T. 1987. "El Mirador: An Early Maya Metropolis Uncovered." *National Geographic Magazine*, vol. 172, no. 3, pp. 317–339.

Maupomé, Lucrecia. 1986. "Reseña de las Evidencias de la Actividad Astronómica en la América Antigua." In *Historia de la Astronomía en México*, ed. Marco Arturo Moreno Corral, pp. 17–64. Mexico City: Ediciones Olimpia S.A.

Meeus, Jean, and Hermann Mucke. 1979. *Canon of Lunar Eclipses −2002 to +2526.* Vienna: Astronomisches Buro.

Merrill, Robert H. 1945. "Maya Sun Calendar Dictum Disproved." *American Antiquity*, vol. 10, pp. 307–311.

Messenger, Lewis C., Jr. 1990. "Ancient Winds of Change: Climatic Settings and Prehistoric Social Complexity in Mesoamerica." *Ancient Mesoamerica*, vol. 1, pp. 21–40.

Millon, René. 1992. "Teotihuacán Studies: From 1950 to 1990 and Beyond." In *Art, Ideology, and the City of Teotihuacan*, ed. Janet C. Berto, pp. 339–419. A Symposium at Dumbarton Oaks, October 8–9, 1988. Washington, D.C.: Dumbarton Oaks Research Library and Collections.

Miranda, Francisco, ed. 1981. *La Cultura Purhé.* II Coloquio de Antropología e Historia Regionales. Fuentes e historia. Mexico City: FONAPAS Michoacán.

Moreno Corral, Marco Arturo, ed. 1986. *Historia de la Astronomía en México.* Mexico City: Lito Ediciones Olimpia S.A.

Morley, Sylvanus Griswold. 1920. "The Inscriptions of Copán." Publication no. 219. Washington, D.C.: Carnegie Institution of Washington.

―――. 1938. "The Inscriptions of Petén." Publication no. 437. Washington, D.C.: Carnegie Institution of Washington.

Morley, Sylvanus Griswold, and George W. Brainerd. 1983. *The Ancient Maya.* 4th ed., revised by Robert J. Sharer. Stanford: Stanford University Press.

Norman, W. Garth. 1973. "Izapa Sculpture. Pt 1: Album." *Papers of the New World Archaeological Foundation*, no. 30. Provo, Utah: New World Archaeological Foundation, Brigham Young University.

———. 1976. "Izapa Sculpture. Pt 2: Text." *Papers of the New World Archaeological Foundation*, no. 30. Provo, Utah: New World Archaeological Foundation, Brigham Young University.

Nuttall, Zelia. 1928. "Nouvelles lumières sur les civilisations americaines et le système du calendrier." *Proceedings of the Twenty-second International Congress of Americanists* (Rome), p. 119–148.

Ochoa, Lorenzo, and Thomas A. Lee, Jr., eds. 1983. *Antropología e Historia de Los Mixe-Zoques y Mayas.* (Homenaje a Frans Blom.) Mexico City: Universidad Nacional Autónoma de México, Brigham Young University.

Oppolzer, Theodor Ritter von. 1887. *Canon der Finsternisse.* Denkschriften der Kaiserlichen Akademie der Wissenschaften, Band 52. Vienna.

Parsons, Lee A. 1981. "Post-Olmec Stone Sculpture: The Olmec-Izapan Transition on the Southern Pacific Coast and Highlands." In *The Olmec and Their Neighbors*, ed. Elizabeth P. Benson, pp. 257–288. Washington, D.C.: Dumbarton Oaks Research Library and Collections.

Peterson, David A. 1990. *Discovery of an Ancient Calendar and Decipherment of the Earliest Inscriptions at Monte Albán, Oaxaca.* Research Report. Institute of Oaxaca Studies, Museo Frissell de Arte Zapoteca, Universidad de Las Américas, A.C., Mexico City. Preliminary ed. (photocopy).

Piña Chan, Román. 1989. *The Olmec: Mother Culture of Mesoamerica.* Ed. Laura Minelli. New York: Rizzoli.

Pollard, Helen Perlstein. 1991. "The Construction of Ideology in the Emergence of the Prehispanic Tarascan State." *Ancient Mesoamerica*, vol. 2, pp. 167–179.

———. 1993. *Taríacuri's Legacy: The Prehispanic Tarascan State.* Norman: University of Oklahoma Press.

Rojas, Alfonso Villa. 1983. "Recordando a Frans." In *Antropologia e Historia de Los Mixe-Zoques y Mayas*, ed. Lorenzo Ochoa and Thomas A. Lee, Jr. (Homenaje a Frans Blom.) Mexico City: Universidad Nacional Autónoma de México/Brigham Young University.

Roslund, Curt. 1979. "Ale—Forntidsmatematiker och astronom?" *Forskning och Framsteg*, vol. 5, pp. 6–11.

Sabloff, Jeremy A. 1989. *The Cities of Ancient Mexico: Reconstructing a Lost World.* New York: Thames and Hudson.

Sahagún, Bernardino de. 1990. *História general de las cosas de Nueva España.* Ed. Juan Carlos Temprano. Madrid: Gráficas Nilo.

Sauer, Carl O. 1952. *Agricultural Origins and Dispersals.* New York: American Geographical Society.

Schele, Linda, and David Freidel. 1990. *A Forest of Kings: The Untold Story of the Ancient Maya.* New York: William Morrow and Company, Inc.

Schöndube, Otto. 1981. "Las exploraciones arqueológicas en el área tarasca." In *La Cultura Purhé,* ed. Francisco Miranda, pp. 16–27. II Coloquio de Antropología e Historia Regionales. Colegio de Michoacán. Mexico City: FONAPAS Michoacán.

Seachrist, Lisa. 1994. "Sea Turtles Master Migration with Magnetic Memories." *Science,* vol. 264, no. 5159, pp. 661–662.

Seler, Eduard. 1902. *Gesammelte Abhandlungen,* vol. 1, pp. 162–300. Berlin.

———. 1990. *Collected Works in Mesoamerican Linguistics and Archaeology,* ed. J. Eric S. Thompson and Francis B. Richardson. Culver City, Calif.: Labyrinthos.

Sharer, Robert J., and David C. Grove, eds. 1989. *Regional Perspectives on the Olmec.* Cambridge: Cambridge University Press.

Shukla, K. S. 1987. "Main Characteristics and Achievements of Ancient Indian Astronomy in Historical Perspective." In *History of Oriental Astronomy,* ed. G. Swarup, A. K. Bag, and K. S. Shukla, pp. 9–22. Proceedings of an International Astronomical Colloquium no. 91, New Delhi, India, November 13–16, 1985. Cambridge: Cambridge University Press.

Spinden, Herbert J. 1924. "The Reduction of Maya Dates." *Papers of the Peabody Museum,* vol. 6, no. 4. Cambridge: Harvard University.

Spores, Ronald. 1984. *The Mixtecs in Ancient and Colonial Times.* Norman: University of Oklahoma Press.

———. 1993. "Tututepec: A Post-Class Period Mixtec Conquest State." *Ancient Mesoamerica,* vol. 4, pp. 167-174.

Stanislawski, Dan. 1947. "Tarascan Political Geography." *American Anthropologist,* vol. 49, pp. 46–55.

Stirling, Matthew W. 1939. "Discovering the New World's Oldest Dated Work of Man." *National Geographic Magazine,* vol. 76, no. 8, pp. 183–218.

Stuart, David. 1992. "Hieroglyphs and Archaeology at Copán." *Ancient Mesoamerica,* vol. 3, pp. 169–184.

Stuart, George E. 1993. "New Light on the Olmec." *National Geographic Magazine,* vol. 184, no. 5, pp. 88–114.

Swadesh, Morris. 1953. "The Language of the Archaeological Huastecs." *Notes of Middle American Archaeology and Ethnology,* no. 14. Washington, D.C.: Carnegie Institution of Washington.

Tamayo, Jorge L. 1976. *Geografía Moderna de México.* Mexico City: Editorial Trillas.

Teeple, John E. 1931. *Maya Astronomy.* Contributions to American Archaeology, vol. 1, no. 4. Washington, D.C.: Carnegie Institution of Washington, Publication 403.

Thomsen, Dietrick E. 1984. "Calendric Reform in Yucatán." *Science News*, vol. 126, no. 18 (Nov. 3), pp. 282–283.

Thompson, John Eric Sydney. 1927. *A Correlation of the Mayan and European Calendars*. Anthropological Series, Publication 241, vol. 17, no. 1, pp. 3–22. Chicago: Field Museum of Natural History.

———. 1935. *Maya Chronology: The Correlation Question*. Contributions to American Anthropology and History, vol. 3, no. 14. Washington, D.C.: Carnegie Institution of Washington, Publication 456.

———. 1950. *Maya Hieroglyphic Writing: An Introduction*. Washington, D.C.: Carnegie Institution of Washington, Publication 589.

———. 1966. *The Rise and Fall of Maya Civilization*. Norman: University of Oklahoma Press.

———. 1970. *Maya History and Religion*. Norman: University of Oklahoma Press.

———. 1972. *A Commentary on the Dresden Codex: A Maya Hieroglyphic Book*. Philadelphia: American Philosophical Society.

Urcid, Javier. 1993. "The Westernmost Extent of Zapotec Script." *Ancient Mesoamerica*, vol. 4, pp. 141–165.

Voorhies, Barbara. 1976. "The Chantuto People: An Archaic Period Society of the Chiapas Littoral, Mexico." *Papers of the New World Archaeological Foundation*, no. 41. Provo, Utah: New World Archaeological Foundation, Brigham Young University.

———, ed. 1989. *Ancient Trade and Tribute: Economies of the Soconusco Region of Mesoamerica*. Salt Lake City: University of Utah Press.

Wallrath, Matthew, and Alfonso Rangel Ruiz. 1991. "Xihuingo (Tepeapulco): Un Centro de Observación Astronómica." In *Arqueoastronomía y Etnoastronomía en Mesoamérica*, ed. Johanna Broda, Stanislaw Iwaniszewski, and Lucrecia Maupomé, pp. 297–308. Mexico City: Universidad Nacional Autónoma de México.

Warren, J. Benedict. 1985. *The Conquest of Michoacán: The Spanish Domination of the Tarascan Kingdom in Western Mexico, 1521–1530*. Norman: University of Oklahoma Press.

Weaver, Muriel Porter. 1993. *The Aztecs, Mayas, and Their Predecessors*. 3d ed. San Diego: Academic Press.

Weigand, Phil C. 1985. "Evidence for Complex Societies during the Western Mesoamerican Classic Period." In *The Archaeology of West and Northwest Mesoamerica*, ed. Michael S. Foster and Phil C. Weigand. Boulder: Westview Press.

Whitecotton, Joseph W. 1977. *The Zapotecs: Princes, Priests, and Peasants*. The Civilization of the American Indian Series. Norman: University of Oklahoma Press.

Wicke, Charles R. 1971. *Olmec: An Early Art Style of Pre-Columbian Mexico.* Tucson: University of Arizona Press.

Xi Zezong. 1987. "The Characteristics of Ancient China's Astronomy." In *History of Oriental Astronomy*, ed. G. Swarup, A. K. Bag, and K. S. Shukla, pp. 33–40. Proceedings of an International Astronomical Colloquium no. 91, New Delhi, India, November 13–16, 1985. Cambridge: Cambridge University Press.

Index

F 1219.3 .C2 M25 1997
Malmstrèm, Vincent
  Herschel, 1926-
Cycles of the sun,